S0-BBJ-320

HARTLAND PUBLIC LIBRARIES
PO BOX 137, ROUTE 12
HARTLAND, VT 05048

All Politics Is Personal

ALL POLITICS IS PERSONAL

BY RALPH WRIGHT

MARSHALL JONES COMPANY
Publishers Since 1902
Manchester Center, Vermont

MARSHALL JONES COMPANY
Manchester Center, Vermont

©1996, Ralph G. Wright
All Rights Reserved

Library of Congress
Catalog Card Number 95-81866
I.S.B.N. 0-8338-0228-3

PRINTED IN THE UNITED STATES OF AMERICA

DEDICATION

I dedicate this book to my mother, Mary Ellen Corrigan Wright, and my wife, Cathy, the two people who have meant the most to me throughout my life. My mother never wavered in her belief I was a good boy, while Cathy, my friend and partner of 38 years, never wavered in her belief I was a good man.

ACKNOWLEDGMENTS

Few books are written without help and encouragement from a host of people. And, in trying to list some of them, I am very much aware I run the almost certain risk of leaving someone out. Nevertheless, I do wish to thank the following people for their encouragement and support in what proved to be a labor of love.

I am forever indebted to my wife, Cathy, and our four loving children: Rick, Cathy Marie, Sheila Marie and Suzanne Marie. I am also indebted to my sister, Mary Wright Hughes, for reminding me there is more than one way to express my thoughts.

An expression of thanks is required for those who encouraged me during those times when I felt all was beyond my doing: Harvey Carter, Howard Coffin, Tom Davis, Peter Freyne, Allen Gilbert, Grant Reeher and Kendall Wild. Thank you to former Governor Tom Salmon for trying to place this story in perspective through its preface.

Special thanks go to my publisher and editor Peggi Simmons and Craig Altschul of the Marshall Jones Company for their steady patience and calmness.

And, finally, my gratitude to David Buckley, who, after I had survived a lifetime of working without the aid of a computer, introduced me to the technological wonders at my fingertips.

–Ralph G. Wright

ALL POLITICS IS PERSONAL: A PREFACE
By Thomas P. Salmon

(Mr. Salmon, a former Governor of Vermont, is President of The University of Vermont.)

It is said we live in interesting times.

Ralph G. Wright's inordinate focus on the years 1979 through 1994 under the golden dome we call the Vermont State House contributes mightily to our understanding of modern Vermont political history.

The author is one of thousands of out-of-staters or "suntanners," as we are sometimes called, who came to Vermont at or about the time the state was discovered. The advent of the interstate highway system made this remote, rural state accessible to those in the Northeast who sought a quieter and more qualitative lifestyle.

What distinguishes this book from so many books on politics and politicians I have read is its unique writing style and its proclivity for unusual candor.

Most politicians are a fairly conservative lot. They are sensitive to their image among colleagues, constituents and the public at large. In *All Politics Is Personal*, the author lets the zephyrs flow in an inimitable manner which, while perhaps lacking in English composition style, earns high marks in informing the reader about the way it was in the lower house of our General Assembly during a notable decade and a half.

The author needs no ghost writer to polish his text. As he has done during so much of his upwardly mobile political career, he just tells it like it is.

Throughout the journey we learn much about the man and the *raison d'etre* of his being elected Speaker of the House in five successive bienniums, thus establishing a Vermont record for longevity that may never be equaled or excelled. We learn of his roots in greater Boston, his hard scrabble youth, the tour in the U.S. Marines, and the events that brought him to the Green Mountain State.

Nothing has more greatly contributed to his longevity and success than single-minded determination and persistence, and the capacity to be patient, which is central to the success of any legislative leader.

As one turns the pages, one surmises that from the early years this "young turk" found his place in an Assembly of many moods and many ambitions, and began to carve out a niche as an unabashed, unreconstructed liberal, with an agenda consistently manifested throughout his legislative career. His self-described finest hours were in helping to mastermind and deliver on a liberal agenda, committed to the simple proposition of helping people.

The book is replete with the battles he fought, and largely won, in recognizing the interests of Gays and Lesbians, providing millions of dollars to refuel the property tax rebate program that has served our state since 1973, providing impressive increases in resources for state aid to education, advancement of a variety of environmental initiatives which solidify Vermont's national reputation, and support for any program that had as its natural beneficiary the least of our brethren. His sturdy comrade in arms during much of this time was Paul Poirier, with whom he developed a seamless political and personal relationship, and whose departure to engage in other political pursuits contributed to fewer political successes in the out years of his stewardship.

Along the way, Wright seemed to take particular joy in taking on the privileged, especially large corporations, and exuded special glee in putting bankers and electric utility types in their place. He seldom encountered a liberal program he didn't like and was, and is, unapologetic about it.

Yet this personal reflective reveals another side of the man. On two occasions, when Vermont faced acute fiscal crises, he rose to become the point person in helping our state do the right thing. The first situation was in 1983, during the special session which Governor Richard A. Snelling called to retire the "Republican Deficit." Abandoned by the leadership of his own party, Snelling was forced to reach out to the likes of Ralph Wright, Democratic leader, who put his shoulder solidly to the wheel in helping Vermont meet its compelling budget cut and tax increase requirements, and then to sunset the tax increases that we then required.

It must have felt like *deja vu* to him, as "King Richard" returned to the scene for a fifth term in 1991, identifying as his Number One priority the slaying of the dragon now entitled the "Democratic Deficit."

Wright became a faithful and loyal acolyte in the cause, providing the hard-nosed political leadership within the Legislature that created conditions for members doing something they desperately did not want to do; namely, voting the largest cluster of tax increases in the history of Vermont. To his credit, and in furtherance of the legacy of Dick Snelling, whom he much admired, the tax increases of 1991 were eventually sunsetted as Vermont approached a condition of sustainable revenue and sustainable spending. The seeming message is the unreconstructed liberals sometimes act in a fiscally responsive manner.

Much of the grist of this book is found in the vivid portrayal of that cast of characters who make up the body politic we call the Vermont General Assembly, the media, lobbyists, supplicants, and a variety of hangers-on. Having come to know and work with virtually all the acolytes who performed at center stage during Wright's time adds value to my personal appreciation of his reminiscences. He mines no words in character descriptions. The heroics of Ludlow's fabled Representative John Murphy and the happenings in the General and Military Affairs Committee have been a road show that has continued for over a quarter of a century. The Murphy stories alone are worth the price of the book. Wright's character portrayals are candid and blunt. He does not hold back.

Candid descriptions of the three Governors with whom he served: Richard A. Snelling (twice), Madeleine Kunin, and Howard Dean, are offered. All receive decidedly positive reviews, although the principal "huzzahs" are reserved for Dick Snelling, in a poignant essay to a fallen leader.

During his years as Democratic leader and Speaker, Wright developed a significant reputation as a person deeply immersed in the political process who knew how to count, and how to deploy his lieutenants in advance of achieving his political objectives. Those who stood in his way were frequently run over. His was a "take no prisoners" style. Sometimes the end seemed to justify the means. It was the style of a hard-nosed, pragmatic politician, who developed a certain mastery about the Legislature and its people. It was the style of a person with a point of view. As all within the media would likely agree. He made good copy.

Vermont's living Governors, and a variety of political scientists, will have difficulty with his proposition that all that went on in the State House was the business of the Legislature. The argument is, of course, correct as respects the disposition of legislation; but arguably much of what happens in Montpelier is reflected in what the Governor proposes. He, or she, has an equal opportunity to exploit their will in advancing the executive agenda in our participatory democracy.

Much of this book is laced with self-deprecating humor, and abundant evidence that the Speaker made his share of mistakes. The author understands that mistakes are simply another form of experience in life, from which one often times profits. The book is remarkably self-critical. In the final analysis, Wright views himself as a lucky person in the right place at the right time. He seems to understand that political leadership is forged on the anvil of one's willingness to compromise. Yet he, too, found it difficult to compromise at times.

His iterations with the Vermont media bear careful scrutiny. What is left unsaid is that it is virtually impossible for a public figure to develop any warm and close relationship with any member of the fourth estate while they are in active service. This is especially true of a leader alleged to have a heavy hand and a capacity for ruthlessness. The role of a political leader is to lead. The role of the media is to aggressively observe this leadership and report on whether or not he or she is fulfilling their stated objectives. Conflict is inevitable.

The "last hurrah" for Ralph Wright, circa 1993-1994, was not a pleasant time. Having a Democratic Governor, and record numbers of elected House Democrats, did not turn the tide.

Health care reform and local tax reform were on his primary liberal agenda. What materialized was the increased decibel level of his critics. As Vermont prepared for election 1994, he stood as a survivor who had helped establish the firm footings of the Democratic Party in the House, through single minded determination and intense campaigning in individual communities of Vermont.

In some respects, Wright's larger agenda in building the Democratic Party may have been a contributing factor to his 1994 legislative defeat at the hands of Gerald Morrissey. Undoubtedly many factors contributed to the end result. He candidly concludes that "it was time for a new face,"

History will remember Ralph G. Wright as a dominant and forceful legislative leader of the twentieth century, whose presence made a difference. Careful scholars will detect a man unabashedly devoted to his family and his colleagues, with a special love of political combat in advance of his cause. Critical observers will also note his more than two decades of special service to the alternative educational program in his community designed to literally save the lives of vulnerable young men and women. It is ironic that this public man, who raised megabucks to advance his party's political agenda in the Legislature, would never accept a dime from anyone to advance his own political campaigns.

As Theodore Roosevelt reminded us, Ralph Wright will never stand among those poor and timid souls who know neither victory nor defeat. His poignant memoir also reminds us that Vermont will not soon forget the member from Bennington.

-T.P.S.

CONTENTS

All Politics Is Personal

1. A TIME TO GO

I sat in the back row of the Vermont House of Representatives for the final time. It was an eerie feeling to realize that these few moments would be my last in this building. I was leaving now. Not of my own volition, to be sure. That decision had been made for me by the people back home in my district. They had chosen someone else to represent them after 16 years.

I knew it was nothing personal, merely time for a change. I couldn't get people to believe me. But, I understood and felt a sense of relief as if a burden had been lifted from me. It was over. My mind was now filled with fondness and my thoughts were on Danny Debonis, my seat mate of more than a decade ago.

Dan had been a veteran of nearly 20 years when I first arrived, and except for the chair reserved for the Speaker at the podium, he occupied the best seat in the House. It was an aisle seat at the very back of the chamber, giving quick access to the cafeteria and telephones, and adjacent to the red seats (those usually reserved for infrequent joint sessions with Senators) where guests, lobbyists, or others could sit and hobnob with him. Each morning he religiously threw his daily calendars and journals into a cardboard liquor box under the nearest red seat. Danny bragged that he didn't read any of that "crap." I suspected he couldn't read well, or perhaps, not at all. But he was a very effective legislator and I was never brazen enough to ask, even during those times when he would flippantly toss a bill or amendment onto my desk, ask me to tell him what this "crap says," and then watch with amazement as he would get up on the floor and articulate what I had relayed as if he had written it himself. Oh, he was good!

Danny was a "good ole boy" and I was smart enough to pay deference to that type of seniority. As part of the inner circle, he could make or break someone with a word or two to the leadership and I made sure Danny had no reason to be sinking my ship behind the scenes.

I don't know this for sure, but I always suspected he made some sort of deference to me for my willingness to be helpful. Danny was a straight shooter who never confused anyone with where he stood. He used me and I used him.

Danny is gone now, a victim of a hunting accident. I reflected on the time we spent together all those years as seat mates with a deep feeling of regret at his passing. I reminisced about him and it now seemed these were the memories that I would most regret leaving behind.

To my right sat Paul Poirier - the *Butch* in *Butch Cassidy and the Sundance Kid* - the handle hung on the two of us. Paul was more than my seat mate. He was a co-leader with me, an inseparable partner and best friend, night and day. It will be a long time before the Vermont Legislature sees the likes of us again. We were young "turks" in the right place at the right time.

Though Paul came two years after me, he was possessed by the same drive that consumed me. He was smart and a quick study. More than once I saw Paul take a half-inch thick legislative bill, disappear for 15 minutes, and then take the floor ready to do battle. And, battle he would. I never failed to sit back with an inner smirk and watch the devastation he would wreak on his bewildered opponents. Paul's brains and superb political instincts were fortified by a courage that can only be described as reckless. We, his friends, had the satisfaction of knowing what the end result would be. His adversaries sat watching the slow disintegration of whomever was their great hope of the moment. Paul was one of those rare creatures that looked at life as a series of struggles, each one having no other purpose than to lead to the next.

Now, Paul, too, was gone from the legislature and I was consumed with a feeling only pleasant memories can bring.

There were hundreds of occasions during my ten years as Speaker that I was asked to address different visiting groups in the well of the House. I tend to look at the world as a stage by nature and I welcomed such opportunities. Though I enjoyed speaking to almost all groups that visited, I enjoyed the school groups most. I could anticipate certain questions: How old are you? How much do they pay you? Do you enjoy being Speaker? What is your job like? It was this last question that offered a variety of answers with which I could respond. I could take them through a formal civics class in a ten minute response, boring the daylights out of them, or I could give them my "*Symphony Orchestra*" answer.

I would ask them to envision the chamber as a Symphony Hall. Where they sat was where the 150 members of the orchestra sat. As the Speaker at the Podium, I was merely the conductor. The talent sat where they sat. There were strings and horns and it was my job as the conductor to know where the various musicians sat and when to bring them in. If I did it right, and anticipated timing and talent, this orchestra produced a symphony of sound, music to the ears, so to speak. If, on the other hand, I as Speaker, brought in the wrong players at the wrong time, all that occurred was noise. It was no different with the peoples' legislation.

The real reason I enjoyed the kids so much was they insisted on honesty, brutal honesty. This was not true with legislators. It's the marvel of youth they have not reached the sophistication that comes with living in a tough world that demands them to always be protecting their flanks. Legislators are long-term inhabitants of that tough world and have perfected the perfect defense to an art form: *The non-answer.* Politics is a part of that tough world. It is a world one learns to perfect only the answer the listener wants to hear. From the novice politician's earliest introduction to campaigning, he or she digests the body language of the constituent, tone of the question, or the follow up. Politicians have molded this into an art form. If they fail-they're history.

Success in the legislature depends on one's ability to read people. Find the hot button and don't be afraid to push it. I learned early in life that fear of failure—in politics or life—is like a shot to the gut.

There's no IQ test to gain admission to the legislature. The place would not be full if there were. On the other hand, there were some absolutely brilliant people I worked with during my tenure. There were others who struggled with the complex. Amazingly, it is the bright that run the risk of going bust. The legislature, like most other entities, works best on the premise of *"keep it simple, stupid."* The members who complicated their effort to the point that nobody could understand what they were talking about ran the grave risk of the rest of the members invoking the rule "when in doubt, vote no."

I was continually amused by the amount of discussion generated by supporters and adversaries alike as to the secret to my success. It actually was simple. I listened to members. I observed members. I paid attention to members who listened and observed other members. It was no different than what I had tried to master as a teacher for 30 years. The difference was instead of 25 young people, there was now a classroom of 149 adults.

In a general sense, it was my job to maintain a semblance of control, to accomplish the day's agenda and to encourage participation. But, it didn't end there. As in a classroom, I had to be ever observant as to the mood of the members, not simply as a group, but as individuals. I had to constantly remind myself these people had other lives which involved spouses, children, jobs, and more. The fact there were 149 people to be concerned with meant I could spend all the time available to me dealing with what had occurred to each of them between the time they left the night before and their emergence back into the legislative world that morning.

If someone bounced up the back stairway leading to the Speaker's Office and cafeteria, then the upbeat mood signified I could push his or her patience with my normal sarcastic banter. If, on the other hand, a member appeared quiet or sullen, a more appropriate response was in order. I would take the complaint or problem seriously. Even if I thought his or her concerns were pretty dumb, I tried to hide those feelings. I ran into some incredible stories. Amazingly, there seemed to be a rule that worked more often than I had a right to expect. I called it the "common cold" rule: Time healed all. If I could delay taking immediate action, the problem eventually would get resolved either by somebody else or, magically, by time itself. Real or imagined problems, like adolescents, tend to mature. If, in the course of the day the conflict festered and grew worse, then it was time for me to get involved. As luck or the rule would have it, it often resolved itself.

This all seemed rather second nature to me, but to some people it appeared I had some magical power. This is not to deny that the office of the Speaker is indeed a powerful office, but there were limits. There exists a thin line between "magic", being good, and plain, simple luck. Most of the time I opted to be lucky, rather than good. It amused me when something would happen in the State House that didn't implicate me. Even if I hadn't the slightest knowledge of what the accuser was talking about, I inevitably would get blamed for things that went wrong. A chorus of angels singing my defense couldn't dissuade my accusers. On the same token, there were numerous occasions I received credit for things I absolutely had nothing to do with. Power has its own mystique and, after a period of time, I stopped trying to figure it out.

But let's, as they say, begin at the beginning.

2. THE LEARNING CURVE

I didn't go to the legislature with the vaguest notion of rising to any level of leadership or power. It never occurred to me I would someday become Speaker when I first entered. I was content to serve on any committee. The good luck of being appointed to the Health and Welfare Committee pushed any such thoughts of power out of the reach of my focus. Besides, my freshman naiveté led to an amusing ambivalence when it came to my impressions of the Speakership. The Speaker, to me, was simply a traffic cop, a person at the podium who had the rather uninteresting task of presiding over our deliberations. This was a lonely sort of figure who occasionally had visitors, but beyond that, he was the only member isolated by post and obligations. The rest of us were at liberty to sit or wander wherever we desired. We could visit with our seat mate when bored, or get up and leave. The Speaker, on the other hand, seemed chained to his post. In addition, I began to realize that the title of "Speaker" was a misnomer. Speakers never spoke. They "chanted." No ad-libbing and no interjecting of their own opinions. More than once I felt I was attending Mass, listening to Father.

I had no conception of the power amassed just above me and to the right. Years later when I personally would be doing the chanting, I came to realize this was the very heart and soul of all that occurred in the building. It was like a traffic control center for a very busy airport. Nothing could take off or land without, at least, the knowledge and often the OK, from the controlling officer. But for now, I was content to believe that as the member from Bennington, seated in seat 23, I was an equal partner in the great American experiment.

My committee assignment came without any discussion with anyone of whom I had knowledge. I was unaware that others probably had plenty to say about where I spent two years of my life, but I, a lowly freshman, was not privy to that. The only occasions I had to even discuss my assignment, beyond filling out my three choice request sheet, was the rather nice gesture from Merritt Hewitt, a veteran Bennington County Senator who, on his own initiative, took me to see Speaker Timothy O'Connor. His purpose was to make sure I got the best possible committee assignment. I should say that was his primary purpose, for I was soon to learn there is always an ulterior motive in the legislature. These ulterior motives were not just for kind or positive gestures of seeming good-will, but even for the opposite. More than I care to

relate, I witnessed sometimes brutal attacks that were just preliminary
to a second move. In either case, Speaker O'Connor received the
Senator and me like there were no people on this earth he was happier
to see. His air said "we couldn't have started without you, Big Guy."
Considering my background, I was sure the Education Committee was
where I could best utilize my abilities. I was somewhat taken back
when Merritt informed the Speaker I really would prove to be a solid
member of the Appropriations Committee. In spite of being as naive as
any freshman had a right to be, I knew such a request was not going to
be taken very seriously by O'Connor. It wasn't. But one would have had
trouble detecting the hilarity the request must have been met with
inside. O'Connor just parried Merritt's solicitous overture and
answered in another direction. He thought I would find the Education
Committee truly a bore. As a practicing school teacher, I was way
overqualified to serve with ten others whose last experiences in school
were as students. He was sure I wouldn't have the patience to put up
with the monotonous, slow pace he knew the committee would
require. But he felt I was perfect for a seat on Health and Welfare. And,
so it was. It was my first experience at having a fellow pol do me a favor
by denying me what I wanted. It wouldn't be my last.

It turned out to be the best thing that could possibly have happened
to me. Each day, each hour, was unique and exciting. It was a whole
new world. The committee received bills dealing with children, the
poor, elderly, retarded and health issues. In other words, we dealt with
all the people and programs about which I cared the most. It was a new
world, with a whole new language or jargon, but it was a world I would
have bought a ticket to enter. It was to be a great four years.

Of greater importance was the fact I was to experience the luxury of
working for perhaps the best chairman possible, Edgar May, the
Representative from Springfield.

May is a New Frontier democrat. He had worked with Sargeant
Shriver during the John F. Kennedy administration and, in fact, had
socially hobnobbed with the Kennedy's. Winner of a Pulitzer Prize as a
reporter, he somehow ended up in Vermont and migrated to the legislature. He is an amazing guy who proved perfect for me to emulate and
learn from. He was half of a rather amazing family. His sister, Madeleine
Kunin, became Governor in 1985, the same year I became Speaker. That
prediction would have earned a raised eyebrow or two in January, 1979.

Here is one smart guy, not just intellectually, but street smart as well.
He never liked to admit he usually always had two agendas going, but
he did. I never questioned his commitment to the right causes, nor did
it ever bother me that May was a master at manipulating people (OK,

using people). "Used" was exactly what I wanted to be. Everyone on the committee felt the May magic. The committee was always under control *(his control)* and we seldom failed to accomplish our goals. If we showed initiative and interest, he would give us encouragement and all the free reign we wanted. I learned a ton about the nuts and bolts of the process during this period, which proved to be a very valuable future foundation. Marking up bills, referencing them to the present statute, amending, total rewrites (called "strike alls") became second nature endeavors. The give and take in the committee could get heavy, but May would see to it that it always rolled to a consensus. His greatest attribute was bringing people together. This was not an impossible task, especially in a committee filled with committed people and, not incidentally, as devoted to the Chair as I was.

May had special roles for each member of the committee. Mine was to report bills out on the floor and, when the occasion called for it, play the role of the "bad cop." Of course Edgar played the "good cop." I had no objection to this as all the parts served to make a whole. When he was Chairman of the Senate Appropriations years later, and his sister was Governor, we got into a showdown over state aid to education. I had made it a very public priority to pump a great deal of new money into the public schools from surplus in state revenues that had befallen us. Under the guise of fiscal restraint, Edgar and his sister took me on; the confrontation became bitter and drawn-out. After several weeks of insisting we'd stay in session until the proverbial cows came home, they finally relented and we got our money. As Paul Poirier and I were departing the building that evening, we chanced to walk by May's committee room in the Senate wing. Edgar spotted us and took the opportunity to let me know just what he thought of our conduct during the past few weeks. I had never seen him as angry as he was that day and I just let him vent. After all, we had won. He ended the entire heated one-way exchange by telling me exactly what he thought.

"Mr. Speaker, I worked and served with Bobby Kennedy and, until I ran into Ralph Wright, I thought I had seen the height of ruthlessness. But you even top Bobby Kennedy at his most ruthless." With that he abruptly turned his back and stormed back into his committee room.

Poirier and I thought the best thing we could do was to get the hell out of there as fast as we could. As we went out the door and started down the steps, Paul turned to me and said with the voice of a child's wonderment, "Geez, Ralph, did ya hear that? He compared you to Bobby Kennedy. Wow! It doesn't get any better than this, does it?"

Edgar May was a mentor to me and I didn't come close to Bobby Kennedy.

The four years flew by. I couldn't imagine wanting to be anyplace else. Health and Welfare was the center of the universe to me and I never longed to be on any of the lesser planets. Little did I know my world was about to be turned upside down.

By the end of my first term Speaker O'Connor had decided to venture out into the world of state politics. His decision to run for Governor after having served as the longest reigning Speaker in the history of the state to date (six years) proved to be ill-fated. O'Connor was a great guy to work for, an opinion shared by members on both sides of the aisle. An eclectic sort, as a politician, conservatively bent, his agenda alienated no one. Some said he never had an agenda. Regardless, he was not one to take himself too seriously (another endearing quality) and, consequently, his campaign had the air of casualness that inevitably spelled disaster.

He displayed this blasé attitude from the very beginning of the campaign. For example, the General and Military Committee held a public hearing on a labor bill in the well of the House. The room was packed to the rafters with people who had bussed in from all across the state, many with packs of Marlboros rolled in the shirt sleeves. Anybody who was anybody got there early enough to get a seat and publicly show his or her concern for "Joe Sixpack."

Tim O'Connor wasn't there at all. He was 175 miles away in Worcester, Massachusetts, watching Boston College beat his beloved Crusaders. Yeah, Timmy O'Connor had a sense of humor.

He was beaten in that September's Primary by Jerry Diamond, the sitting Attorney General. Diamond was administered a sound thumping by incumbent Richard Snelling two months later. None of this meant much to me as my legislative life was going just fine. I was hardly aware of Governors, let alone Speakers. In fact, I had never visited that inner enclave of the Speaker's Office, nor did I deem it important to do so. Edgar May handled those matters and as long as O'Connor was there, he always appeared to get what he wanted. But now in 1981, O'Connor's decision to run for Governor meant there was a Republican Speaker and, though I was unaware of it, things were changing for May. That meant things were going to change for the rest of us as well. They changed slowly and, at first, barely noticeably, but something different was happening.

The new Speaker, Stephen Morse (he liked to have it pronounced Steffen), was a handsome, thirtyish young Republican from Newfane, a small picturesque town in the southern part of Vermont. A relative newcomer to the legislature, he had become Party Whip in only his second term. He was elected Speaker in his third term. I didn't vote for him, but I remember he won by a much larger margin than his majority. I found this interesting and tucked it away as another lesson learned. Marshall McLuhan said "the medium is the message"; in politics this gets translated to "power is the impression of power." People like to be with the winner. I was mostly troubled that Democrats had crossed over for personal gain of some sort, a thought that was alien to my Marine background.

It didn't help that the Democratic candidate opposing Morse was a liberal from Norwich named Norrie Hoyt, a bright, committed and humble man. It was this last quality that doomed him. He refused to campaign; the most we could anticipate was a call. Actually, I called Hoyt to let him know he could count on my vote. He was dealing with an aggressive opponent who had the numbers (Republicans outnumbered Democrats 86-64).

This was all occurring as I began my second term and though a new Speaker takes some getting used to, it wasn't in the areas one might expect. To me it was merely a new priest saying Mass.

The chant was different, the process more deliberate and perhaps sloppy, at least in the beginning, and one could not help notice different "good ole boys" clustered around the seat of power. But the Speaker was still, in my mind at least, simply the traffic cop who made things orderly enough for the rest of us to change the world.

Unfortunately, Edgar May was not finding the Speaker's Office as accommodating as in the past. Perhaps it was simply that Morse was a Republican and Edgar a Democrat. In the animal world, no matter how well the dog and the cat get along, eventually instinct takes over and the dog can't resist chasing the cat. So it is with political parties. They were created to confront one another. Actually, it was more than that, as May and Morse's background and chemistry were poles apart. Edgar gave the air of good breeding, while Steve was a country boy. One had the benefit of a world class education, while the other had hardly ventured beyond Vermont's narrow borders. May managed to hide his ambition in a facade of class, while Morse wore it on his sleeve. In either case, clash was inevitable and one of them had to go. I wasn't smart enough to know it then, but it wasn't going to be Morse.

❖ ❖ ❖ ❖ ❖

One learns early in legislative life many people come and go, but the system continues. There's no place like a legislature. I say this with admiration in the sense that if continuity is the very essence of life, then a legislature is eternal. Only the local Post Office can duplicate the persistence and tenaciousness of process. I had to listen to incessant complaints from all quarters about the incompetence of the delivery of mail. My response was simple: "When was the last time you didn't get an electric bill?" Look, there are systems that work. The Post Office happens to be one of them. The system of representative democracy is another. Personalities may color a General Assembly with different tints, but they are just passing through. The process is more permanent. It is why we are so reluctant to change our Constitution. *The system works.*

And so it was during this, my second term, the beat went on. Things were changing but I hardly noticed any impact on my life.

We all got used to the new Speaker. We grew more comfortable as Morse's self-confidence developed and he rode the crest of acceptance that a newly elected Speaker generally experiences. Everybody was paying deference to the newly crowned king. Bi-partisanship was rampant. This Speaker was no single vote victor. Accompanying this was a Governor, not only of the same party, but a father figure who several years later was to administer the vows of marriage to Steve and his new bride. This tandem, coupled with an overwhelming majority in both houses, placed the Speaker in the inevitable position of a two thousand pound gorilla who could do anything he pleased. Meanwhile in Health and Welfare, we kept pumping out "dopey do-gooder" bills, such as creation of the Independence Fund for elderly shut-ins, expansion of programs for mentally retarded people and the foundation of a statewide system of group homes for abused and neglected adolescents.

It was during these times I learned it took courage to show courage. It is so easy for the politician to find a multitude of ways to hide inside the political process. Here we can lay in the reeds beyond the sight of our public, emerging only when we feel it is safe. Pols go to great pains to leave everyone confused and often bewildered as to where they stand on any given issue. It is a matter of survival to most. Not attractive maybe, and the public will side with me on this point, but it means we live to serve another day. This is a paradox in a process called democracy that will eventually change the system-or perhaps destroy it. If truth in lending is a social good, then truth in voting is a political good.

There are three ways you can keep track of what your local Representative is doing, presumably on your behalf. The first two are next to impossible for most citizens to ever be aware of because it would take his or her actual presence in the well or arena of the House. Voice votes are just that: you vote by calling out "yes" or "no" in unison while in your seat. Even the members would be unaware if you sat silent, or as in some cases reported to me, answers of both "yes" and "no" on the same question. I haven't the foggiest idea why someone would do that, however. In the second instance, a member can request that the Speaker ask the members to rise and be counted, a "division" in legislative parlance. This is a little less secretive, as the members must stand to record their opinion and the clerks must count while they remain standing. Even the quickest eye would find it difficult to keep track of, or remember, those who were on their feet and how they voted. Obviously if you weren't actually there, you wouldn't have a clue as to what your local representative had done. It happens fairly fast and even the members present have difficulty making an accurate mental note of just how each member performed. The folks back home would not have any better idea of their legislator's conduct than they had on a voice vote.

The third manner is the roll call vote. This one is for posterity. The whole world knows what you're thinking because you have to answer "yes" or "no" (no maybes) and it is recorded. The press can, and often does, run it in the next day's paper. It is also readily available to anyone down the road who wants to go to the "journals" and dig out your votes to use as they see fit.I was called disparaging names by weak-kneed members for allowing somebody to get a "roll call" vote on tough issues. Some members would break into a cold sweat at the thought of going on record.

It didn't take long to be put to the test. It came at the end of the session when the last minute scrambling reached a crescendo and the women in the House discovered they had lost funding for their Woman's Caucus. It was a relatively small amount, perhaps $30,000, but it was at a time the women were fighting for the smallest advance on the long road to equality. It was buried in the big appropriation bill as a little noticed line item. The Senate, being more conservative and showing no apprehension in preparing for equal rights for women, simply cut it out, but the House conferees had gone along with the Senate's wishes and kept it out of the final budget. It was another sign of just how tight a hold the "good ole boys" had on all that happened in those days. The only hope women in the House had was to threaten to refuse "rule suspension"* on the Appropriations Bill until they took it back into conference and restored the funding to the cause.

* *Our founding fathers set out to make democracy an extremely deliberative process. There were to be no "hunch bets." All legislative proposals have a series of three readings that normally take three days to move from one house to the other. It's based on the logical concept all decisions should be "slept on." To "suspend the rules" simply allows the entire process to be accomplished in one sitting. It is an infrequently used tactic to move the process along, generally only used in the waning days of a session when the Assembly is driving toward adjournment. It takes a three-quarters vote of those present to pass instead of a simply majority.*

Speaker O'Connor tried to bring up the appropriations bill and moved the first time to suspend the rules and bring the "Big Bill" up for consideration. The 30 or so women, anticipating such a move, countered by uniting to block suspension of the rules. I had committed to hang with them.

O'Connor tried rules suspension the first time on a voice vote. This was no problem as I could simply sit in my seat and keep the commitment I had given the women by voting "no" in as low a voice as possible. Even my friend and seatmate Ray Poor, who was hard of hearing, gave me a surprised look. Ray was too nice a guy to say anything, but he realized I was taking a treacherous path with the power structure in the House. The Speaker, trying to decipher if he had a majority to suspend, welcomed the request from one of the members that we be asked to stand in order to count the votes. I was in a section that was surrounded by male members, many of them with no necks and gnarled knuckles. When I rose with the "Nays", I felt like I was naked on stage at Carnegie Hall. But I stood and my only salvation standing with all the women was, as I looked to my left, there in the front row also standing was Rusty Sachs the representative from Windsor. He, like me, was a Marine, but he was a decorated Vietnam veteran and a law school grad. God love you, Rusty.

It took the clerks the longest time to count the 30 of us standing. "I hope I don't ever have to do this again", I thought, as I could feel the eyes of the Neanderthals on Sachs and me. It was a telling moment in my new life as a legislator. Hang tough, Ralphie Babe. I then began hoping we'd lose. I wanted us to come up short in our effort to block the rules and let the bill get brought up without the women's funding and pass. We won. Damn. No sooner had O'Connor abided by the rules and brought up another bill, than the request came to try once again to suspend the rules. Sachs and I got up again. If not losing our masculinity, we were relinquishing at least our right to borrow the power tools or sit in at the Wednesday night poker games.

It seemed like they tried rules suspension a half dozen times during the course of the day, each with the same results. Finally they gave up and put the women's money back in the budget amidst an outbreak of very feminine cheers. I received a note:

"Congratulations. A victory well deserved by 30 women and two queers." Of course it wasn't signed. But I had my suspicions of its origins and there were plenty of suspects.

Hanging tough isn't all it's cracked up to be. But a decade and a half later, I'm proud enough to tell *you* about it.

The new Speaker didn't much care for me and the reasons went beyond party politics or different philosophies. In fairness, Steve Morse was more politically liberal than O'Connor had been. It was just that where O'Connor had been a "hands-off" Speaker, Morse was a take-charge kind of guy. He had an agenda and he meant to push it through. If one's agenda was of the opposite bent, he'd attempt to kill it. I didn't vote with his side very often, but as we were always on the losing end, this never mattered a great deal to either the Speaker or his followers. It went beyond philosophy. *All politics is personal.* It may have been the natural defense mechanisms inherent in all people in power to take stock of one's colleagues and categorize them into threats and non-threats. Most everybody has a dream and it's the rare freshman who, upon arriving in the legislature, doesn't glance up at the podium and picture himself or herself standing tall wielding a heavy gavel. That's an innocent enough response from the starry-eyed, but there are times when it's not a passing fancy and the signal is not often unnoticed by those that are in power. I am an "issues" kind of person, so the pinnacle of power to me was to become a Committee Chair. Getting elected, in itself, is a high. Joe and Jane Average can be transformed quickly from humble everyday folk into the "People's Choice." The strut can become overbearing. If it's noticed by those who have fought their way to the top, it can place the "upstart" in a combat role.

My personality all by itself had proven to be a turnoff to more people than I dare count over the years. Or, it may have been the only significant press coverage I managed to get during my first few years. Within weeks of my freshman year, an article appeared that designated Ted Riehle from Burlington and me as freshmen to watch. Any veteran would have paid little attention to it. The road to stardom in a legislature is a marathon, not a sprint. It was nice, as I remember it, but unfortunately, all it managed to do for those who read it, or bothered to remember it, was to place me in the "threat" category. Members have long memories. One learns to forgive, but not forget. So Morse had placed me in his mind in a category that didn't spell good news for me. Steve ran unopposed for his second term as Speaker (a luxury, incidentally, I never experienced). There was no suspense surrounding the opening day of my third term. But that doesn't mean that things weren't looking up for me. Edgar May had made the leap and decided he had no future in the House. He was now Senator May from Windsor County. That meant we were going to have a new Chair in Health and Welfare, and I fully expected it would be me.

The ride to Montpelier was an especially happy one. It was shared with my youngest daughter Suzanne, who being an eighth grader, had been chosen as a Page. We both felt the excitement during this second week. Suzanne, poised to enter a unique and powerful experience of the world of government, and me, entering what promised to be a turning point in my political life. It was a turning point all right...right over the bridge.

As we swung right and headed up over Mendon Mountain out of Rutland, the radio commentator was predicting that I was rumored to be the new Chairman of the House Health and Welfare Committee. Great, I mused. Before lunch I'd be introducing myself to my new committee members and laying out the committee's schedule for the session. By the time we settled into the State House, a handful of members had begun to congratulate me in anticipation of committee assignment announcements. By tradition, Committee assignments had been read by the Speaker on Tuesday of the second week. This gave him the weekend to sort out the members' requests and hopefully make everyone happy. In theory, this was supposed to mean each member would be assigned according to his or her ability to each of the 14 committees.

Of all the Committee Chairs I appointed as Speaker, only a few failed to commit his or her vote for Speaker to me. When I appointed a Republican on merit alone, I was praised to the heavens for my bipartisan fairness. Unlike most other states, Vermont makes a rather pretentious effort at being bipartisan. It is a weak refute of "to the victors belong the spoils." Generally, of the 14 standing committees, there are three or four chaired by a number of the opposite party from the Speaker. This just means the Speaker has some "friends" on the other side of the aisle. They voted for the Speaker and he rewarded them.

In response to the energy crisis, Morse created a new Energy Committee that promised to be just another "dump" committee in the sense that few would want to serve on it. It seemed a given it would be sent few bills. But the more obvious signal this was a committee to be avoided was it didn't even have a place to meet. It had no committee room. Eleven people, like Charlie on the MTA were destined to spend two years wandering the crowded State House forever searching for a place to perch. I didn't give it much thought as I was certain that legislative life held out more promising prospects for me.

A new twist had been added to my prospectus. One of the dailies was predicting I was going to be the new Chairman of the Education Committee. It was not something I would have thought of, but it was not a bad second choice either. If I had been thinking more clearly, I would have reflected on a rather unpleasant scene I had been a part of about four days earlier. It might have helped to bring me back to some sense of reality.

One of the more mundane and preliminary duties of the House upon convening each biennium is the responsibility in conjunction with the Senate of re-affirming the state-wide elections from the previous November. Beyond the boring nature of the task, it's a clear signal of the mundane to those selected to do the counting, something reserved for the lowly freshmen. Poirier and I had been kibitzing up in back just prior to the Speaker making the announced assignments to the Canvassing Committee and ragging Dave Shaffe, the member from Bennington, about a junket he had taken the previous summer to San Francisco. We had not been part of that "good ole boy" network and were not part of the entourage. We quieted down a bit while Morse began droning out the names of the members to report to room 11 immediately upon adjournment, but the teasing of Shaffe went on. Suddenly, amidst all those freshmen being named, I heard "the member from Bennington, Mr. Wright." I couldn't believe my ears. I was headed downstairs to count ballots with the lowly freshmen. Of course, now the ragging beamed in on me. Perhaps out of embarrassment, perhaps out of anger, I reacted in a less than soft voice. "Right, Shaffe," I said rather loudly, "The son of a bitch sends a zero like you to San Francisco for a week and I get to go to Room 11 to count votes with the freshmen for the rest of the day."

The section broke up in laughter, but a number of members on the other side of the well of the House weren't amused. I didn't have to look up to the podium to feel the glare of the Speaker bearing down on me. Nice going, Ralphie.

But that had been four days ago. And what's a little humor? Besides, I rationalized, Morse probably didn't hear what I said anyway.

The bang of the gavel quickly brought the excited members to a resounding quiet and Morse began reading the committee assignments. This was done alphabetically, by committee. Agriculture, Appropriations, Commerce, Education, Energy, Government Operations, Fish and Wildlife, General and Military, Health and Welfare, Judiciary, Municipal Corporations and Elections, Natural Resources, Transportation, and Ways and Means. I didn't have to begin listening until he at least got to the Education Committee and that was thirty or more names away.

"The member from Guilford, Mr. Hunt." He was reading the first name for the Commerce Committee. The first name read is Chair, the second name read is Vice Chair and the third name read is so-called Ranking Member. The remainder of the members to the committee were simply recited in alphabetical order. Get ready, Education would be next.

"Education," he continued in a monotone.

"The member from Charlotte, Mrs. Morse."

O. K. No problem. Not my first choice anyway. I relaxed a bit. There were still a bunch to be read before he gets to the Health and Welfare Committee. I tuned out.

Then it happened. Or did it? Did I hear my name? Can't be . Where the hell is he? I swung around to Poirier.

"Did I just hear him read my name, Paul?"

Paul, stunned as I was, said, "Yeah! I think so."

"You sure?" Heads were turning.

"Yes. I'm positive he said 'The Member from Bennington, Mr. Wright.'"

"Where the hell is he?" I was about to find out.

"Health and Welfare," came the chant. Morse had started the Health and Welfare assignments.

My name had already been read.

"Jesus H. Mahogany Christ, Paul," I said, "I'm on the God damned General and Military Committee. The last member named."

So much for fame. I hadn't fallen off the bridge. I had been pushed.

There were a lot of members who were going to have a bad day. Poirier was dumped on Municipal Corporations. Peter Youngbaer ended up on Energy, as did Wayne Kenyon from Bradford. Michael Obuchowski, who many years later would replace me as Speaker, took a dive. Even though he wrestled out a Chairmanship, it was Chair of Energy. Quite a plunge from Chair of Education. He might still have had a Chair, but he didn't have a room to put it in. We were all liberal Democrats. We were all labeled "Young Turks." And we were all about to be tested unlike anything we had experienced in the past. So this was how it worked. Not exactly as Miss Cheney had described it back in eighth grade civics.

I did the best I could, stiff upper lip and all that. What hurt the most was while all this was going on, my daughter Suzanne had been standing right in back of me. She had not failed to see my noticeable embarrassment and was extremely shaken. She had only been in the legislature for less than a week, but she was smart enough to know her father just had been dumped. It made her cry and my anger multiplied ten-fold.

It was a long walk to the General and Military Committee room and though I knew where it was, I had never been in it. I was about to meet the "infamous" Mr. John Francis Murphy, known to many as simply "the General", and though I never would, in my wildest dreams, have imagined such a thing, I was about to embark on a friendship with another person I've never equaled before or since.

Because I had to spend some time with Suzanne, soothing her and trying my best to assure her everything was going to be all right, I was the last member into the committee room. I took the only empty seat remaining and fixed a glazed stare at the bulletin board across from me. Nobody seemed to be paying any heed and I was grateful for the small share of privacy. I wasn't noticing anyone, either.

Eventually I turned my attention to Murphy. He sat leaned back at the head of the conference table that served as our desk. Though the session had hardly begun, the table was littered with junk. Papers, bills (leftover from the last session), law books, a couple of cheap paperbacks and, barely discernible under the heap, a big, old tape recorder. Murphy appeared relaxed and very much at home amongst this mess.

If I had ever seen "Paddy's Pig", Murphy was it. He seemed as wide as he was long, short legs that didn't touch the floor even when he wasn't leaning back in his chair, hands that barely connected when across his belly, topped with a full head of thick beautiful hair. His face was the color of a perpetual blush.

I watched him as he went around the table asking everyone to introduce themselves. Since the General and Military Committee was reserved by the Speaker for "unknowing" freshmen and the "unruly" (like me), a majority of its members needed introductions. Each intro produced an intense stare from Murphy as if he was sizing everyone up. I later came to realize that was exactly what he was doing. After each spoke his or her name and where they were from, Murphy would mumble "Nice to have ya."

Across from me was a man, perhaps in his late fifties, smoking a pipe. He had a 1950s crew cut. Somehow it seemed an appropriate symbol for how far I had regressed.

To my left sat Bob Harris, one of the true characters in the legislature. He was now a returning veteran, having been defeated two years earlier by the same man he had just defeated and from whom he had taken away his seat. This was no small feat, for incumbency is as instrumental in the Vermont Legislature in maintaining the status quo as it is elsewhere. Harris had done it the hard way. He ran a campaign based on issues and his opponent's voting record. Frankly I had never seen this done before, nor have I seen it since.

I'll say it many times in this book, but all politics is personal. The vast majority of candidates can carry the day on personality alone. Districts are so small that the normal media used in other states is unnecessary here. Everybody tends to know everybody else and most know what issues one cares about. Yet, it still has to be worked at very carefully.

Members are survivors. Their true feelings are not always reflected in the voting record available to the public. Harris' target was a rock-ribbed conservative and his vote in committee reflected such. It didn't matter if the cause was assistance for the poor, blind, disabled, or veterans; it all met with a resounding "no" when taken in committee by this deliverer of doom. What the folks back home didn't know wouldn't hurt this guy, as up until now, committee votes had never been made available to the public.

Vermont is a small state with barely over 550,000 people. That's the total of men, women, and children, not voters. Each member consequently only represents about 3,750 constituents. I remember during one visit to Boston talking with Billy Bulger, President of the Massachusetts Senate, a true "Last Hurrah" if ever there was one. After mentioning to this re-incarnation of James Michael Curley that my District only contained 3,700 or so constituents, he, serving a district of tens of thousands came back with, "My God, I could take that many to lunch."

Day after day, during Harris' onslaught, his opponent had to defend his Neanderthal voting record in public. What he couldn't get printed in the *Windsor Chronicle,* Harris would never fail to bring up at a local forum. His opponent was bewildered. For if he tried to deny it, Harris was quick to pull out his committee voting roll call. There was a great difference between that record in committee and his opponents' floor votes.

A member's true thoughts are saved in the protective semi-privacy of the committee room. Many a card-carrying conservative is quick, for self-serving survival reasons, to cover their back ends on any vote taken on the floor. The folks back home get to know their Representative a lot better if they can read in the local paper how that Representative voted yesterday. Many local weeklies would carry that information. Thus a member who was quick to protect the taxpayers dollar like it was his own when the issue was in committee, started acting like a FDR Democrat when the same veteran's issue hit the floor. It didn't take long for Harris' victim to realize he was between a rock and a hard place. Harris had conveniently bypassed the more moderate vote on the floor and used the recorded committee's roll calls, generally thought to be hidden in the darkest recesses of the committee file cabinet. He had made the crucial mistake of underestimating Harris' comfort level with dark places.

But now as I watched Murphy, I became painfully aware, once again, I had my own dark place to deal with and it was called the General and Military Affairs Committee.

After introductions, Murphy explained how pleased he was with his new committee.

"There's a lot of very capable people on this committee" he began, though there were none here more capable than he, "and I want to make clear that each of you will be respected and utilized (by Murphy, of course) while you're a member of this committee. Everyone should feel they are an integral part of this entire process, and if there's anything you want to bring up, or any bill in which you're interested and feel this committee should bring up, all you have to do is raise your hand and speak up. Nobody's suggestions are too insignificant to get a fair hearing as long as I'm your Chair."

Harris' hand shot up.

"Ah! Mr. Harris. Nice to have you back. What can I do for you?"

"I move there be no smoking in the committee room."

The sudden tension in the air made me look up.

Murphy, glaring out of half closed eyes, shot back, "Mr. Harris, I'll make like I never heard that motion."

"Well, I'll say it a little God damned louder, General," Harris said, and he repeated the motion. You could cut the air with a knife as Murphy's chair slammed down on all four legs.

"Mr. Harris, you were trouble when you were in this committee two years ago and I can see that your little hiatus didn't serve to teach you very much. Why the people of your district get it all screwed up every other term only the good Lord knows, but we'll have none of your shenanigans in here for the next two years."

"Mr. Chairman, I believe I have a motion on the floor here. And let's make something perfectly clear before other members get the wrong idea. I consider my assignment to this committee a sentence to be served. I didn't ask to be here and I'm not too happy that I've been remanded here. Now, Oh Commandant, I respectfully request that you call the roll."

"O. K., Harris that's it. I'm going to see the Speaker," and he got up and stormed out of the room.

Well, I thought, this was certainly going to be different than Health and Welfare. I wondered if there was a back exit to this place.

3. MURPHY'S LAW

The irony of my appointment to the General and Military Affairs Committee was that this was going to prove to be the most enjoyable two years of my entire legislative career. John Murphy and his antics were worth the price of the ticket, and I looked forward to going to his committee. Even when I became Speaker and found myself with time on my hands to move around the building and visit with people that I normally would not have had time for, I always seemed to be drawn to Murphy's room. The committee itself was filled with characters right out of Li'l Abner. Harris and Murphy were the stars of this Off-Broadway comedy, and they never passed up an opportunity to torment one another. When they weren't after each other, they would team up against some other poor soul. Both were absolutely politically amazing. I swore they could be dropped at any City Hall or legislature in the country, and not only survive, but like cream, would rise to the top. Murphy was the more amazing of the two, and I never ceased to be impressed by an almost daily display of a new instinct or talent that came forth from him. Edgar May once explained to me Murphy had an uncanny ability to read the mood of the floor unlike anyone he had ever seen. He not only possessed that unique ability to read people, but he was able to assess the moods, desires, and motivations of large groups. I witnessed this first-hand dozens of times over the years, and I always was amused at those who underestimated Murphy. I never tried to guess what he would do in any given situation until he had made his intent obvious. That way, I might have ended up disappointed, but never surprised.

Several years later when I was Speaker, we were fighting to pass a gay rights bill and I had taken the unusual step to lobby the members myself. Normally the process would have been run through the Democratic Caucus with the leader and the whip taking responsibility for rounding up votes. Of all the duties of leadership, that was the primary one. The issue was an emotionally explosive one and it promised to divide the caucus in two, no matter what our efforts to avoid it. Even the liberals, who could be counted on to support the bill, were more than a little nervous about being on record in support of a bill guaranteeing equal rights in employment and housing for gays. Other members had religious or conscience objections. The major problem was that a large number of the caucus simply resented the bill as it aroused a homophobic atmosphere one literally could feel throughout the building. This was the second time we brought the bill out on the floor. Two years earlier the tension and animosity had grown to such proportions, I had the Chairman of the committee that was reporting the bill out pull it back. I truly felt for the only time in my tenure in the legislature an air of violence was evident. This time there would be no turning back. The bill was out of committee (you guessed it, Murphy's) and up for third reading. As Speaker, I could delay it for a day or two, but eventually it was going to hit the floor of the House and it didn't take a rocket scientist to predict there was going to be one hell of a debate and a roll call vote. Everybody, for better or worse, was going to have to stand up and be counted. It didn't help that Murphy's committee had voted it out adverse by 5-4. In addition, Murphy and the Vice Chair had voted against it. So here was this already badly crippled bill and one we could expect little help on from the members of the committee. In fact, Murphy had quietly vowed to get on his feet during debate and to fight against his own committee's bill.

Though the odds seemed stacked, I had a distinct advantage as the person responsible for garnering the necessary votes amongst the members. First and foremost, we were right on the issue. I believed gays were entitled to all the rights enjoyed by others. Secondly, I was the Speaker and had the leverage to buttonhole* the members.

I do not believe it is enough to simply be right on an issue. We had to be good and then it helped a great deal if it turned out that, in addition, we were "right." It never was enough for my little impatient soul to win the debate on the floor, only to end up with 45 votes. This was something over which I never stopped tearing out my hair. I had a large number of Democratic members who felt victory simply encompassed raising an issue. It didn't matter whether they won or lost. To many of them, the measure of the event was in the level of engagement. If that were true, Lee would have become President, not Grant. And, I might add, slavery would be a recent memory, not a distant one. In either case, I usually managed to talk some sense into my "Library Liberals", and we seldom ventured into deep waters as far as assuring ourselves that not only were we right, but "we had the votes." Votes didn't just show up at our door; we had to roll up our sleeves and go out and work for them. In legislative parlance, we had to work the floor. Members created every conceivable defense against my onslaught.

---

* *Buttonholing, in legislative parlance, refers to the Speaker's making it known to members that he or she has a commitment to a particular bill. On other occasions, it could mean that the Speaker's seeking out individual members, and with eye-to-eye contact, asking them to help on a particular item. Few members would ignore this type of "in-your-face" request.*

Common sense told me to stay away from some members. I knew their vote was coming from their conscience, and it didn't matter how wrong I felt their conscience was, I still had to respect their right to be wrong (only in America). On the other side, an equally large number agreed with the bill, and though they might be nervous about the political fallout, they would vote for it in the end. The battleground rested with the remaining members who felt in their hearts people shouldn't be discriminated against, but the politics of the situation were so explosive they were going to vote no. These were the members I sought.

Within 24 hours, I was in the mid-sixties. Passage required a majority of those present. If there was full attendance, 75 votes would do it. The Speaker, as one of 150, only voted to break or make a tie, which in the latter case meant the bill failed. No one ever could guess correctly what the attendance would be on any given day, but our exercise as a leadership team was to begin a running count the day of the vote. This would begin early in the morning and be updated constantly as to who was there and who wasn't, right up to the moment the roll call began. Missing members would be tracked down, assuming they were going to vote with us, and calls would go out to their home, business or car phone. We were diligent about it and this extra effort often made the difference.

Sixty-five or so votes weren't going to cut it, as the bill had generated such emotion that few, if any, would be absent. We were going to have to get our count into the low 70s if any measure of security was going to occur. It was common knowledge someone could get 40 or so votes in the House for any crazy idea. Getting to 75 was indeed a different task that took a good deal of effort. Usually this fell on the leaders' shoulders, but this time it was my sole responsibility. It was my rear end on the line and it didn't go unnoticed by the members or by the Press. The betting was it couldn't be done and, quite frankly, though I said nothing, I didn't disbelieve the handicappers. It was the tensest of times and I was pulling out all my tricks.

There were very few members I hadn't bailed out of a tough situation as Speaker. Whether it was a choice committee assignment or simply helping them move a bill from a reticent committee, a Speaker's day is filled with dozens of occasions for his or her power to be helpful to other members. A large majority of the delegation never failed to run to the Speaker when they thought the power and persuasiveness of the office could serve their purpose. I made it a rule I would never let even the most mundane of demands for help go unanswered. My criteria to judge just how far I would go to help a member was simple and straight forward: As long as it wasn't against the law, didn't require that I go to confession, or wouldn't break up my marriage, I did it. Thus it was it took a steely-nerved member with a short memory who could deny me a request for reciprocal help. This coupled with the fact I made it a point to ration the times I would do this, made my pressure all the more effective now.

More important than all of this was the image that had been created for me. The press, and many of my critics, never missed an opportunity to paint a "tough guy" picture of me. They were constantly referring to my background as a Marine and my upbringing. I was just a wise guy Boston Irish kid to many, who brought his street fighter style to Vermont politics. Though I died a thousand deaths with this noose, it was now proving to be helpful. Nobody dared get after me as they might have gotten after others with a more genteel background. Nobody dared call me a "queer lover." Some, I'm sure, thought it, but they were careful to keep such slop to themselves.

As I got closer to the magic number, the list of those I felt might be able to turn around grew smaller. Time was growing short and my frustration was building.

" Billy, can I talk to ya for a minute?" I said, as we bumped into each other just outside the Speaker's office. (Billy is a fictitious name.)

"Sure, Mr. Speaker," came the less than enthusiastic reply. Billy sensed he was about to be buttonholed.

"C'mon in the office for a second," I said. He followed like a kid headed for Mother Superior's shed.

"Now, Billy, you know I've been working my ass off trying to get enough votes to pass this gay rights bill and I need your help. I wouldn't ask you, but it's going to be an extremely tight vote. What do you say, can I count on you?"

"Geez, Mr. Speaker, I just can't give you a hand on this one," he said. "My district is dead set against me voting for something like this." He was nervous.

"Oh, for Chrissakes, Billy, you know as well as I that by the time next election comes around no one's going to remember this vote.* We're a year and a half from the next time you have to put your name on a ballot," I argued.

"They'll remember this one, Mr. Speaker. I've been getting a lot of mail and calls. This is a tough one." He said it with the confidence of a man winning an argument.

---

* *The public has about a 30-second concentration span and unless the Press reminds people 18 months later, something like a vote is seldom mentioned again. The Press, being generally liberal, would let it pass.*

"C'mon, Billy, I really need you on this one," I pleaded.

"Mr. Speaker, you know I'd do anything to help you out if I could but you know it isn't just my folks back home. Frankly, the bill just isn't right." That was the killer. He spoke now with the conviction of a used car salesman closing a deal for a lemon with sawdust in the transmission. He repeated this plea.

"It's just not right." Now at his best, his was the voice of an innocent alter boy.

Suddenly my mind flashed back to a rather famous "Tip" O'Neill tale and I ended the conversation by lashing out at him, paraphrasing the legendary U.S. House Speaker from Massachusetts:

"Billy, you ass, I don't need you when I'm right. I need you now."

I was up to 66.

I often would have trouble sleeping, especially if we were in a tough fight and we were counting votes. This was one of those times where I found myself waking up at four or five in the morning, often finding myself in the State House as early as 6 A.M. So it was the day of the vote on gay rights.

My efforts paid off in the sense I felt if every vote held, we'd win it. But there was no doubt it was going to be extremely close. There would be little margin for error. Attendance became important in a situation like this and I began counting as soon as I arrived at my office. As usual, only Michael "Obie" Obuchowski, my Appropriations Committee Chair from Bellows Falls, was there. I don't believe I ever beat him, no matter how early I arrived. I wandered through the building looking for members to buttonhole, the anticipation of the fight providing all the energy I needed. I was like a boxer in the locker room awaiting the call.

The debate was as contentious as any I had ever heard and I felt no sense of comfort over the entire two or three hour period. My practice of allowing the members to carry on until their hearts' content probably extended the arguments. I have little recollection of most of what was said, or by whom, but I do recall the eloquence of Francis Brooks from Montpelier, one of only two black members in the House. Francis stands out in my mind as a man of great integrity. Blessed with an imperturbable demeanor and a sense of fairness that was not that common among the rest of us, he commanded a respect from Democrats and Republicans alike. He spoke that day of the specter of fear...fear of being judged by others, not for who you were, but for your superficial characteristics. This fear of being judged was a lonely road few had traveled. The quiet that overtook the House said it all. It was apparent the members were moved by Francis' passionate plea.

I was feeling upbeat for the first time, but no sooner had Francis finished than my darkest nightmare came true. Out of the corner of my eye, I saw Murphy jump to his feet and heard the dreaded beckoning: "Mr. Speaker." God damn, Murphy. I don't think I had ever been as upset or felt a greater awareness of betrayal as I now felt towards John Murphy. He was going to bring the bill and us down, all by himself.

The liberals in the House groaned in apprehension as they braced for the anticipated gay bashing onslaught. I stood at the podium, and for a brief moment considered ignoring his request to be recognized. This was out of the question, of course, and I did the only thing left in my repertoire. I stared at him with a look of anger that he caught and reflected on, all in the same moment. Though we had no agreement he would stay out of the fight, he was well aware of all the effort I had made. Murphy had been quiet for over two hours and I was convinced he was going to pay me the courtesy of letting me win or lose it on my own. As close as I knew the vote was, I was certain this was a debate where crucial votes could be swayed by arguments from the floor. This didn't happen often, but there were rare examples of it occurring in the past.

"When Murphy jumped up, I said to myself, 'Oh, no, we're dead,'" Brooks reflected afterwards. As for me, I would have strangled him, if I could have reached the little sucker. I recognized him and he began his dialogue in, what was for him, an unusual, even voice. Murphy's words are worth repeating here:

"Mr. Speaker," he said, "I've always been a person of courage and conviction. As I listen today, I have searched my soul and found that I've been wrong. Very seldom have I come to that conclusion. In the past, I have done everything I could to kill the gay rights bills. In the past, I've been on the wrong side, Mr. Speaker. I've changed my mind. Today I hope to do what is right. I'm going to support this bill. I can assure my colleagues this bill isn't any different than those that I helped to kill in the past. It's me, Murphy, who's different." With that, he sat down into his seat.

The entire House sat in stunned silence.

I swore if I ever got to Ireland, I would fall to my hands and knees and kiss the sod that had grown John Murphy.

We went on to enact that bill into law and it stands as one of my proudest memories.

Later the Press tried to find Murphy's reason for his change of heart. They were half convinced that a deal had been made with me. Murphy had made a deal, that was a fact. But it was with someone a helluva lot more powerful than the Speaker.

4. THE RIGHT PLACE; THE RIGHT TIME

One soon learns life is filled with surprises. Perhaps this is the one ingredient the legislature offers that explains the addictive nature of politics. No day is exactly the same as another. In fact, days don't even come close to duplicating one another. Tim Corcoran, one of five other members from Bennington, and I, usually rode up together each week as he was experiencing a period of living with a one-car family. I would pick him up each Tuesday morning for the two and a half hour drive.

Of all the people I met during my years in Vermont, Corcoran was, without doubt, the most unforgettable character I came across. A fellow Democrat, he arrived in the legislature two years after I did. He lived, breathed and died politics. And, I swear, he was delivered on this earth that way. He didn't hang pictures of Mickey Mantle on his bedroom wall as a kid. He plastered his bedroom with John F. Kennedy posters. A Vermont native, he was an Irish Democrat who didn't know it and wasn't concerned about it. He never talked about his family, but I learned enough to decipher that his roots in Bennington over the generations were what would be considered "shanty Irish." Grandma Hogan changed bed sheets in aristocratic Old Bennington 50 years earlier and Corcoran unknowingly was destined to make amends. He wasn't a liberal Democrat, but rather what I refer to as a 1940 democrat (fiscally conservative and socially progressive on certain issues). He once told me he never read anything that didn't have his name in it. He has a high IQ, a near photographic memory, intensity and a love for a political battle. Elected a town selectman at the age of 21, his life was one political battle after another. Everything he did was calculated toward the fight to get re-elected. Most of the time he drove me crazy with his "no-tax , no spend" votes, but I learned over time I could get him to vote for something if I could place the problem right smack in front of him. I don't mean the issue, rather the person who would feel the impact of a vote. If I wanted his help on a foster program, for example, I would arrange for him to coincidentally run into a foster kid whom I just happened to have with me. People touched his heart, not theories. Corc could be trusted, not if WE believed in the deal, but only if *HE* believed in it. I would have to be smart enough to decipher whether he was truly committed or not. He'd make any deal, but only to where *HE* was headed. If we got left behind, it never really bothered him. If we responded angrily, he'd simply turn on his Irish charm. He might explain he didn't remember the arrangement or he might go do a nice deed for you or somebody you loved. Once, after an angry exchange, he bought my son a garden rake and a hoe. It didn't matter to him my son was living in a rented apartment, with no lawn, and had no notion what was occurring. That was Corc's way of saying, "I'm sorry." Few people managed to stay angry at him for any length of time. It drove us crazy. He was always scheming and he always had an angle.

One morning, about three weeks after I had been "dumped" into Murphy's committee, Corcoran came out of the house. He threw his clothes in the back seat and got in front.

"You can win it." No "good morning." No "hello."

"I can win what?"

"You can win the Caucus race for Democratic leader." Then, he opened the *Bennington Banner*.

And that's exactly what happened. A lot of politics is luck. That's a fact. Being in the right place at the right time makes up for a lot of deficiencies. I believe this was my basis for finding a respect for almost all but the most disreputable. I never hid my admiration for those who showed a willingness to grab the moment, perhaps risking all, and go for the "brass ring." Serving in the legislature only required one to be a resident of the district he or she represented and have reached the age of maturity. There are no IQ tests or beauty contests. It took something to get yourself elected, if only it was hard work or the courage to enter the fray. It often boiled down to simply being in the right place at the right time. So it was for me.

We weren't a month into the new session when our Democratic leader from Burlington, Judy Stephany, announced she was throwing her hat into the ring as a candidate for Mayor of Burlington, Vermont's largest city. This would be the second member of our leadership team to have stepped down since the session opened. Several weeks earlier, Althea Kroger, the Whip from Essex, had accepted a seat on the Appropriations Committee. This was one of those offers she "couldn't refuse" as the " good ole boy network" was intent on seeing to her removal as assistant Democratic leader.* Kroger's departure had witnessed a host of candidates for Whip, with Paul Poirier emerging the winner. I wasn't thinking in those terms at the time of the new Whip's race, as I was still trying to cope with my new committee, but a month's passage of time had gone far to heal my wounds and I was ready for a new battle. A battle is too soft a word for I was the sixth or seventh candidate to declare my candidacy.

* *They were still working on the "women's place was in the home" theory. Althea Kroger was young, smart and (God forbid) liberal. She was a Democrat, born and raised in Chicago.*

My biggest obstacle to winning was Paul. He decided after three weeks as assistant Leader, he was now ready for the top job. Paul never suffered from shyness or a sense of inferiority. It was Corcoran who put a quick and sudden end to Poirier's candidacy. Announcements, such as this, occurred in caucus, and Paul and I were two of the half-dozen who were present with our various backers at Tuesday's weekly meeting of Democrats. All of us made the announcement with no problem, or comments from our colleagues, except one. When Paul announced he failed to mention he would vacate his Whip's post in order to pursue the higher position, it was Corcoran who rose to his feet to protest that if Paul wanted to run for leader, in fairness to those of us who might reconsider and take a shot at the Whip's post, he should vacate his present position. Take one or the other, Corc said, but make up your mind. Paul was surprised and for a moment you could see he was weighing whether "a bird in the hand is worth two in the nest." He also was well aware there were six of us ready to do battle for the higher position.

Fate took control. Paul was every bit as talented as I, and a case can be made that even though it was only three weeks, he had a leg up with seniority. We had struck up a friendship those past few weeks, and I'm positive had things been reversed, I would have proven as loyal to him as he later proved to be to me. But Corcoran's quick move eliminated Paul as he chose to maintain his safe seat. I went on to win the leadership post, but it was a discouraged and disparaged minority I inherited. Sixty-five members in this rag tag army ran the gamut from despair to uncaring.

It wasn't a unanimous victory as not everyone thought I had leadership qualities. Beyond that, the Caucus, which had been controlled by this "good old boy" network for as long as anyone could remember, had grave worries about my "reliability." I wasn't someone whom they felt confident they could trust to do the expedient thing. I had shown a great propensity to push my own ideas, and my willingness to make politics a partisan war at every opportunity, left many with a great feeling of apprehension. Besides, I made no secret I was a liberal through and through, whose idea of government was to have no purpose other than to help those in need. This, to them, meant high crime.

I only added to their misgivings with my reputation as a fighter. This was constantly evident during my first four years in the legislature by my willingness to rise to my feet on the floor of the House at the slightest provocation.

I carried this to an extreme one night by actually engaging in a fist fight with one of the multitude of state workers who would frequent that lounge. (There's no point now in naming him.) It was just one of those things neither of us should be proud of, and I mention it only because it was a factor in my gaining a reputation of a man who was always on the verge of being out of control.

We had been the minority party for just short of 200 years. Vermont was known as a Republican state and Democrats in the House acted like the Washington Generals, the team that loses to the Harlem Globetrotters year after year. Patsies. I hadn't articulated it in my mind at this point in my political journey, but things were changing. Actually they had changed already, but no one had gotten it yet.

My Caucus consisted of three groups:

Group #1: "Good ole boys." This group went along to get along. They had no agenda and no partisan fighting. They were not unhappy to be second level partners with the Republicans. Group #2: "Young Turks." They were relatively young and combative and loaded down with agenda.

Group #3: "Grandstanders." This group encompassed all the rest. They were not terribly interested in issues, but always had their fingers to the wind. Cause and country were bound by day-to-day loyalties. They enjoyed a good fight as long as they weren't involved.

I saw an excellent example of how familiar some of the Dems were with "rolling over" shortly after I became minority leader. The Republicans had a bill on the floor that loosened up a handful of regulations for the benefit of the electric power companies. It was a fight made for us as it was so blatantly slanted to profit big business. The power company lobbyists didn't make any attempt to hide their disdain for our point of view. This only served to motivate us to a higher level of combativeness.

It was a glorious battle. I don't believe I ever carried myself nobler in a floor debate. Back and forth we went with the two Republican leaders receiving delivered notes from lobbyists sitting in the gallery. Their cannon was direct at me. I put up the fight of my life parrying their interrogations with target striking points. I murdered them that day and after an hour or more of debate I slumped in my seat, exhausted from battle, to await a decision I was certain meant a well-deserved victory for the good guys. When they called the roll, I had been trounced something like 91 to 55. Give me a break! We had 65 Democrats.

I was devastated and hot as hell.

After any fight such as this, the normal procedure is to accept the "good try, better luck next time" compliments and then go off to lick your wounds. On the way out, Carmel Babcock, a Democrat from Burlington, came by and embraced me.

"Oh, Ralph, you were wonderful. I wish I could have expressed myself as eloquently as you did. You won every point and I was moved to tears when you mentioned the poor, especially the children."

"Thanks, Carmel." And then it struck me

"Hey ! Wait a minute, Carmel, you voted against me. Why'd ya do that?"

"Ralph, you were going to lose anyway. I thought I'd go with the winner."

Welcome to the real world, Ralphie. I might have had 65 Democrats in body, but there were only 55 in spirit. I didn't have to know higher math to realize we had more than just a numbers problem. I could safely add to this undeniable and unpleasant fact that we had a defeatist attitude to go with it.

Paul Poirier and I became close friends over the next two years, a friendship that has grown even stronger over a decade later. But again, it was fate or luck that brought us together. We sat next to each other. This meant little, prior to our becoming leaders within a three-week period, but once it occurred it proved to be bad news for the opposition. Now we constantly had two minds working all the time. Instead of one of us having a thought and waving for a page to send a note to the other, we simply had to turn in our chair. This was important, for unlike Congress, all the floor action in the Vermont Assembly is with near full attendance of the members. It's where the action is and I've always felt the members of Congress were missing out on the vitality and knowledge that assembling each day as a group would afford them.* I know I learned to follow the members or, better still, the handwritten notes as both moved through the well of the House. This human inter-action, if observed, closely went far in explaining what was happening—really happening—amongst the members. A knowledge of body language also was invaluable. Little things meant a lot.

I was sitting up in my back row seat late one evening and I was alone, except for Murphy, who sat almost directly across from me on the other side of the hall. I slipped in quietly through the side door and he, being pre-occupied with something at his desk, didn't notice my presence.

I was writing and noticed Murphy getting up and waddling along the raised platform that was situated on each side of the podium. He

*This is one of the vital ingredients that makes up one of America's last "citizen legislatures", as compared to professional lawmakers in most other states and Congress. This has the same "eye-to-eye" impact as any other communications between people.

turned at the rostrum to exit out the ramp leading to the back of the building where the Speaker's office was located. He didn't just turn and exit, but halted prior to pushing through the red curtains. He was looking around. I could see him, but because of his short stature, the podium blocked me from his view. He then moved back, approaching the podium. He reached down under the podium, grabbed something, and in one quick motion, stuffed whatever he had taken into his coat pocket and left abruptly through the curtains. Curious? I certainly was.

I waited a moment and then got up and headed for Murphy's committee room which was just a few yards through a hallway in the west wing of the building. He was sitting, facing me as I entered the room, filing through a small pile of crumbled up notes. I put two and two together.

"Murphy," I half shouted, "I saw what you just did. Let me see what you got there."

Murphy grabbed the notes and stuffed them in his pocket, reacting defensively.

"What are you talking about?"

"Never mind the bullshit, Murphy. I saw you take those notes out of the Speaker's wastebasket." I had him and he knew it.

"Listen, Wright, keep your mouth shut. Close the door. C'mere, I'll show you what I've got."

I spent a minute reading. "What the hell are you doing going through people's trash? These are just all the crap notes Morse gets from his ass kissers during the day."

Murphy responded with that air of excitement that came over him every time he was into the devil. "Wright, if you're going to amount to anything in this place, then you better learn how things work around here." He was lecturing to his student.

"The Speaker knows everything, that's why he's powerful. That podium is like the great communications center in the sky. Nothing happens without it going through the Speaker. If they're dumb enough to put things in writing, then he's dumb enough to throw it in the basket. That's what he does every day and that's what I do every day. I know everything he knows and he doesn't know anything I know. I know who's sending him dumb jokes, who's passing love notes to him (Morse was single at the time), who's asking when they should get up to speak, what the arguments are going to be and so on. I know as much as one can know without actually being Speaker. Information is knowledge and knowledge is power." A big Cheshire cat grin exploded across his red face.

I never threw a note in the basket once I became Speaker.

Paul Poirier and I didn't win much of anything over the ensuing months, but we were learning a great deal.

The next two years flew by. Leadership was in many ways a seat-of-the-pants operation, at least for us. Paul and I took each day one at a time and often we were totally unaware of events until they were upon us. This is where our friendship and proximity in seating paid huge dividends. Our personal bond meant we felt a deep enough trust for each other that allowed each of us to give the other free reign to use whatever talents we possessed. We were constantly observing and questioning whatever was in front of us. Being seat mates, we had the opportunity to discuss and analyze what we heard and saw. As was his style, Morse made sure we were never privy to what was really going on in the back room cabals that were a constant in the Speaker's office and the corner office occupied by the Governor. Still, not much got by us.

Our only brush with the rich and powerful came at Leadership Meetings. Protocol called for a Friday morning Leadership meeting with the Governor and the House leaders. Senate leaders met at another time. We would all gather together around the huge table in Gov. Richard Snelling's ceremonial office in the State House and spend 30 minutes or so under the pretense of listening to each others views. The meetings really amounted to Gov. Snelling giving us his views on the "state of the state." The Speaker never failed to pay deference to him nor did Susan Auld, the majority Whip. Bob Kinsey, the Republican leader, was a different story altogether. Perhaps it was something in the chemistry, or maybe it was a matter of divergent philosophy, but those two could light up each others tempers. Snelling was renown for his short fuse. In any case, it all served as an omen for future events, as Kinsey was eventually going to break with Snelling on raising taxes to help pay off a deficit. It was a bold move by Kinsey to be sure, but I think, with the privilege of 20/20 hindsight, it was this breaking of ranks that cost Kinsey the Speakership two years later.

As for Paul and me, we had little to say at any of these meetings, mostly because we weren't privy to information Morse and Snelling had and consequently didn't know anything. I should have realized not knowing anything about a topic never kept a politician from talking at great length, but we enjoyed watching them get into discussions that inevitably ended up in heated arguments. Snelling would always win, but not before interrupting, or in some other way embarrassing Morse or Auld. Kinsey, always more willing to talk back or disagree, often angered Snelling and/or the Speaker. Auld for the most part, sat quietly or tried to please. The end result was we never resolved anything of substance. We took it for the measure that it was worth, entertainment, and thus looked forward to this weekly exercise in bickering. We simply leaned back, said nothing, and watched the sparks fly.

We had a numbers problem, being in the minority, 85-65. There was nothing Paul or I could do about that until the next election in November, 1984 but the attitude problem was another issue and we searched desperately to try and reverse this acceptance of losing that permeated the souls of too many of our members. It was no light task and we needed a break somewhere along the way. We got one shortly into the first year of the biennium: The University of Vermont (UVM) Trustees election.

Morse made a classic mistake and broke one of what I consider the cardinal rules of power: *Never put your name on any more secret ballots than you have to.* If you're lucky enough to have won a seat of power, then be grateful for what you have. Enjoy and nurture it. To most of us, power is like love in that people can never get enough of it. The Speaker announced he would be a candidate for the University of Vermont Board of Trustees. This election occurred every year at a joint meeting of the legislature. Of all the different ways a politician can get himself in a pickle, this type of election would serve as the worst. It was an exercise with dozens of moving parts, each one, if not understood, certain to suck a pol into a cavern of defeat. All 180 members had a vote, Senator and House member alike. There might be six or seven candidates running for perhaps two seats. We could withdraw or withhold our candidacy at any time depending on our strategy, or the deal made with another candidate. The unwritten rules, not always adhered to, said that if there were two open seats, tradition dictated one went to a Republican and the other to a Democrat; one to a senator, the other to a house member. Entering this contest was like taking the place of that guy who keeps all the dishes spinning on the tops of the sticks. You'd better be fast or prepare for the crash of dishes.

Speakers are powerful creatures. Their very stature high above the crowd up at the podium is a constant reminder of this special place they hold in the political world. Deference is paid at every turn or, as my grandson Matt characterized it, "he's the man with the hammer." Woe befall those who openly attempt to bring him down.

But this was a secret ballot, a matter between only you and your priest, an instrument of God to insure a semblance of humility in mankind.

There are members who absolutely hate the person in power simply because they resent people who have power. Even among one's loyal brigade there can be a certain solace to the mighty being humbled from time to time. Therein lay Morse's dilemma. All we had to do was find an opponent envied less than Morse, and time our entrance onto the ballot that coincided with our attributes concerning party affiliation and house.

We found the perfect candidate in Senator Edgar May. Once we called him on his sick bed and convinced him that not only could he win, but he could continue his recovery from the flu as Paul and I would do the bulk of his campaigning for him. He gave his somewhat reluctant "OK" to our pushing his candidacy. He stayed home and recuperated and we went to work making sure that we got a House Republican elected first. Lots of members took a silent joy in knowing this was not just another Trustees election, but a real political battle.

When the smoke cleared, we had vanquished the mighty. The morning headline reported *"A Rising Star Had Fallen."* I suspect Morse always regretted jumping into that contest, but even the most bitter of defeats dissipates and life returns to normal. But for us, the Democratic leadership, we had proven, given the right circumstances, we could win. That attitude change we so desperately were looking for was beginning to turn. A slow laborious turn, but like a huge aircraft carrier at sea, it was turning.

5. The Great Number Plate Caper

Maybe it's the Irish in me, but my last refuge in tight situations is humor. Speaker Morse didn't have much humor in his repertoire. Perhaps he didn't see us as very funny people. The great number license plate caper helps to better explain .

Each member of the legislature is assigned a numbered seat. They are numbered, not because, as some have claimed, most of us need it to find our way to our seat each day, but rather as one of the few perks that is afforded by Vermont to its citizen legislature. Our license plate corresponds to our seat number. Mine was House 132, Paul's was House 133 and so on. The Speaker was assigned House 1. Members would actually vie to get into a seat with a low number and, thereby, to their way of thinking, increase their prestige on the byways of the state.

I found the opposite to be true years later when I proudly displayed "House 1." I began getting the middle finger salute from perfect strangers. I stopped displaying that symbol of high rank after my wife, Cathy, reported angrily from North Carolina her travel south that day was uneventful except for the rude gentleman on I-95 who gave her the same greeting I had been receiving in Vermont. Within days I got rid of the plate and my car went back to being just an ordinary vehicle.

Someone with a rather different sense of humor took it upon themselves to remove Speaker Morse's plates. This caper was done at night and to add to the Speaker's dilemma, he didn't notice it until days later when he had returned to his own district. Someone pointed out he didn't have any license plates on his car. To protect his decorum, Morse said nothing about it, but quietly chose to replace the plates. This was a simple matter for a Speaker, as all he had to do was have his assistant call the Motor Vehicle Department and the new plates were hand delivered by one of the clerks. It did cost an additional $32 and that, I'm sure, didn't do much to lighten Morse's mood.

Everything was fine for a few weeks. Morse took special precautions, diligently checking to be sure his plates were where they should be each morning as he left his apartment and rechecking each evening as he left the State House. As an added measure of security, he took pains to keep secret where he and his car would be each evening. It all seemed to be working quite well until the night of a Judiciary Committee party when his assistant received a rather urgent call shortly after the Speaker left to rendezvous with a few friends to car pool out to Stowe for the committee dinner party. The caller was from a TV station asking where they might find the Speaker. They hoped to get a statement on a legislative matter for the 6 P.M. news. Though the assistant was reluctant, she told the caller if he hurried, he could catch him at Rep. Ed Zuccaro's apartment, where they were shortly departing in order to meet the rest of the group. Zuccaro was a Morse lieutenant. The culprits, safely ensconced at one of the local pubs, ordered another drink, and after a leisurely delay, they casually made their way up the hill to Zuccaro's rented apartment. Morse's car sat there in all its splendor. The House 1 plates, in the eyes of the petty thieves, might as well have been in flashing neon. Out came the burglar's tools of the trade and off came the Speaker's brand new number plates.

These guys were not your normal run of the mill burglars and, with the plates in hand, they hustled off to the exclusive restaurant in Stowe. Under cover of darkness, the culprits methodically removed a plate from two other legislator's cars, who at that unsuspecting moment, were inside enjoying the comraderie, and attached one of the Speaker's plates as a replacement on each and then proceeded back to Zuccaro's apartment. There, they promptly put a House 7 plate on the front of Morse's car and the other plate on the back of his car. They returned to the local watering hole and settled in to a well-deserved after dinner drink.

Upon discovery the next morning, the repeat theft was more than Morse could endure and he immediately took the unusual measure of rising on a point of personal order. This was not funny, he assured us all from the podium. In fact, it was beyond the point where it was any longer just a prank. It came close to being a crime and he was going to get to the bottom of it all.

Early morning is not the best time to catch a crowd on the floor of the House, but the small group of members who were present were somewhat taken back by the angry and accusatory tone of Morse's tale of woe. Some hadn't the foggiest idea of what he was talking about; others were amused. Most had their curiosity piqued, and spent the day joking and laughing about the incident. The case of the missing plates was beginning to compare favorably to Captain Queeg and the missing strawberries.

It didn't take long for Evie, the Speaker's assistant, to find me in the cafeteria, and in a solemn voice, announce the Speaker would like to see me in his office—*Pronto.* To be so beckoned to the Speaker's office didn't happen often and I quickly hurried up the back stairs and entered only to find Poirier already seated. This was something special indeed.

Having no idea what calamity had struck, I waited for Morse to explain. I caught a faint smirk on Paul's face.

"O. K. You guys know why you're here."

"As a matter of fact, I don't," I answered .

"Well, as a matter of fact," he said, sarcastically, "I want to know where my number plates are."

No response. We both sensed if we had dared look at each other we'd burst out laughing.

" Look guys, a joke's a joke," he said a bit softer, " and I can deal with a joke that's all in good fun as well as the next guy, but this has gone too far. I'm missing a set of plates and it cost me $32 to replace them. But it's become more serious than that. If this keeps up, we'll have half the members riding around with somebody else's plates. That's illegal and worse still, it's embarrassing to this body. I've asked the State Police to get to the bottom of this and if they find who did this, and I'm sure they will, that person's going to have some serious legal problems." Then in his best impersonation of a junior high school principal, he said, "I know you guys had something to do with this."

It was time to act. Leaning forward in my chair and speaking in an angry tone, I responded.

"Listen here, Morse, I resent being dragged in here like we're a couple of seventh graders and being accused of some high crime you've dreamed up. I don't know about Paul, but I've got better things to do than sleaze around lifting your, or anyone else's, number plates. The fact is Zuccaro or one of your other buddies are probably the guys who ought to be sitting here, not us. If this is all so embarrassing, it's you that's made a mountain out of a mole hill. You've got everybody buzzing around the building giggling and laughing."

I could tell he had calmed down and he quickly recanted.

"Look, I'm not accusing you. I just thought if you heard anything you might tell them enough's enough. I'd like to get my plates back and that will be the end of it."

"Well," interjected Paul, "I feel just the same as Ralph. I resent being accused of this."

"I didn't mean I think you did it, Paul. I just need some help in putting a stop to it." He was almost pleading now.

"We'll keep up eyes open," I said, and with that we got up and left.

 The next day began like any other. The guest clergy took four or five minutes to lead us in religious services. This was followed by the normal four or five minutes of housekeeping between the Speaker and the Clerk as they got the resolutions and bills in order for the day's agenda. Meanwhile the House was filling up faster than normal. This was unusual and only happened when the word would spread that something was happening on the floor that was not the normal sedate beginning of a day's session. Members filed in, took their seats, and leaned to their seat mates inquiring as to what was going on. Morse stood preoccupied, conferring with the clerk. Then, as if a message from heaven were forthcoming, all eyes slowly moved to the upper corners of the hall. There, hanging from the necks of the twin statues, were two plates with the number *HOUSE 1*.

6. A CHANGING PLACE

Steven Morse was a good Speaker. He was bright, aggressive, and understood the principles of power. He was also the last Speaker in what was to become "old Vermont." The Green Mountain State had a centuries old reputation of being a hardscrabble backwater place people had to endure simply to survive. But Vermont was also recognized for its fierce independence and rigid conservatism. Things were changing now; perhaps not rapidly enough to be noticeable to the politically untrained eye, but critical scrutiny detected a shift and this meant a drastic change.

The government was still dominated by the Republican party and that was evident in the clear majorities that party held in both the House and Senate, but these were no longer overwhelming majorities. Where once a description of a Democratic meeting hall was depicted as a telephone booth, it was now something requiring a bigger space.

Any analysis of this evolutionary change that was becoming apparent in 1983 was clearly traceable to events that occurred in the 1960s and early 1970s. A major breakthrough hit like lightning in 1962 when Phil Hoff, a young and handsome liberal Democrat, astounded the placid and staid Vermont political scene by eking out a narrow victory over the Republican "kid Governor" Ray Keyser. "King Philip", as the upstart and fledgling Democratic party dubbed him, was the first Democrat to become governor since before the Civil War. His path had been paved four years earlier by the surprisingly strong showing of Bernard Leddy. Democrat Leddy lost that year to then-Governor Bob Stafford, but many were surprised by the closeness of the race.

Now Hoff had won and the Republicans, had they been more astute, would have been smart to drop everything and analyze the problem. Instead, they dismissed the entire affair as an aberration, a one time misfire a slight correction in windage would serve to bring all back on target.

There was, if not a simple explanation, an explanation which took shape during the early part of the 1962 campaign. Squabbling within the Republican party over a race track in the southwest town of Pownal took form in the creation of two or three different groups. Gov. Keyser jumped in with one of the groups, thereby leaving the others out in the cold. One of those groups was led by T. Gary Buckley, a Bennington local, who later became Lt. Governor. He bested (by one vote in a legislative run-off), the Democrat who had won the popular vote in

November, but had failed by a handful to get the necessary majority required by the state constitution. Buckley was no novice local pol, but a streetwise guy who thought in huge dimensions. But that wasn't his greatest asset, as he had shown time after time he enjoyed the fight as much as the cause. He was absolutely fearless when it came to engaging the opponent. And now, his group set out to respond to the sitting Governor. Maintaining their cloak of Republicanism, they formed a third party. Unfortunately for Governor Keyser, the upstart Hoff snatched this Independent Party's nomination and had his name on the ballot as both a Democrat and an Independent. When the results were totaled in the early morning hours after the polls had closed, it appeared Keyser had won a narrow victory, but this was turned into bitter defeat when the 1,500 or so Independent votes were added to Phil Hoff's totals. That was the end of Keyser, and the beginning of a revolution that is still playing out in Vermont.

To many people, the shock of Hoff becoming Vermont's first Democratic governor in over a century didn't register as anything more than an anomaly in the Republican scheme of things. Indeed, things seemed to return to a period of "normalcy" after Hoff left the governor's suite in 1968 and was replaced by Republican Deane C. Davis. But even this showed portents of an undercurrent that was fermenting just below the Vermont political surface.

Though Davis seemed to be a "safe Republican", he was anything but, as he danced to no political party tune. He pushed through a realignment of government that further dispensed the "old way", and then startled even those who knew him best. Davis forced through Act 250, a protective device to Vermont's cherished environment in statute that placed this tiny state in the forefront of the nation's effort to protect all we knew to be beyond replacing.

Lightning struck again in 1972. A young and attractive lawyer from the small river town of Bellows Falls announced his candidacy for governor. The fact that Thomas P. Salmon was a socially conscious Democrat wasn't what startled the inner ranks of the political hierarchy; it was that Salmon barely beat the deadline for filing that caught people by surprise. To say he was a late entry to oppose the Republican choice, Luther Hacket, was an understatement. Consequently, few gave him a prayer of upsetting his opponent, including Democrats.

Nobody, that is, but Salmon himself.

Norrie Hoyt, who served in the Davis Administration as a deputy commissioner in the tax department, was also a close friend and avid supporter of Salmon. It was Hoyt who recognized the growing pressure on the average Vermonter's wallet, placed there by the ever-demanding property tax. He felt certain the high cost of education and its subsequent drain on the local property tax had to be addressed. Salmon knew an issue when he saw it. His response to this major problem was what we now know as the Property Tax Rebate Program. Salmon, recognizing its simplicity and promise, took it "on the road" to the people.

The rebate program has been a winner for over 20 years, and on election night in 1972, so was Tom Salmon—the second Democrat to be elected governor in over 100 years.

As I was a world away during these events, I had no idea that 20 years later all these happenings were going to make it possible for me to become the only minority Speaker in the country.

It's safe to say the 1960s changed America and changed Vermont no less. It was during this period that Vermont witnessed a great in-migration from south of its border, primarily Massachusetts, Connecticut, and the urban and suburban New York City areas. The population of Vermont in 1960 was 377,747. By 1995, it was 562,758. Who were these new Vermonters?

For the most part, they were young, restless and looking for a simpler way of life. Raised in urban areas, they were the beneficiaries of a good education and a family tradition that believed fervently in the premise that each generation, committed to hard work, could provide a better life for their children. Their parents worked hard to guarantee they would get the education that Mom and Dad couldn't. This hard work, coupled with the G.I. Bill, fostered opportunities for them beyond their parents' dreams. But as opportunity increased, it was accompanied by the collapse of the cities. What was once a relatively safe haven for their own young years, no longer seemed to serve as a good place to raise their children. This was the generation that composed the brigades for the New Frontier, and issues beyond Vietnam and civil rights were important. There were other things that made a life worth living and few came without an agenda that placed issues such as education and environment at the fore- front. Besides, Vermont was an uncrowded oasis where one could still lean over the edge of a brook and drink from the water, or walk the dog along thousands of miles of dirt roads. It was a safe place, seemingly free of drugs and crime so prevalent in the hot-topped cities. All that was required was the courage to pack up and go, and a job.

The job made all the difference. Nobody ever moved to Vermont who was earning $11 per hour in a factory in Lowell, Boston, or Bridgeport, only to find the same job paid $7 per hour in Brattleboro or Bennington. One might ride the wave of security and prosperity afforded by a union in New York City, but Vermont was devoid of union activity. Those who crossed into Vermont had employment waiting for them. They were, by a huge majority, professionals, or college educated budding entrepreneurs. A small inn or a vacant loft to create arts and crafts were just what they were searching for, and the fact they could have 20 acres attached made it all appear to be a dream come true.

Some came to the crushing reality a college education didn't make the local help any more responsible and a maid who failed to come into work didn't mean the toilets didn't have to be scrubbed or the beds made. Regardless, this was a land of town meetings and small schools that concerned citizens could delve into with all their heart and know they were making a difference. Life couldn't be better and one person *did* count. Only in Vermont, or so it seemed.

Their parents' politics followed them. They may have failed to register as a voter back in the city, but here it was a community responsibility that was embraced wholeheartedly. Surprisingly, no one asked them what party they belonged to and it became popular to profess with pride when cornered, "I'm an independent- with a small I." But history dictated differently. Many never lost their Boston or New York accents, and despite the change in scenery, they were the children of their parents' politics, and this meant they were Democrats. They were enlightened and educated Democrats to be sure, but when forced to make a public declaration, they were Democrats. They might be waylaid and non-practicing Catholics. That's what they were born to be and that's how they would leave this world. So it was with a political party, and though it might take some special effort, or a heated political discussion over wine and candlelight, they stuck with what they felt comfortable and had been taught by their parents. There were some that had undergone a revelation or simply had a need to think differently about how government ought to work, but these few served as the exceptions to the rule.

To the large majority of newcomers, government was good, and if not good, then certainly necessary. This was especially true if concerned citizens were going to muster the muscle to protect themselves from the large corporate entities that were, through their bigness, threatening the things they held close to hearts. Only Uncle Sam could match the corporate bulk and they attached a faith in their government's willingness to get involved.

Even if they hadn't gotten involved to the degree that freed their conscience, hadn't it been but a small group of their very own that changed the course of history by bringing even the colossal government around to its way of thinking in Vietnam, Civil Rights, and the war against poverty? Government might have to be kept in check or constantly watched, but it was always thought to be an ally that could stand by the side of those who needed it.

Native Vermonters, if shaken at this great influx of flatlanders, seldom appeared alarmed. It was they who were reaping the profits on the sale of this hardscrabble land. An acre of pristine Vermont land in the Northeast Kingdom was selling for as much as $60 as late as 1965. And if that was an outrageously high price for you, down in the southern part of the state you could find city folks who would pay as much as $500 per acre.

Farmers, tired of scratching out a barebones living from the rocky soil, finding their children leaving by the droves to more populated centers offering a nine- to-five jobs, and always doing endless chores, were more than happy to sell newcomers a hundred acres or so. Aiding and abetting this trend were the developers who bought large plots from the same farmer with an eye to a patchwork of one acre lots and the clink of the cash register. The farmer consoled himself it wasn't just the endless toil that was breaking him, it was the plain and simple arithmetic of running a small dairy farm. A farmer just couldn't make a living anymore, that is unless he was willing to modernize and keep up with the big farmers who owned the Hood's bulk milk trucks. That took investment capital this prudent farmer wasn't willing to sign on the line for. It must have seemed that all of Vermont was for sale to the casual eye traveling through Vermont in the 1960s.

Little noticed, but destined to have an impact on Vermont's future, was legislation working its way through the General Assembly. If ever small bills carried a great wallop, it was the ones requiring bulk tanks, and its legislative twin designed to clean up the unsanitary conditions that existed in the dairy barns.

The bulk tank bill was aimed at keeping the bacteria count at acceptable health levels. It required standing milk be kept refrigerated while awaiting the milk producers tanker that would carry it to the processing plant. The bulk tank was not inexpensive as the cost could go as high as $5,000. For many small farmers, this was equal to a year's income, thus the hundreds of farms milking small numbers of cows found themselves with a lose-lose decision. The only solution was to go to the local bank, hat in hand, and talk their way into debt. Or, they could show those cityfolk the back forty. Many chose the latter.

The second bill, no less devastating, was referred to as the cement floor bill. Every farmer with a wooden floor barn in Vermont was affected. Wood, it was argued, was the great carrier of waste and germs as it is difficult to wash down. Within a set circle of time, farmers were going to be required to replace their wood floors with newly laid cement. Expensive in its own right, it was impossible in 100-year-old barns that utilized ramps to house cows on the second floor. The weight of the new flooring could not be withstood by the old timbers shoring up the barns. Nobody knows the number, but the casualty rate among dairy farmers grew larger.

It wasn't easy to decipher, but the old Vermont line about being a place that "had more cows than people" was about to become passé.

There was one last segment to what now appears to have been a great upheaval in the Vermont tradition that had held fast since the beginning of its recorded history. In 1965, the Vermont General Assembly held its longest legislative session. (I was to come recklessly close to that record in 1994 as Speaker.) It re-apportioned, under the threat of Federal mandate, its House and Senate. Nothing would prove so instrumental in overcoming the Republican way of life as this momentous effort.

Throughout its history of electing its legislators, Vermont followed the rule of "one town, one legislator." Now the law of the land dictated "one man, one vote." It was to change the face of Vermont politics forever.

I was not a member of the Legislature when re-apportionment took place, but veterans of that era described it to me in heart-tugging detail. A member's district is as sacred as his homestead. Like a man's land, the politician spends every available moment roaming over it making sure all is well. Broken fences have to be mended. The tenants of this measured political parcel have to be forever aware that the sire cares about their welfare.

Across the nation, those involved in politics and government knew the law was to cause grave repercussions in the way things were done in the electoral process. No one could predict with any degree of certainly how drastic the change would be.

Vermont, with its citizen legislature, was hardly immune. Beyond mastering the art of political campaigning, the Supreme Court decision demanding that all elections be based upon a premise of "one man, one vote", forced a tidal wave of change on the human make-up of the legislature.

When the 1965 legislature convened, the House members knew six months hence, upon passage of the re-apportionment act, the size of their membership would be reduced from 246 (the number of incorporated Vermont cities, towns and hamlet) to 150 members. Ninety-six of them would bear witness to their own political demise. Grown men actually wept on the floor of the House to save their political souls.

While the personal price paid for re-apportionment was high, it did not match the price paid by the small towns, for the most part perched alongside the north-south ridge of the Green Mountains running through the entire state. They lost much of their voice in Montpelier and the state was now run by the bigger towns and cities where the bulk of the population was centered. Burlington, the state's largest city, went from a lone representative intuitive to 11 others. Others cities like Rutland, Bennington, Brattleboro, White River Junction and a few others, saw their political numbers grow proportionally. The political repercussions seemed endless.

I did take part in re-apportioning as a member, but it was to draw up 150 new districts for a sitting group of 150. This meant drawing new lines to fit the latest census and though it brought about bitter partisan in-fighting, the entire process didn't change more than 30 percent of all the districts. Less than a dozen were affected to the degree that a member was at risk of losing his or her district. That wasn't the case in 1965.

The only members guaranteed to maintain their districts as they were during the previous election, were the handful that represented a town that happened to have almost exactly the number of men, women, and children as required by federal law. There might have been four or five such lucky ones. All the rest were thrown into what, to them, was a foreign land. Some found their little piece of power (the town in which they lived), only might represent 10 percent or less of the total inhabitants of the entire new district.

If a member was lucky in any respect, it might be that he or she shared a district with a neighboring legislator who was in the same boat. At least in these uncommon cases, they shared an equal spot behind the "eight ball." The major problem for not quite 100 of the 246 members was they were not going to be returning, no matter how the new map was drawn. Districts they had ruled for years because they were popular or prosperous no longer existed. Now they often found themselves poised to compete in areas where, in some cases, they did not know a soul. If they weren't familiar with the politics of campaigning, and many were not, they found themselves pondering retirement. Nothing in Vermont political history would prove equivalent to this as far as changing the nature of getting elected was concerned. Members were going to have to familiarize themselves with the art of campaigning if they were going to survive.

I recall getting involved in redistricting in 1981 during my second term. In compliance with federal law, the legislature was required to draw a new map every 10 years in accordance with the census. At that time, each district was approximately 3,400 men, women, and children and though the Congress allowed for a 10 percent variance, they referred to it as the deviation factor, it was a task that, at best, could be described as tedious. If one liked map drawing back in elementary school and could couple this with a Machiavellian political nature, then they'd love drawing political re-apportionment maps. I was interested in maps, politics, and Machiavelli. This, coupled with the fact that the preliminary draft had my home district losing a seat to the benefit of Speaker Morse's county, supplied all the motivation necessary for me to get involved.

As it turned out, we managed to save the Bennington seat and short circuit Morse from gaining at our expense over the mountain in Windham County. I also recall that, in so doing, we forced two sitting Republicans into the same district, thereby inciting one to call me a very dirty name after losing the fight for survival on the floor. I spent many enjoyable hours drawing dozens of maps and the hard work paid off.

The knowledge gained was going to reap even greater benefits 10 years later, as for the first time in the history of re-apportionment, Democrats were in charge of the process. As Speaker, I chose the committee responsible for drawing up the bill to be presented to the entire body and I chose carefully. The major effort was left to the Government Operations Committee which had a 7-4 Democratic majority. I appointed Don Hooper as Chairman and made sure the other Dems were aware of the once-in-a-decade opportunity that had been handed to them. I guess the best way to describe the year long process is to ask you, the reader, to imagine a group of 11 master chess players pitting their expertise and cunning against each other. The minority of four knew, in the end, the majority of seven would out vote them. There were limits to how far one side could run off with the bacon as Federal guidelines made it clear districts had to have a set number of people. In Vermont, the number had risen to 3,700 by 1990, give or take the 10 percent deviation; districts had to be contiguous, and there should be as little disrupting of present districts as was possible. This last criteria was easier said than done. We learned very quickly a district which had grown rapidly since the last census and had too many people in it, required the committee must give some to an adjoining town. That district in turn might have to do the same, creating a ripple effect sweeping across the map. It was never as simple as giving the surplus to a neighboring district. That surplus had to fit. If it didn't, we were forced to move to another choice. Like squeezing a balloon filled with water, it could get very nerve-wracking and frustrating. Those with the patience and the motivation to create districts that were politically beneficial could harvest great rewards for their party over the next decade. And, it was all legal as the high court had ruled re-apportionment was a political exercise as well as a Constitutional exercise. We were determined to take advantage of this opportunity and we did.

We didn't match the tears or contentiousness of 1965, but there were moments we must have come close.

7. THE DEFICIT DEBACLE

Phil Hoff's election, re-apportionment, and a changing Vermont landscape demographically didn't do much to make life any easier for the Democrats in Montpelier. We were still saddled with a minority in spite of our victory in the UVM Trustees contest, an attitude problem. We were aware there was little we could do to change the numbers problem as that would encompass, at the very least, an election 18 months away. A 20-member minority was no small hurdle and Poirier and I, having little experience in campaigning for an entire party, conveniently pushed it aside in order to deal with what was in front of us, such as trying to win anything. This was easier said than done as no matter how right we felt we were on an issue, it was a different matter getting enough of our colleagues across the aisle to come on over and vote with us. As the member from Burlington had made so alarmingly clear, our own Democrats were reluctant to stay in rank on any given issue. So, we had to search for another way. We got lucky as it appeared at our door early in the 1983 session in the form of a looming deficit.

This was the Ronald Reagan era and it was "Morning in America." No tax or program cuts were beyond "trickle down economics" and the mid-1980s bore witness to massive income tax cuts and gigantic deficits. This has a major impact on Vermont's budget as we were one of only three states that remained piggy-backed onto the Federal tax system. If Federal taxes went up, Montpelier experienced a sudden windfall in additional revenues. Unfortunately, the reverse was also true. Washington, in its infinite wisdom, was slashing the Federal income tax at a rate unprecedented in U.S. history. Since we were "piggy-backed" onto the Federal tax system, each cut in the Federal income tax of 10 percent, and there were to be three such cuts, slashed our revenues in Vermont by 10 percent. Something had to give and the pop we heard echoing out of Washington across the hilltops of Vermont was our state budget buckling under severe deficits. We spent the entire 1983 session arguing over how best to deal with the shortfall and, in fact, though we were unaware of this in the winter and spring, we would be forced into an emergency summer session, specifically to deal with the specter of an economy falling apart. In retrospect, one can see clearly now that we in Montpelier were much more capable of dealing with mushrooming deficits than the gurus in Washington, for to this day, the cancer of fiscal irresponsibility eats away at our Federal government on almost a daily basis.

I'll give Gov. Richard Snelling credit, as he was the first to bring the deficit to public attention. He was quite wrong as to the extent and depth of the problem, but he set out early to find the solution. His original estimate was just over $8 million. *(It was to end up well over 60 million.)* Eight or 60 million might appear as "chump change" elsewhere, but to the Vermont budget eight million, at the time of $300 million budgets, represented 3 percent of the entire revenue expenditures for the state over a 12-month period. It wasn't anything over which to jump out the window, but a signal that a correction was in order. Sixty million was something else for this represented over 20 percent of the state budget. Now that might call for a leap out of something! It sent alarms ringing through Wall Street, warning that measures had to be taken or our bond rating would suffer.

Want to find a defining difference between the two parties in America? Look no further than how each approaches a solution to a deficit. It's as fundamental a difference as night and day. The Republicans immediately set out to slash spending. On a brazen day they might even couple that with tax cuts. The Democrats, on the other hand, begin the search for new taxes yet unwritten and raise them. Never suggest to a Democrat a few dollars in cuts to a program would serve to alleviate the problem. To cut a program is parallel to making an incision into a Democrat's heart. Diplomatically and soundly, Snelling set out to do a little of both, thereby guaranteeing both sides of the aisle would be equally upset. Snelling was good at a lot of things, but he was a master at upsetting people by telling them the truth, and to rub it in, he never gave a hint at caring how upset they became.

Poirier and I were now part of this setting. If ever there existed two people who knew less about economics, revenue projections, or Wall Street idiosyncrasies, I'd like to know who they were. But that didn't matter as we spoke for 55 members, and if the majority of Republicans were going to get after each other, it just might turn out that we would be needed somewhere along the line. Much to our amazement, that is exactly what happened.

A couple of things were going on simultaneously. First, Gov. Snelling had made it known he was serving his last term and most likely could not be talked into running for an unprecedented fifth two-year term.

At the same time, Morse revealed he would, upon the conclusion of his second term as Speaker, be leaving to take a job at a southern Vermont foundation. Morse, though a UVM graduate, had made his living as a house painter. A noble occupation, but nowhere near as financially lucrative as director of the prestigious Windham

Foundation. They both were looked at as lame ducks by many. It was not exactly the setting for decisive leadership.

Then there was Bob Kinsey. As Republican leader, he was forced by both role and personality to be forever in the background. Speaker Morse could call on his authority at any time to muster the troops. Consequently, he didn't need Kinsey, or so it seemed. Snelling's personality was sufficient to dominate any situation.

I don't know what went on in Kinsey's mind during this period, but it was a situation that presented the opportunity for him to cut his own path. I do know this path at least led to the podium. Kinsey wanted to be Speaker and it appeared his road was cleared by his election as Republican leader. He had seniority as he was an eight-term veteran. His second term as leader had commenced without mishaps. Kinsey was the epitome of all that 200 years of Republican Vermont Speakers had been made of: conservative farmer, soft spoken, and patient. A keeper of the torch.

But he had his liabilities. He had an inability to present himself well on the floor. He tended to speak in a monotone that the members had difficulty understanding. This was not a good omen for a future spokesperson for the entire assembly. In addition, he had a characteristic that would prove to be his downfall: He was a very stubborn man. Once committed to a position, he seldom backed off it. This was a troubling aspect of character to carry in a body that demands constant half-loaves and it has been the downfall of a multitude of good people. If there's one necessary criteria required of leadership while trying to govern, the vital one is the willingness to compromise. But compromise was not something that Kinsey found easy. This set the stage for the Democrats to become players in the oncoming crisis.

After much haggling and in-fighting, Snelling managed to push through a small increase in taxes. This was to offset what he felt was a deficit that could be handled with a combination of his tax increase and careful scrutiny of an already tight budget. Much to his credit, he paid no heed to the ax wielders who looked with joy on deep cuts to programs that Snelling felt were vital to government's obligations to people in need.

But the ominous cloud of recession, coupled with federal tax cuts, kept pressing down on Vermont's economy. With each Reagan slash, our state finances grew smaller by 10 percent. What may have appeared to be *"Morning in America"* was bringing the darkness of *"Twilight to Vermont."* As the session was winding up in April, the projected deficit had risen to $28 million. Now it was a serious problem. Snelling was threatening a special session if the last months' revenues failed to bail us out. As there was little chance of that, we left Montpelier in April with the full knowledge a summer session appeared inevitable.

Some were now predicting a $50 or $60 million shortfall and we hadn't returned home for very long before the call went out to return in July to deal with the emergency. Special sessions by dictate of the Vermont Constitution can only be called by the governor, but the agenda can only be determined by the legislature. The legislature possesses the constitutional power to adjourn, thus how long an assembly meets and what the agenda consists of can only be suggested by the governor, not mandated. The potential for a free-for-all session is always present, but in this case Morse made it clear, and the leadership agreed to comply, we were here to raise taxes to meet the crisis, not to delve into any members' pet bills.

Preliminary meetings were held in order to lay the groundwork for the incoming members. Money committee chairs and others were invited to these meetings with the leadership with one exception: they failed to ask the Democrats to attend. We raised a little hell in the Press about this snubbing, but it became clear Snelling, Morse, and company felt confident their large majorities would prove sufficient to get the job done without our help. That was not all necessarily bad, as we weren't in any big hurry to raise taxes. Obviously, as dyed in the wool liberals, we weren't going to cooperate in cutting programs, but as Paul had been quoted, "This was a Republican deficit."

Letting the big guys twist slowly in the wind was fairly high on our list of interesting things to do on our summer vacation.

Politics is a vocation filled with fate and the unexpected, and no sooner had we arrived at the capital, than we were summoned to a leadership meeting in the governor's ceremonial office on the second floor corner of the State House. It was a typical Dick Snelling meeting. He was cordial and accommodating. Morse tried desperately to display a command of his own. Kinsey sat quietly, knowing he was working without the comfort of being included in all that had been discussed, or decided prior to our arrival. We knew he would be called upon to rubber stamp what others had decided was the best course for the state to take. We could see Kinsey's growing exasperation with the course of the conversation and the air soon became heavy with resentment. Within seconds of a forceful summation by the governor that left little room for how we were going to respond to the shortfall of funds, what tax would be raised, and when it would be raised, it was Kinsey's turn to respond.

"I can't support you on this." Pause. "Nor will my caucus."

I stared in wonderment. This was going to be different. The air was tense.

Then, all hell broke loose. Snelling blew his top and there was little anyone could do but let him vent. There was always the option of getting up and walking out, but Paul and I were glued to our seats with both fear and fascination. This guy just didn't explode; he did it with big-time, major league anger and ferocity.

Kinsey picked up his option. He got up and casually walked out, leaving the governor screaming at people at whom he wasn't even mad. It dawned on us, if not on Snelling or Morse, that if Kinsey could hold his caucus to no new taxes, we were all the governor had left if he was going to deliver the necessary votes to pass his tax package.

There comes a time in every politician's career that he or she has to rise above politics and do what he or she thinks is right. We discussed the other options, which amounted to a simple "let them twist slowly in the wind", but dismissed it quickly. It was clear to us, as well as everyone who had a pulse, Vermont was in a very serious situation that couldn't be ignored. It wasn't just that Wall Street would take drastic measures with our bond rating and all the resulting repercussions, but that people's lives would be affected in an extremely negative way. That was as unacceptable to Paul and me as it was to Gov. Snelling and Speaker Morse. This was a situation where there was a right thing to do and that was it. No other options were acceptable to us.

We delivered the necessary and deciding votes from our caucus. The deficit proved even greater than anyone had imagined, but it was Gov. Madeleine Kunin, succeeding Snelling, who was able to let it take its course. Two years later, as she presided over the executive branch, she was the one who got to bust the deficit balloon. By that time, Snelling was sailing somewhere in the Atlantic, the captain of another ship.

This was an opportunity Kinsey missed. Certainly the 35 or so Republicans who joined with us Democrats to pass the tax package that July day in 1983, must have pondered his commitment to act responsibly during a crisis. Whether it was his dislike for the governor, or simply his dislike for taxes that forced him to the position he took, I never knew. But it took a stubborn man indeed to lose the Speaker's race by one vote and not second guess a previous action of this magnitude.

On Friday, July 29, 1983 an editorial ran in the *Bennington Banner* titled "The Heroes of Montpelier." It read, in part:

"The governor singled out Ralph Wright of North Bennington, House Democratic leader, and Senator Jane Gardner...for the roles they played in breaking the stalemate that ended this special session of the Legislature."

I was soon to learn that in politics, as in most every other aspects of public life, "fame is fleeting." Within eight months, Dick Snelling was referring to me as an "irresponsible tyrant."

8. Delaying The Love Boat

We finally won one. It was not the greatest of victories, as raising taxes often gave people like me the longevity of a Marine 2nd Lt., somewhere in the Pacific, dateline 1943. But we won, and that was something we had not experienced very often yet.

This had been a unique experience and one I was to remember the rest of my days in politics. It brought to life the old adage, "That one can get a lot done if he doesn't care who gets the credit." The next victory was a personal one. Up to now, I had taken events as they came to me. Leadership was a vast area I had never traveled before, and any response I might have had was merely instinctual and not one I could explain. There is no textbook to prepare one for the multitude of situations in which we find ourselves. Each occasion or circumstance demands a reaction, not always of the "smart" nature.

We were wrapping up the session nine months later in 1984. The waning days of a legislative session are always filled with an energy and confusion unparalleled to anything I can relate to in the everyday world. The rush toward adjournment brings out the worst in members. Bills that have been lying dormant for months suddenly spring to life with an urgency that far outweighs their importance. Members who profess to absolutely despise confrontation, become Tartan hordes trying to rescue bills held hostage by former friends and colleagues, now described as "swine." Conference committees announce almost hourly they are at hopeless impasse.

It is here a leader gets the opportunity to shine and I never fail to bring to mind the first verse of my favorite poem by Rudyard Kipling:

> *If You Can Keep Your Head When All about You*
> *Are Losing Theirs and Blaming it on You,*
> *If You Can Trust Yourself When All Doubt You*
> *But Make Allowance for Their Doubting Too;*
> *If You Can Wait and Not Be Tired of Waiting,*
> *Or Being Lied About, Not Deal in Lies,*
> *or Being Hated Don't Give Way to Hating,*
> *Nor Don't Look Too Good, Nor Talk Too Wise.*

Nothing describes the necessary traits demanded of a leader during the closing of a session better than the words of Kipling.

These were the last days of both Snelling and Morse. We were going to have a new governor and a new Speaker when we reconvened in eight months, though no one had the foggiest who. And though I wouldn't describe them as lame ducks (especially Snelling), we could read in their eyes the anticipation they must have held to exit this craziness and get on with their lives. It was a whole new world for Morse. He was to "retire" before the age of 40 to the life of a country baron (my description, not his); a simple life, surrounded by his sheep, and disrupted only occasionally by the necessity of administering grants to worthy causes as dictated by his overseers. Snelling and his wife, Barbara, were headed back to the quiet life of bank board meetings and administering the estate. But prior to getting down to not doing much of anything, they were scheduled to take a cruise. We dubbed it the *Love Boat,* behind his back, of course.

The session had been anything but easy. By February, the proclaimed estimates for the deficit had reached $40 million and showed no promise of stopping there. Once again, Morse and Snelling got little help from their leadership. Not only did Kinsey break out in a rash every time new taxes were mentioned, but now he was joined by some of the more prominent Republican members, including Peter Giuliani, the Chairman of the House Ways and Means Committee.

Giuliani, a wizened old veteran of the process, refused to move the latest tax increase out of his committee, and only a public threat by Morse to remove him of his chairmanship forced his hand. Kinsey, his eyes still locked on the podium, played the tune of "No New Taxes" to an election year Republican caucus. Once again, the Democrats rode to the rescue and supplied the necessary votes to save the day.

It was all over but the tumult and the shouting. Or, so everybody thought.

We were scheduled to adjourn Saturday night, April 14. All that was left to pass were a half-dozen small bills, and what was referred to as *"the big bill."* This latter was the appropriations bill that contained all of the necessary authority to run government for the next fiscal year. Tradition always allocated the "last bill passed" slot for appropriations, as once passed, members could adjourn with a sense of responsibility. If someone had a pet bill, he or she had to take heed that it beat the "big bill" to passage. Buried in the small pile of so-called "unimportant" legislation was a consumer credit bill that lifted the ceiling credit card companies could charge consumers for interest. If taxes made Republicans break out in a rash, then a bill such as this threatened to send liberals to intensive care. We refused to suspend the rules in order for the Speaker to bring up the bill. That did it.

I've already described rules suspension is necessary when it's incumbent upon speeding things up. In some cases when there is low attendance, 30 people, well organized, can bring the speeding train of adjournment to a screeching halt. And that's what we did.

This can be a dangerous political game to play. It is not done on a whim. It is usually done for a cause that, for different reasons, can't get heard. But if you've got tickets for a cruise on a *"Love Boat"*, and know they're not going to hold the boat at the dock for you, then all defenses of your cause become lame ones. The governor wasn't going to call Captain Stubing and explain that he was tied up "here in Vermont by a Machiavellian demagogue named Ralph Wright." Instead, he called a press conference and did the next best thing. He called me a tyrant and a bully. I heard he got really nasty in private. Like the rest of the members, I went home for the weekend.

I was as scared as I had ever been. Prior to entering politics, my name had been in the paper perhaps a half dozen times, never for anything negative. My prior newsprint amounted to no more than a "a marine saying good-bye at South Station or a group picture of kids as city summer league playground champs." This was certainly something different. I did plenty of thinking that weekend and, for the life of me, I couldn't figure a way out of what I was coming to think was close to a felony. I look back now on this as just an amusing incident. Since then, I have been called a lot worse and have been though episodes of derision and name calling that put it all in perspective. But, for that moment in time, I was sure I had committed a crime that if it didn't put me in prison, was going to bring a halt to what I considered a promising career. I did what any smart con would do: I called my lawyer Monday morning..

In this case my lawyer happened to be Bill Russell, chief of the Legislative Council.

Vermont government and its citizen legislature is one of a dying breed in America. Members, on top of being paid $485 per week and expenses, have no personal staff, nor do they have office space. Instead, a pool of staff is provided by a Legislative Council that over the years, due to demand, has grown to 10 or 12 lawyers who draft bills and generally advise members in a non-partisan manner. On the rare occasion when a member finds him or herself in a legal bind deriving from a legislative entanglement, the legal staff serves as counsel. There is an additional group of clerical staff of 20 or so that are the backbone of the entire process. All of this limited assistance is on a first-come, first-serve basis.

I took a shot in the dark and asked Bill if he would mind thumbing through the old journals and seeing if any leader, or anyone for that matter, had "abused" rules suspension in the same manner Snelling was now accusing me of having done. I didn't think there was a chance he would be successful in finding it.

It wasn't 15 minutes later when he called back and said he thought he had found something.

"It's been done before, " he exclaimed, sounding incredulous.

"You're kidding," I responded, with the excitement of a child who's just realized his brother has just repeated an act on which he's awaiting his mother's judgment.

"Yeah! Back in 1975, the Republican leader held a group together and they refused to suspend. The entire assembly had to adjourn and return the following week to finish business. "Actually this was a worse scenario, in that this same leader made the motion to suspend the rules and then voted against his own motion along with enough of his fellow Republicans to block suspension," he continued.

"Who the hell was arrogant enough to do that?" I asked.

"You won't believe this, Ralph. It was Republican Leader Richard Snelling."

Here's what Bob Sherman wrote the following Tuesday in the *Rutland Herald:*

"House Democrats gave Wright a standing ovation when he appeared at the afternoon caucus. Most all 65 had signed a card, commemorating his Saturday night clash with Snelling and advising that he 'grin and ignore it.' Democrats view Wright as a conquering hero for standing up to Snelling."

We went home that week feeling secure we had left our "bad attitude" behind us. Now it was time to take care of this numbers problem.

9. THE NUMBERS RUNNERS

Politics in the Green Mountain State is a rather laid back endeavor. At least it was at the time that I was entering into it. People didn't campaign for office. They *"stood"* for office. We were going to change all that in a way neither Paul Poirier nor I had any notion of what would be considered a political campaign plan in another place. We approached the 1984 general election by a seat-of-the-pants approach, the same way we struggled through our first two years in leadership. That's not to say that we weren't aware of the problem. We didn't have to be too bright to realize we failed to win much of anything with an 85 to 65 minority, but what to do about it was an entirely different matter.

There was no background material we could turn to, so it became a simple choice for us to set off hacking away in a political wilderness.

The road for a veteran campaigner probably would have proven so rough that the odds of winning enough seats to make a respectable run for the Speakership would have appeared beyond hope. We were just naive enough not to recognize all these obstacles when we sat down to "organize" a campaign strategy. It went something like this, " Brother Paul, you hit em high and I'll hit em low." Paul would recruit, train, and get elected all the Democrats north of Montpelier and I would handle all those south of the capital.

Actually, it became more complicated than that, but not by much. The first problem we had to measure was how to find candidates. Vermont, as I've noted, was filling up with a lot of bright, young activists who certainly were making their impact felt at local school board meetings and in town affairs. But attending meetings and voting at the local town hall wasn't the same as putting one's name on an election ballot.

I've often said that nobody should go through life without running for political office. I can't thing of a scarier or more humbling experience. It's one thing to pick up the local newspaper each morning and get a morbid sense of satisfaction out of reading an attack on some poor soul who happens to be your local pol. Next time you're taking special joy in this type of sport, try a simple exercise: Replace your name with the pol being brutalized. It takes on a whole new demeanor, doesn't it?

I'm sophisticated enough after all these years in politics to know this isn't the army, Mr. Jones. You don't get drafted onto the ballot. It's a choice you make, probably against both your and your spouse's better judgment. The political bug carries a big bite and I've always been amazed by the lengths politicians carry themselves to be allowed the privilege of participating.

Political figures will simply do the most outrageous things in an effort to be successful that the typical voter has every right to question his or her suitability to not just hold office, but to remain free and walking around the community. Though I took more abuse than I ever gave, I'll admit I did and said things about my opposition across the aisle that, had I done the same things to family members, my mother would have seen to it I never attended another Thanksgiving dinner. At the very least, she would have made me sit at the folding table with the rest of the kids.

Recruiting in the past had not been what I would have classified as a scientific affair. There's a good reason for this. Politics is a people game, and you have little more chance of applying the soundest of principles to a campaign than you do to guessing what any given individual will do in a certain set of everyday circumstances. It's possible to guess right nine out of ten times, but it's the odd one that has you throwing up your hands in utter frustration. To add to this jumble of confusion, there is simply and absolutely nowhere you can go to ask for help or read a "How To" plan. What occurs in New Jersey or California has little bearing on the situation in Vermont.

There are, of course, underlying principles that make a difference. Like any endeavor in life, hard work and perseverance pays off. Paul and I fanatically set off to change the numbers in the House. If all that was necessary to accomplish this end was hard work and perseverance, we weren't going to be found lacking.

I admired Paul, not so much for his political smarts, as for his tenacity. He loved the fight! Time after time, Paul would get himself in over his head, but I don't ever recall him showing the slightest sign of surrender no matter how hopeless the situation. He'd emerge from any struggle bloodied and battered, but with the grin of a victorious alley fighter.

I often made comparison of the two of us with the great Boston Bruins teams of the early seventies. (Paul was an outstanding hockey player at Norwich University in Northfield; whereas I skated on my ankles.) That great team had a roster of stars unparalleled in Boston Bruins' history: Orr, Stanfield, and the team's prolific scorer, Phil Esposito. But it was a spunky wing that made that team go by the name of "Pie" McKensie. He was forever going into the corner with the big bodies, scrapping along the boards for the evasive puck. Inevitably, and often miraculously, the puck would emerge radar-like to find the hulking figure of Esposito, stick at the ready. Goal Boston. So it was with

Paul and me. He did the scrapping and I stood by ready to slap the puck home. We were a great team for six years and I often have reflected that once he made the decision to venture into state-wide politics, it quickened the day my end would arrive, too.

We must have put 50,000 miles on our cars that summer and fall. Although I did this every two years for the next decade, it never was the same as that first effort. I enjoyed every minute of it. We rumpled through towns and villages we never heard of before searching for candidates for the House. It was a difficult task, for we often found ourselves in isolated backwaters where we didn't know a soul. That wouldn't stop us though. More than once while grabbing a sandwich or wandering around the village, we would strike up a conversation with one of the locals hoping to come across a person we could run down and convince to join our team and run for the district's seat. It wasn't the best method of recruitment, but even a blind squirrel finds an acorn every now and then. The quality of the candidate was foremost on our mind, but the nature of the district ran a close second.

That was a subject on which we could do a little research, and we worked it to the hilt. The trick was not simply to find a candidate, but to find one in a district where we had a chance of winning. There are districts in Vermont so rock-ribbed Republican, we could have run a John F. Kennedy clone and taken a bad beating. One that comes to mind is the town of Lyndonville in the Northeast Kingdom. This was a two-member district* that had three or four smaller towns joining Lyndonville to comprise the whole. I swear there weren't 50 Democrats among Lyndonville's 3,500 or so living creatures. We spun our wheels in our effort to find a brave soul who would run on the Democratic ticket, but it was to no avail.

We left that community a half dozen times totally devastated by our failure, only to keep returning, hoping against hope, our luck would change. It never did, not in that election year or in any future year. I don't know what made us persist, as we were well aware Lyndonville hadn't ever sent a Democrat to the legislature as far as we could discern. Maybe it was just being conscious of who they had been sending to represent them in Montpelier that brought about our huge effort.

One was a joyless old bachelor who had represented the district for years. He wasn't much older than I, but he acted like he belonged in the last century. I'm sure he had some good points, but he voted like an Industrial Age Republican *all* the time. The issue didn't matter to

---

Approximately 25 percent of all districts had two members.

him: programs for children, *No*; programs for the elderly, *No*; even programs for Lyndonville, *NO*. He outlasted both Paul and me.

Our research didn't fail us all the time and we eventually were able to put forth a stable of Democrats to march into the November, 1984 battle. Our approach was different than any previous effort made by a so-called recruitment team. Past leaders had made an effort, but it never equaled what Paul and I now were setting out to do. There were three major differences between what had gone on in the past and our approach.

First, and probably most vital, was that it was our asses on the line, particularly mine. We made no secret by the time we adjourned in April that we intended to take over the House. That announcement met with derision from many, but still it was public knowledge and that meant that we'd better not fail. There would be no committee so low to deserve our presence if this pre-emptive strike failed. It was an "all or nothing" effort. The real fallout would have been within our own caucus where failure to grasp the golden ring placed their complacent, but comfortable rear ends, in jeopardy. Our right to lead would have come into serious question. There is no fall so far as a fall from leadership, as they say. From a Republican standpoint, we were making life miserable for a lot of incumbents, some of whom had run unopposed for years. We might not have been successful in places like Lyndonville, but we were in dozens of other districts. If the Republicans survived our onslaught, they were sure to show up in Montpelier loaded for bear come January. There would have been no end to their clamor for our heads. Though we needed little motivation, this in itself, kept us running and trying to do more.

I learned as a young kid to do everything within my power to stay out of the alley as only bad things happened there. But it also was a very strict tradition that once in the alley, I'd better get my hands out of my pockets. We were wandering in dark allies and nobody had to tell us to be ready.

Unlike our predecessors, we weren't just after numbers of candidates. We targeted districts. We saw little purpose in having a Democratic candidate in all 150 districts, if many of them didn't stand a prayer of winning.

We did a little research before traipsing around the state, provided by the Secretary of State's office. Past election results were available in a specially prepared booklet published just after elections every two years, but they failed to reach down into the individual legislative races. We could find out all we wanted to know about the major statewide races in terms of numbers and results, but we would have to make a special request to get the legislative or, further down, the local Board of Civil Authority or school board results. They were there, but one had to take the initiative to get them.

We did this and it proved an invaluable source of budding young political junkies venturing into political waters for the first time. Now it was up to us to sweet-talk them into a bigger pool. We got better and better at this as the weeks rolled by.

We recruited women. We didn't set out to do it, but it wasn't long before we realized there was a big political difference between the sexes. We understand other differences, obviously, but I don't believe many noticed the political implications previously. Simply stated, women made much better candidates than men. One reason was political; the other philosophic. They were candidates uncorrupted by the process. Many had never sought political office before, so they didn't have to unlearn bad habits.

I had experienced this once before years ago when I arrived on Parris Island as a boot recruit. There wasn't much of anything happening that I remember with any sense of fondness, but of all the trauma we were put through, none measured up to qualifying with the M-1 on the rifle range. A bigger smattering of American youth couldn't be imagined, and none were abused more than the poor country boy who had been raised with a rifle by his side. The fact he could hit a rabbit between the eyes at a hundred yards amounted to a peehole in the snow as far as the Corps was concerned. He was a Marine now, and there was only one way he could do it...the Corps' way.

I saw days of torture as lads attempted, often furtively, to unlearn all they had been taught and pick up the proper way from scratch. As a city boy, I never so much as laid my eyes on a rifle, let alone had one in my hands, and everything taught was new enough to be retained, at least to the point of qualifying. The poor and unfortunate farm boys, try as they might, kept reverting to the proven measures of a quickly fading childhood memory. Their punishment was to wear the dress reserved for those old dogs who couldn't learn new tricks.

We would often recruit a "good old boy" who had grown bored of service as a selectman where his good name, or the good name of his descendants, had served him well. He was one of those that "stood" for, rather than "ran" for, election. In too many cases that was not enough, and the broader perimeters of a legislative district required that he get out and meet the people in the new areas of the district. Failure to do this often meant the race went to the swift. Remember, Vermont was changing and, unfortunately, there were those that couldn't or wouldn't change with it. To our Democratic advantage, I'm not sure the Republicans get it yet.

This was the first venture into the world of politics for most of our women candidates and that meant there was no cleansing that had to take place. When you suggested something, they took that advice and did it. They often returned in half the time asking, "Now what do I do?" Women had untold energy as, for the most part, they were young recruits. Coupled with an ability to stay organized in an endeavor such as a seven-week campaign blitz almost always kept them competitive and often guaranteed a win. God help the complacent incumbent who laughed at the "little lady" and her "big city" campaign tricks. More often than not, she had the last laugh.

As important as her energy and willingness to take advice was her perception or reason for running. She, inevitably, knew why she ran. She had a "raison d'etre" that often took the form of a people-centered agenda. One doesn't have to look any further than this to explain the liberal, or people-oriented nature, of the present legislative make-up. Woman after woman arrived in the General Assembly, especially the House, over the next decade intent on getting something done. Slowly, but inevitably, it changed Vermont philosophically as it pertained to making law.

It peaked during the Madeleine Kunin years, when Vermont emerged as a national leader in progressive legislation, especially in the areas of health care, education, taxation, and the environment. I was extremely proud to be a major part of that sea of change. But at this point, we were just after numbers. The rest would take place automatically.

Finally, it should be mentioned that we did almost all of this on our own nickel.

This got to be an expensive proposition and only our commitment to winning the brass ring allowed us to overlook just how expensive. Our wives, who barely tolerated the political world anyway, would have cut us both off at the knees if they were aware how much we were taking out of our own pockets on a daily basis. And, this was in the days when candidates were on their own to raise or finance a campaign. We didn't give them checks, as we had all we could do to pay for the gas and the telephone calls. Years later we learned the attributes of power, such as being able to get people to pay $500 to eat dinner with us.

My wife, Cathy, upon learning that 40 lobbyists and friends had coughed up $500 to sit and break bread with the great Speaker, looked up and in her most matter of fact voice said, "Ralph, there were nights over the past 35 years I would have paid $500 not to have to eat with you."

Recruiting was just the first phase of our intended quest. We did a pretty good job, at least by previously set standards, though we continued to get better and better at it as we became more experienced. The July filing deadline pushed us into our second stage, the training of candidates. Most of this took the form of one-to-one counseling, but we did bring the candidate training seminar to Vermont that is copied by all parties in the state now. This consisted of two different sessions where we would rent a central meeting place, usually in Montpelier, always on a Saturday, and spend the day teaching the rudiments of political campaigning. It centered on the normal things such as leaflets, advertising, phone banks, and door-to-door canvassing. We tried to emphasize the latter as the one thing that was a must. A candidate who wouldn't knock on doors, and there were some who couldn't overcome their fear of such personal close encounters at a stranger's door, soon found our enthusiasm for them waning. We didn't believe a candidate who was afraid to meet his or her constituents belonged in the legislature. We didn't have to worry about their presence on opening day, as they would fail on their own.

Poirier and I kept at it all through the fall. We were going to accomplish that which Democrats had never seriously attempted, let alone brought to fruition. We would win the House and then conquer the podium. We knew that as sure as we knew we existed. I never remember being tired and I can't recall Paul ever complaining of being tired either. We were wired.

Election day came all too fast. We had the feeling we hadn't done all that was possible, but that's the way it is. You're happy it's over, but nervous you haven't done quite enough. Now it was up to the people. Our fate was in their hands.

We won seven seats that election day. Not a majority, but a giant step in the right direction. Our numbers, now at 72, had us within striking distance, but obviously we were going to have to get a little help from our friends across the aisle if we were going to capture the podium.

10. MR. SPEAKER!

We surprised a lot of unsuspecting people on Election Day, 1984. We had moved from 65 House Democrats to 72, placing the Democratic Speaker candidate within striking distance. Republicans still had a 75-72 advantage. There was no guarantee and, in fact, the Democrat chosen to vie for the Speakership had to face the raw fact there was not a minority Speaker in power in any of the 50 states. Before any of that, however, I had to win over the Democratic Caucus and be nominated.

I hit the road intending to see every Democrat on his or her turf. There were approximately four weeks between election day and the first Saturday in December when our caucus would meet to select the Democratic candidate for Speaker. This was going to prove difficult, as my opponent was John Zampieri, a fellow Democrat from Ryegate in the Northeast Kingdom. He was a 20-year veteran who chaired the Transportation Committee for the past four years. He was in the inner circle, having befriended Speaker Morse sufficiently enough to be appointed to that prestigious post in a Republican regime. I didn't take him lightly.

My strategy was simple. Hold my liberals (Zampieri is a conservative) and work hard to win the trust of the moderates who made up the bulk of the caucus. The new members were obviously going to support me as I had been their lifeline during the campaign and could take some credit in their being where they were.

I campaigned with the same energy that had carried us through election day with Paul Poirier by my side every step of the way. At caucus time, I felt I had the votes. Secret ballots are a scary experience and the nervousness that accompanies you into these frays doesn't leave much in the way of pleasant memories.

When the votes were finally tallied that day, I won 45 to 27.

All 72 Democrats fought lousy weather to get to Montpelier to cast their ballots and I was never again going to be on a ballot that didn't have full attendance. This may seem insignificant, but what it really denoted was the importance of these votes in the decade to come. It showed the extent of the effort members would make to cast their votes for and against me.

Immediately after the results were read to our caucus, Zampieri was on his feet pledging his support to me and urging the members to put this inter-family fight behind us and unite in an effort to upset the soon-to-be-selected Republican candidate. John was a man of his word and I never had any reason to doubt he did exactly what he asked the members to do.

We scheduled our caucus at the earliest possible date in December in anticipation of finding it necessary to mend fences and heal wounds. The greater the time frame between the caucus and the floor vote for Speaker on opening day in January, the greater the opportunity for me, or whomever the candidate proved to be, to move around the state soothing hurt feelings. This didn't prove necessary, thanks to Zamp's magnanimous gesture, but I was pleasantly surprised the Republicans didn't see the importance of leaving this window of an extra week open to themselves. They carried on with their tradition of holding their caucus the week after ours, much like the best of company making sure they are the last to arrive at the gala ball.

I looked forward to the Republican caucus with almost the same anticipation I had awaited my own. It promised to be a donnybrook as they had four announced "wannabes" and several rumored. The favorite was Bob Kinsey, the two-term Republican leader. I'm not sure he spent a good deal of time doing much more than telephoning his members, but I was equally certain his opponents took the same course. Elections, again, were for the most part something a Republican "stood for." It might appear unbecoming to seem too anxious or nervous to the point of practicing politics by embarking on a full-fledged campaign.

Besides, a 78-72 majority still edged the comfort zone and even if it wasn't as comfortable as 85-65, it appeared safe enough to maintain the status quo. That, coupled with the rather pleasant surprise to the Republicans, it seemed the Democrats had seemingly self-destructed by choosing the least strong of their two candidates. Me! To their aristocratic eyes, Zampieri, as a conservative, held out the greatest threat in enticing members on the other side of the aisle to cross over and vote Democratic. John, a congenial fellow, had proven a welcome member to the "good ole boys club." There might actually prove to be a rush of conservative Democrats across party lines to ward off the election of anyone who might disturb the level of security that permeated the legislature's hallowed halls. It was bordering on the incredulous to think of a liberal with a Boston accent presiding over a Vermont House. If you were Jimmy the Greek, you weren't going to take bets on me.

Still, I was certain I was going to be the next Speaker. It wasn't going to be any landslide, but it was going to be. Looking back, I had a lot of nerve to be thinking like this, as there were already forces at work to head the "upstart" off at the pass. Nevertheless, like young men who march off to war, life is forever, and it's always going to be another who falls victim to the enemy.

I hit the campaign trail once again, this time with a potential constituency of 14. Actually it was easier than that, as I could break the membership into three general categories: those who were going to vote for me because they thought I was the best man; those who weren't going to vote for me because they thought I wasn't the best man, and all the rest, who were up for grabs. It was the last group that represented the ground on which the battle would be waged. But first, I had to know who my opponent would be.

I arranged to keep an open line into the State House, calling a friend who was then serving as Assistant Sergeant at Arms. There was no chicanery involved in this, for all my friend was doing for me was reporting over the phone lines each time the Republicans took a vote. It was no secret a deal already had been struck that Kinsey would step aside and allow Susan Auld, his assistant leader from Middlesex, to fill his vacated leadership post. In return, she most certainly had to commit to his candidacy for Speaker. The other candidates had to be a little more than chagrined at this cozy alignment, but these are the types of side problems that occur in the heat of a campaign.

The only problem with the alignment was Auld had enjoyed the advantage of running unopposed, in no small part to Kinsey throwing his support to her, while Kinsey had members lining up to run against him. She was sitting with a guaranteed seat of power, while Kinsey had to fight for his. He had to hope her measure of enthusiasm for his quest didn't fade with a equal measure to her sense of security.

A week earlier I managed to convince my people it was only fair that we select our leaders after the Speaker's vote in January. After all, why should I be sent up on the floor at great odds into a David vs. Goliath battle, and if the oddsmakers were right and I had my head handed to me, I would find myself out of my leadership position.

This would prove to be an exciting morning, a watershed in our drive to the Speakership. All but one of the 78 Republicans showed up, thus a vote of 39 was all that was necessary to go over the top. Back in Bennington, Corcoran, my son Rick, and I, sat waiting for the results. It didn't take long. We were startled to learn no winner had emerged. Kinsey was one vote shy at 38, followed by John Hise, an elderly and highly respected veteran of the Appropriations Committee at 21 votes. Bringing up the rear were Gretchen Morse (no relation to the Speaker), Chair of Health and Welfare from Charlotte, with ten votes, and the surprise candidacy of Ed Lucas, best described by some as a loose cannon. He had eight votes.

The second round saw Kinsey drop by four to 34 and Hise gain three and bump to 24. Morse stayed in front of Lucas. She now had ten supporters; Lucas had nine.

"God damn Kinsey, he'd screw up a high Mass," I cried in frustration and anger.

"That's not good," Corcoran said. "We don't want to have to run against Hise."

He added this more for Rick's benefit than mine, as I knew full well the dire consequences of having to pit myself against Hise.

Kinsey was the opponent we wanted. We didn't discuss it, but I had felt all along, if we were going to have any hope of winning, Kinsey would have to be the one we went up against. Lucus and Morse weren't the threats Hise was and the procedure for selecting their candidate required that after the second round, the low vote-getter would have to drop out. So, where would Lucas, who was low vote-getter, direct his nine votes? Kinsey needed five desperately. We were 130 miles south and there was nothing we could do about Kinsey's (and my) plight.

It wasn't that I didn't have a friend in caucus. I did, as Harold Weidman, the Republican Rep from Wallingford, was sitting in the caucus room. We entered the legislature together back in 1979 and struck up a friendship that was to grow with the passing years. Our bond as friends was already strong enough that Harold was one of the committed Republican votes I would need in January. He was a stand-up guy and one who could be relied on to stand up beside me, no matter how tight the situation got. But now I could only guess at what he was doing.

"I'll be a son of a bitch. Weidman is sitting there voting for Lucas." I threw the Republican roster up into the air in frustration. "He hates Kinsey and I'll bet he won't be smart enough to throw him a vote on the next ballot. Hise is going to win this."

To make matters even more dismal, Morse withdrew her candidacy, leaving her ten votes and Lucas' nine, up for grabs. Of the 19 votes now available, I was leery of Morse's ten as she, being a liberal, had probably garnered the more left-leaning Republicans, and they certainly were not likely to jump into Kinsey's column. If Hise grabbed all ten of those Morse votes, he'd only need five of Lucas' nine to go over the top. "C'mon, Weidman and company, do the smart thing and vote Kinsey," I said.

On third ballot, Kinsey pulled it out, winning 41-36.

I looked over at my son, who by this time was totally confused, and said in a boastful manner:

"Rick, your dad just got himself elected Speaker."

❖ ❖ ❖ ❖ ❖

I hit the road again. This time with the "pot of gold" in my sights.

The strategy seemed simple" keep my 72 Democrats and steal four Republicans. It was simple on paper, but it was a plan filled with a lot of "ifs." I had no guarantee I could hold all my Democrats and the lists that I was constantly preparing never turned up less than ten or so Dems about whom I had every reason to worry. This was the group that I referred to as the "good ole boys" and they had little motivation to abandon their comfort zone the Republican regime had afforded them.

I don't think they ever felt a Kinsey Speakership was going to change their life very much. But a Wright Speakership threatened to be a very different atmosphere indeed. To start with, I was 180 degrees to the left of Kinsey which meant issues that rested in the committee "black holes" in the past were going to hit the floor for debate. The comfortable life of the conservatives and their lobbyists friends would certainly change, and not for the better.

A lot of these same people just didn't like me for much more personal reasons. I told you, all politics is personal. I couldn't be trusted to do the right thing in their minds. They watched, with a high degree of chagrin, as I constantly jumped to my feet wading in against the corporate interest.

Though they always emerged the winners in these battles, the Speakership with the power to rearrange the entire process promised to present a problem for them of a much greater magnitude. I could turn out to be very dangerous character. Their predictions proved accurate, for years later Howard Dean, then Governor and on speaking terms with the corporate inner-circle, told me they had concluded I was, indeed, a "very dangerous man." It was obvious I had my work cut out for me.

I immediately set off for the Rutland area, for it was here that I could test my support on both sides of the aisle. My first stop was Ab Wilson's barber shop in Fair Haven. Ab, a Republican, had a mind of his own and the courage to do what he thought was right. A real Vermonter. I found him at home and got right to the point.

"Ab, I'm here to ask you for your support in my run for the Speakership. I think we're close enough friends for you, hopefully, to agree I would be the better Speaker to represent us all." I waited, fearfully anticipating his response.

And the simple response nearly floored me. "I'll vote for you."

That was it.

Then he added, "But I don't want to read about it the papers. They'll get mean if they find out. They won't even talk to Harold Weidman."

Several days earlier, Weidman was asked by his local radio station reporter who he was going to support for Speaker. He answered he was going to do the "old fashioned thing" and vote for the best man, Ralph Wright. They jumped him good and flooded his line with calls trying to convince him to reverse his decision. "I don't need the hassle," Ab said.

"I hope you won't change your mind, Ab. They know we're friends and they're not stupid. They'll put two and two together and you'll be hearing from them."

"That's fine. I can deal with that. I gave you my word, and you don't have to worry about me changing my mind."

Coming from Ab, I didn't spent any time worrying about it. The next person I sought out wasn't going to be quite as easy.

Tom Candon was a poker-faced veteran of 20 years or so in the legislature. He was the godfather of the Democratic minority in the House. I desperately needed his support. He hated all I stood for and I strongly suspected he felt no different about me personally. He had given up the Democratic leadership post just after my first term, but he still held tight reigns on the Democratic caucus. It had been passed on to me he thought the Democrats made a huge mistake by nominating me as Speaker and, by inference, there was no way I would get his vote or support in January. I couldn't win without his support. Maybe I could do without his vote, for I didn't believe there was anything I could do to get him to like me, but not without his support. I knew I would lose a small number of Democratic votes, but I hoped I could keep it a small number, as there simply was nothing I could do about somebody who either liked Kinsey a lot or disliked me a lot. I was smart enough to figure out there remained a fairly significant number of Dems who wouldn't dare go against Tom. They didn't call him the "Godfather" for nothing. It was vital that Tom was in my corner. So, I walked up four flights of stairs to accomplish it.

This was a scene right out of a Sam Spade movie.

It was not the cleanest of hallways I walked down, trying to read the writing on the smoke glassed door windows by the light of a single 40-watt bulb. I tapped gently on Tom's door and was beckoned in. He certainly wasn't expecting me. I could read that on his surprised face as I entered. I got right to the point.

"Tom, I know I probably didn't have to drop by" I stammered, "and I don't want to sound like I'm taking anything for granted...Well I want you to know I care enough to ask you for your support. You know not taking anything for granted or...."

He interrupted, "Well, you didn't have to waste your time stopping here, Ralph. You can count on my vote. How's it going?"

"Great," I lied, "I've got enough Republicans. If I can hold the 72 Dems, I'm pretty certain I can beat Kinsey. Tom, I need you to talk to a few of the members for me. As you know, a word from you will go a long way. Guys like Bud Keefe, Walter Moore and maybe Jack Candon, though I think I'm OK with Walter, as we get along and all. Vote a lot alike. But Keefe will feel more comfortable if you tell him it's OK. You could help me with Danny DeBonis and Joe Reed, too."

"Sure," he returned the lie, "I'd be happy to help. Of course, you're gonna take care of them. I mean you're not planning on takin' away their Vice Chairmanships, are you?" (referring to Keefe and Walter's committee assignments).

"No, of course not. They should stay right where they are, unless they want to go to another committee. Where do you think Jack would be happy?" I asked, referring to his son Jack. "I can put him on Ways and Means with you, if you feel that is where he'd be happiest. Of course, Tom, we haven't talked about this but Peter's not coming back (I was referring to Peter Giuliani, the long-serving and powerful Chairman of Ways and Means, who had been upset in the November elections), and you obviously can have the Chairmanship of Ways and Means. If you want Jack there, too, just say the word." The chairmanship of a "money" committee always put one into the top levels of power.

He totally ignored my solicitous offer for the chairmanship and moved instead to Jack's situation. "Oh, no! We shouldn't be on the same committee, he'd start bossing me around in front of everybody." He hesitated, "I'm going to miss Peter."

Giuliani's defeat was no calamity to the Democrats when we heard about it back in November. In fact, there was cause for celebration as Amy Davenport, a young lawyer, had pulled off the upset of the year by beating him. At the time, we were overjoyed to get rid of Peter, for he was what a lot of us young Turks thought was the problem (I later became "fast friends" with Peter and grew to admire and respect him greatly). Amy, a bright liberal, was going to contrast just fine in our minds. She later served as my Chair of the Judiciary Committee and then was appointed a Family Court Judge by Madeleine Kunin. And finally, "Jack probably would be happy with a seat on Commerce. But, you should ask him."

"No problem, I just want to make sure I don't put any one where he doesn't want to be." I got up to go and walked past the expansive, dirt-stained window. All I could see was the brick of the building next door and a couple of pigeons perched on the ledge.

"Quite a scenic view," I joked sarcastically, as I opened the door. Suddenly I stopped and turned looking straight at him. "Oh, by the way, Tom, no big deal, but I'd like you to nominate me."

I thought his teeth would fall out.

"I, uh. I can't do that." And then he caught himself. "I mean I'm not the best one to, uh, you know, be, uh...", he struggled to find the right excuse. "You should get someone else. I don't speak very well on the floor."

"You'll do just fine, Tom. Just fine."

"I'm really no good at speech writing. Get somebody who can do you more good than I can."

"I'll write the speech for you, Tom. You just deliver it." And now the haymaker. "Look, Tom, I need you to do this so the members won't have any doubt the Democrats are united. Now if you won't, then I've got to tell you, all deals are off. We can't afford to be running around in different directions. It's going to be tough enough, even with all of us pulling together. Whatta say? Will you do it ?"

"OK, I guess so." The pain was almost visible.

I skipped down the same stairs I had trudged up. Candon might vote against me, but his followers would see him on his feet singing my praises, and that would be all the signal necessary for them to follow and vote for the liberal Democrat with the funny Boston accent. As for Tom, I knew him well enough to know if he sinned against me on the secret ballot with his own vote, it would be something not even his priest would ever be told.

❖ ❖ ❖ ❖ ❖

I worked hard the next four weeks and if I did slack off, Poirier and Corcoran were right there to make sure I made that extra trip to meet and speak to members personally. They, as I, felt the real possibility of our pulling this off . No call went unmade, as we divided the list and kept counting. If I had any doubt as to the sincerity of a member's commitment, Paul or Tim would follow up. Both were uncanny in reading people's voices and Corcoran, especially, wouldn't hesitate to tell me when he thought someone was lying. If that happened, I would have to make a special effort. More than likely that meant a second visit. This served to not only send an alarm to the guilt ridden soul he or she had the pleasure of my company for a second time, but I seldom showed up without knowing just what it was that was bothering him or her or what he or she wanted. Inevitably, there was something that they wanted and, more than likely, Kinsey had already promised to them. Often I couldn't top Kinsey's offer, but I could at least attempt to match it and put myself back on a level playing field. Politics simply isn't a spectator sport.

People lie. I guess the qualitative difference between the honest and the dishonest is one of degree, not abstinence. We soon, as kids, learn life is full of temptations and the struggle to responsible adulthood is walking away from those things that don't add up to who you want to be. Most of us do a pretty good job at this and as we grow in stature and age, we start telling it like it is. This can get one in a heap of trouble in the political world as one's forced to learn fast. Survival depends on being careful not to say or do anything we don't want to read on the front page of tomorrow's newspaper. This was a tough lesson for me to learn, as I had trouble stopping what was in my head from rolling out my mouth.

There were many nights I lay awake trying to imagine how what I had done or said that day would be depicted in the soon-to-arrive morning newspaper. It was usually as bad as I imagined. While I found it a valuable teaching tool to be brutally frank to a class of high school juniors, the same truth told to a fellow member, who in turn would tell it to a reporter, read like a grand jury winding up a three week session with Jack the Ripper. When one is running for Speaker, 80 percent of support is right up front and represents commitments that can be taken to the bank. They may feel strongly about their support for you; or they may just be staunch Democrats who wouldn't think of voting for a Republican. Whatever their reason, these are people who a candidate soon grows to love. They tell you something, that's it. You can turn your attention to the next member in an effort to gain additional support. But no matter how good of a counter you might be, you could never be absolutely certain as to how that other 20 percent voted in a secret ballot on opening day. If one made a promise, perhaps of a committee assignment, to get a vote from a resistant member, it had better be delivered as it represented something they either got or didn't get. I never broke my promise to offer a certain committee to anyone without undertaking the unpleasant task of calling or seeing personally whom I was disappointing. But there were plenty of members over my five elections for Speaker that failed to do what they had sworn to do. And there wasn't a damned thing I could do about it, at least not at the moment. Let me give you an example of the extent of this problem.

One day, I was hustling votes in the central part of the state, when I pulled into a parking lot, just missing Bob Kinsey. He had just finished visiting Mike Obuchowski at his place of work. Now Obie was a Democrat I had absolutely no reason to distrust, but this is politics, and just to be sure, I pulled to the end of the parking lot and busied myself reading the local paper. After 15 minutes or so had gone by, I felt Kinsey and I couldn't possibly run into each other, so I entered Obie's office. He hadn't even bothered to say hello before he blurted out, "Jesus, first Kinsey, then you."

Obie passed with flying colors but that's not the gist of why I'm telling this. Of course, I wanted to know all that Kinsey had said during his visit. In addition, I was curious to know where he was coming from, and where he was heading next. Obie said Kinsey had volunteered that information. It was helpful for me to keep track of Kinsey's travels as well as his helpers, for knowing this type of data gave me some idea who he was working on as I hoped to gain his support. I emphasized this point to all my Democrats, both at our campaign kick-off meeting and in writing. If Kinsey calls or comes by, I want to know about it.

I put it out of my mind until I got home that evening and took my messages. The Democrat whose house Kinsey was going to from Obie's promptly left a message he had been there, but not to worry. My guy was emphatic in his pronouncement for his support of me, and Kinsey had left heading home himself after only staying an uncomfortable few minutes. What was strange was I didn't hear from the guy whose place Kinsey had left before he came to Obie's. I let a few more days go by expecting the call, growing concerned. I was angry, so I called him.

"Hey, how's it going? What do you hear?" I started out.

"Nothing. Absolutely nothing."

"Nobody's called or tried to get in touch with you?" I pushed.

"No one. Of course I'm not here most of the time as I'm out straight trying to clean up several jobs before we have to go back." Now I was fit to be tied. Here, I knew Kinsey had spent over an hour visiting just three days earlier, and this guy couldn't remember any of it.

"I'm about an hour north of you and I've got to swing through town. You don't mind if I stop by, do you?" I lied, as I was sitting in my kitchen 90 minutes away.

"Well, no. Be my guest. I guess I can get Mary to rustle up a piece of pie and some coffee. See you in an hour or so."

I drove through an ice storm to reach that bastard. Of course, his memory came back to him once I confronted him, but he swore, "Kinsey just happened to be coming by. And he couldn't have stayed very long."

I would have bet the mortgage I didn't get his vote, but because there was no way of telling, I was forced to return him to his plum assignment. I'll bet you this, if Kinsey kept a list of people whom he had commitments from, you wouldn't have to look far to find this guy's name.

Kinsey was paying the price for his late date, holding caucus, as the defeated have long memories. I don't care what is said publicly by a loser in an election. Losing hurts, especially if defeat is suffered in front of all one's friends. I recall attending only one of my high school reunions and I've never been to another.

I was having the normal difficulty of recognizing very many of the 500 or so who attended, and feeling awkward amidst all the strange faces that for the life of me I could not attach to a name. I suddenly made eye contact with a familiar face. With hand extended and my broadest smile, I walked hurriedly to the other side of the bar and embraced my old school chum. I was greeted with less than enthusiasm and after a brief bit of somewhat embarrassed chatter, he finally said, "You've forgotten haven't you, Ralph? You don't remember the wicked brawl we had in the fourth grade after school." He was smiling now, but I could tell this was not his real feelings. Somewhat embarrassed I answered back, "Yeah! My mother nearly killed me when I came home with that rip in my pants." He was not placated and his stare said it all. Our conversation had no place to go and we conveniently wandered off in different directions. Pleasure moves quickly; pain lingers a lifetime.

The session opened on a bitter cold January day. Everyone showed up, as was to be the case in all the elections for the next ten years. I must have entered the State House minutes after the janitor unlocked the doors because it seemed like an eternity waiting for the gavel to fall at 10 A.M. I don't remember a whole lot of that three-hour period, but I'll bet I greeted and shook a thousand hands. This type of anxiety can lead to big-time embarrassment, for it was something I never felt comfortable doing. I often compared politicians to people on the stage fully capable of performing in front of thousands of people, but shy and intimidated in a crowd of one. The drive for both is the need to be loved and it can lead to some embarrassing moments. It occurred, without fail, whenever my name was on a secret ballot.

I once found myself walking on Main Street nodding and smiling at people as we approached each other on the sidewalk. I almost always recognized their faces, but I couldn't place a name with the face. Generally it didn't matter, as the folks in Bennington knew who I was, and by this time I had mastered the art of talking to totally unfamiliar people for extended periods of time without revealing I didn't know who they were.

A middle-aged couple approached and I extended a pleasant "good morning" to them. After continuing down the street and doing a few errands, I returned to my car, encountering the same couple.

This time we chatted briefly about the weather and, as we parted, I gave them my standard parting line: "Remember, if I can ever do anything for you, just give me a call."

I felt just a little foolish as they pulled away, no doubt discussing the strange people of Vermont. The license plates were from Kansas.

Rumors had been flying back and forth that each side had been twisting arms and threatening members who were showing an air of independence. The Press took full advantage of the backbiting and name-calling, and they never seemed to have any trouble getting a quote from one or the other side's lieutenants. Word had even spread a secret coding system had been designed by the Democrats to reveal just how members had voted. I'm sure the Press had to be aware that whoever originated the secret code would at some point have to have access to the ballots *after* they were marked in order to acquire the information for which they were looking. The problem with that was neither Kinsey nor I never had any access to any ballot other than our own. Jim Douglas, the Republican Secretary of State, presided over the House election and he was the only one who actually would have them in his hands after the vote was counted and announced. What he did with them we will never know.

Republicans were beginning to show great concern we just might pull this off. They weren't talking publicly about this worry, as the day before the vote Susan Auld was boasting that Kinsey had a guaranteed count of 80. They admitted to losing two Republicans, but they bragged they had at least four Democrats. That's the math they used to get to 80. I, too, felt I would lose that number of Democrats, but what they didn't know was I was just as certain I had eight Republicans. If I could count better than they, I was going to win 76-74. Not a landslide by any means, but like in baseball, a dribbler down the third base line shows up in the next day's box score just like it was a wicked shot off the wall. One for three is still one for three.

"Bang. Bang. The House will come to order. Bang. Bang. Bang. Bang. The House will please come to order." Douglas implored the members, who began the scramble to find a vacant seat. All I remember going through my mind was, "If you lose, remember, no tears, no show of anger, but you haven't even prepared a concession speech. What'll you say? Do you walk out to meet Kinsey on his way to the podium? It'll look so clumsy, so stupid."

Now the Clerk was calling the attendance roll. "I haven't even prepared an acceptance speech. What if I win? What do you do, Wright, just stand up there looking like a jerk?" I turned to Paul.

"Paul, we didn't prepare a speech. What am I gonna say?"

Paul was little consolation, as his sage advise came back, " No problem, just wing it."

"Wright of Bennington", the monotone as the clerk neared the end of the roll. Here goes, and I swear my mind passed into a semi-conscious state for the next 30 or so minutes while nominating speeches were given for both Kinsey and me. I don't remember much of what was said. I do remember Candon delivering the speech of his life. His voice rang out in his praises for me and he had members believing that we were being witnesses to an historic moment. I never felt certain Tom voted for me that day, though a member who sat just in back of him, swears he saw Candon's ballot and he "x'd" the box next to Wright. He was at his best, that's for sure.

It seemed like a thousand years we sat and waited, while the eight members supervised by the clerks, counted and recounted the 150 paper ballots. I couldn't tell anything by their movement or actions as they huddled around the conference table situated in the very center of the House. Then the word passed up the rows, and I turned anxiously to Paul.

"What's going on?" I asked, my voice nearly breaking with both alarm and excitement.

"They're counting them a third time," he hurriedly responded. "It's tied up."

"Tied up?" I said in too loud a voice. "How can it be tied up? All this and it ends in a tie?"

"I don't know. Maybe somebody didn't vote, or voted for somebody else."

And then with visible anxiety, "Paul, I'm dead if this is tied up and we have to re-vote." We had talked about this before and concluded if anything like that happened and forced a re-vote, the Republicans would surely call for a caucus and that would be the end of us. They'd have beaten the truth into the handful of "traitors" until they harangued them into coming back up on the floor and voting for Kinsey.

The rumor of a tie was wrong. But, it was a very close race. That's why there was a recount. Another two lifetimes passed and I still couldn't read a thing from the group on the floor. Finally, a single piece of paper was handed to Secretary Douglas. And words from the seat next to me.

"I think we're OK." It was Paul's comforting voice. "Douglas doesn't look too happy."

"Christ, he's smiling, Paul."

"He wasn't a second ago when he was reading the results."

Then the gavel banged again.

"The House will come to order." Instant silence.

"Please listen to the results of your vote."

"The member from Craftsbury, Mr. Kinsey, 74."

"The member from Bennington, Mr. Wright, 76. The member from Bennington having obtained a majority of votes of those present. The Chair declares *Ralph Wright Your New Speaker of the Vermont House.*" I went totally numb. We had done it.

11. HOLDING HOSTAGE

The closet-sized Speaker's office was jammed the next few hours with well wishers and supporters. The telephone rang constantly from people I had not heard from in years. One call stands out.

"Hello, Speaker's Office," I answered.

A gruff voice responded, "Let me speak to the Speaker."

"This is the Speaker."

"This is Speaker Kerverian's office in Boston, Can you put me through to Speaker Wright?" There was less patience now in the voice.

One more time. "This is Speaker Wright. How can I help you?"

Silence. And then, "Look, this is Speaker Kerverian's Office and he wants to speak to the Speaker. Now will you put him on?"

Finally, I realized what was happening in this conversation, "You don't believe this is really the Speaker. Do you want me to say *cahr* or *pahc?*"

"Jesus, it is you. What the hell you doing answering your own phone, Mr. Speaker?" There was a new respect in his tone.

"Well, it may come as a real surprise to you guys down in Boston, but when the phone rings up here we answer it. Simple notion, huh?"

By mid-day, I must have had 110 members congratulate me with enough enthusiasm to have an innocent by-stander believe they always had been my biggest boosters and supporters. That's the way it is in politics. Victory has a thousand friends, as they say, while defeat is an orphan.

I don't believe anyone comes to the Speaker's job prepared, because I don't know where one would go to gain the insight or gather the data required just to stay on top of things. It doesn't matter whether we're talking about California, the largest state government, or Vermont with its citizen legislature. The same ingredients that are required to make up what we know as government in one are, necessarily, a part of the other.

The art of survival necessitates that the person in charge has to deal with members and their different agendas, an executive branch, the Press, and a ritual of process than must be followed. I recognized early, a new suit and a constant smile weren't going to be enough. I'd like to have a dollar for each time over the next ten years I was going to be faced with a problem or situation that I had, at least in the beginning, absolutely no clue as to how I should handle it. Without exception, I simply listened to all the advice that time afforded, and used the best judgment I could muster. The old standby attributes of character, such as honesty, concern and sensitivity to others, generally served to resolve the problem. There were times when these characteristics only made things worse however, and I soon learned to regret I never did learn the difference. I got better at it, but never mastered it. I paid the price.

Looking back, I often wonder how I lasted as long as I did. I served ten years as Speaker of the Vermont House, longer than anyone in Vermont history. Longevity counts, especially as it relates to how long we are going to stick around on this earth, but it shouldn't be one's only claim to fame. We all pass through but once, and the length of our stay is not the measure of our level of acceptance at the "Gate." Almost from the beginning, the Republican Party took up the chant that I was a "Boston Irish politician", a northern New England James Michael Curly, a destroyer of the quaint and civil way Vermonters had gone about their business in government. Of course, I didn't agree with this characterization, but I learned there was little I could do to stop it.

I felt no matter how tempted I was to return the name calling as Speaker, I held a position that demanded a higher level of public conduct. That didn't mean I never vented my frustration and anger especially in the private confines of the Speaker's office. It simply meant I had to try and maintain a level of decorum and follow the old adage if "one didn't have something nice to say, then remain silent." I was Speaker of all the members, whatever their political persuasion, and often found myself fighting partisan politics with one hand tied behind my back.

There were to be unfortunate exceptions to my ability to restrain myself over the next ten years, and it never failed to embarrass me and others. I once called a member an "asshole" from the podium. I thought the microphones all were off, but they weren't, and the castigation rang out across the hall. I apologized for it, even though I felt I had been on target in my characterization of this dupe, and I received a half dozen notes complimenting me for my ability to tell it like it is. The Press jumped all over me for it, and I had to read it in the next morning's paper.

Added to my unique ability to attract lightning, was the fact the Press found me one of those "good quote" characters, and once I was "tagged", it was like asking a fan to change his 50-yard line seat for one in the end zone. It just isn't going to happen. The Press never stopped running to me, and I never stopped running my mouth. It made great stories for them and a precarious political career for me. I brought it on myself, as I always knew when I said something stupid.

I could read the signs with an expertise after a while. In retrospect, I probably should have mastered the politician's greatest defense: "Think before you speak", and nurture to a level of perfection the ability to speak on any subject for great lengths of time without saying anything worth printing.

Toward the end of my second year, I was certain I had jumped into the crevice and fallen to my political death. We were performing the annual end-of-session ritual and the normal "hostage" taking of bills was going on between the House and the Senate. It didn't appear to be out of proportion to anything that had happened in the past, thus I felt a measure of confidence in threatening the Senate with a promise not to move their priorities unless they agreed to move those of the House. In particular, we were concerned with an environmental bill that attempted to protect the fast disappearing "open" land that symbolized most everyone's idea of what was right about Vermont. It was referred to as the Current Use bill. We had worked extremely hard on it while it was in the House and had to fight to get it through and over to the Senate. The Senate was now making excuses they didn't have the time this late in the session to deal with the bill properly and were refusing to suspend the rules to expedite the matter. The fact was they had had more than ample time, but simply tried to kill the measure by not dealing with it. The whole rebuttal to our efforts was led by the presiding officer of the Senate, Lt. Gov. Peter Smith. He managed to rally his minority of Republicans, and with a few Democratic Senators, he hung the matter up on the last day of the session. I looked at their actions as a matter of arrogance. I was certain they had to have a certain level of uneasiness with their limp excuse and were simply being unfair. I had no intention of putting up with it. But, they were in a position to carry out their threat, since rules suspension required a three-fourth's majority, and they had the votes. It was a case of tyranny by the minority.

The Press reported I targeted the Senate bill I set out to hold hostage, but this just wasn't true. It was simply a matter of coincidence the next bill moving through the House happened to be the Interstate Banking bill. I promptly took the bill itself out of the "pending bill" box and stuck it in my pocket. And that's exactly where I intended it to rest, until they unlocked the cage that held the Current Use bill. Unknowingly, I had pocketed the "flagship" of the entire Republican agenda for that session. It was the Republican agenda, but it seemed to be everybody's darling. Gov. Madeleine Kunin liked it, seeing it as a token for the business community as part payment to the ton of liberal legislation we passed in our first biennium as a Democratic swat team. There were Senators and House members alike who were in love with it, if only for personal reasons. Many held bank stock that promised to rise, even skyrocket, if certain smaller Vermont banks were to be given the right to merge, or be taken over by larger out-of-state banks. Finally, there was the whole contingency of bank lobbyists and executives who, in anticipation of the sure-fire passage of this relatively unnoticed bill, gleefully watched as their bank stock rose ever-so-consistently with each stage of the bill's passage. The gleeful atmosphere came to a screeching halt as I slipped the bill into my suit pocket and went off down the back stairs to dinner with Leigh Tofferi, the member from Ludlow.

It probably didn't help that when I was told the Senate would not cave in to what they considered an act of my arrogance, I responded with my best Clint Eastwood imitation: "Make my day."

I had gone too far; pushed the "system." But, I also felt strongly that the Senate had crossed that same line into an area unfair to those of us who had worked our tails off to pass a bill that we felt was vital to braking the over-development movement we thought was real.

The underlying motivation behind my action was I felt what the Senate was doing was no different than what I witnessed the bully doing in the schoolyard when I was a kid. If you just hand over your lunch money without a fight, it's never going to stop. You might just as well have your mother send the creep a check. The only answer to that type of threat was a good right to the nose. Even if you took a beating, the guy was smart enough to leave you alone next time. All this made perfect sense to me, and once I decided on my course of action, there was no turning back. If I backed off, I would have sent an eternal signal what I was saying was different than what I intended to do, that I would not fight for what I believed in. That type of wavering can end careers in a hurry. But, so can what I had just done.

I talked to dozens of people that night. "Don't do this, Ralph," one pleaded. "It'll be the end of you and as sure as I'm sitting here, your political career's over." I listened politely and, with more than a little realization, that what Harvey Carter, my friend from Bennington, was saying probably was true. Others showed up at my office door angry as hell. They arrived at the same conclusion that my friend had, except they expressed it in a louder tone. As for the Governor, I refused to even see her, as there was little I could do that would make her happy. It wasn't going to be the last time she would become extremely unhappy with me.

The pleading of my colleagues for me to relent and do the reasonable thing was unending and, at one point, I did waiver.

Earlier in the day I had handed the bill to Tim VanZandt, a Democrat from Springfield, whom I could trust and whom I had named as Chair of the conference committee. I gave him the simplest of instructions, "Get lost." If they don't have the bill, or the chairman of the conference committee, then they can't discuss it.

By evening, I was beginning to have some second thoughts. "OK, someone go find Van Zandt."

We searched all over the building, and then systematically made calls to all the places where he might be: his room in Montpelier, his best friend's room, and every watering hole in town. No Tim.

Finally, in exasperation I asked my assistant Nancy Mason to get me his home phone, even though I couldn't imagine him or anyone else leaving on the last night of the session. The phone rang a couple of times and a man answered, "Hello."

"May I speak to Representative Van Zandt, please."

"Hey! Ralph this is me, Timmy," he responded in a extremely upbeat manner. I couldn't believe it. He was home. A hundred miles away, with the bill.

"Timmy, what the hell ya doin' home? Where's the bill?"

"It's right here on the kitchen table. You told me to get lost. I always do what my Speaker tells me." And he broke out laughing.

Well, that was the end of any thought of caving in and bringing up the Interstate Banking bill, but it's not the end of the story. Four months later, I received a card postmarked York Beach, Maine, from my good friend Rep. Peter Allendorf of Underhill. It read as follows:

Dear Mr. Speaker,

As you can see, we are on our annual trek to the great beaches of Maine. We happen to be stopping at your favorite resort when who did we run into but none other than the member from Springfield, alias Tim Van Zandt. He sends his regards, and asked if you might relay, through me as an intermediary, just when he can come home.

Regards, L.T. Allendorf

P.S. I'll bet you a case of beer that you can't kill the Interstate Banking bill again next year.

We adjourned that Saturday night without the Interstate Banking bill or the Current Use bill. I hurried home and the next day found myself driving a big yellow school bus with my program* kids on a prearranged trip to Washington, D.C. Shortly after arriving, I called to tell Cathy we had arrived safely. Rick answered the phone and as it

---

* The "Bennington Program" is an alternative school for potential drop-outs that I directed for 23 years.

happened to be 6 P.M. on the nose, the Channel 3 news was just coming on. The lead story was the precipitous fall of bank stocks in all the major banks in Vermont. A lot of people who had anticipated the passage of the Interstate Banking bill had taken a bath. Rick hung up joking that I should check under the hood of the bus before starting it up in the morning. I didn't think he was funny.

I survived that episode and lived to see another four elections as Speaker. I didn't know it then but, like life itself, I was too caught up in the living to realize I was participating in that revolution that I have written about in an earlier chapter. With both Houses controlled by the Democrats, and only the third Democratic Governor in nearly 150 years, the Republicans were constantly fighting a retreating action. We set the agenda and we passed the agenda and it wasn't long before the Republicans threw up their arms and admitted they were now a "minority majority" party.

12. THE PRESS

The Speaker had total authority over more than committee assignments and the moving of the daily process. The Speaker also has the power of appointment to a multitude of subsidiary commissions, boards and conferences. In this capacity, he or she can give authority to members to attend conferences all over the country and, in the case of the Eastern Regional Conference, as far away as the Virgin Islands, which happens to be a member of that group. I had never been asked as a member to attend any conference of more importance than the group I called to verify the General Election in Room 11. This had changed the final year of my leadership, and Morse's final year as Speaker, as he asked both Paul and me to attend the National Conference of State Legislatures (NCSL), an annual event. It was being held in Boston. It was a great experience, as over 5,000 fellow legislators, their spouses, and Lobbyists attended these happenings and, for a week, it was non-stop meetings, banquets, and late evening cocktail parties that everyone was welcome to attend.

I'm not making a case for those who would want you to believe it is all work and no play. I will try to dispel the idea espoused by political critics that these conferences are not a necessary part of being a legislator. Perhaps participation is not vital, but we wouldn't operate the same without this travel and fellowship.

As Speaker, I followed my predecessor's guidelines and sent the same number of members to the 1985 NCSL meeting in Seattle that had gone to the Boston event. I tried to keep it bi-partisan and named an equal number of Republicans as Democrats. I decided to take Cathy and my youngest daughter, Suzanne, with me. As I hadn't flown for nearly 20 years I arranged reservations for the trip to Seattle via the Trans-Canadian Railroad. Over the years, I heard this was truly one of the great train rides in the world. Intending to make the trip a family affair, we made arrangements that allowed Cathy and me the extra days to venture leisurely out and back across the continent. We arranged for Suzanne to fly out with others in the group. I paid for Cathy and Suzanne out of my own pocket. All together, there were 35 legislators and staff members who would attend.

The Press never misses an opportunity to make some hay out of any type of legislative endeavor they consider to be a "perk." This was certainly no exception and the fact they're not held in Nome, Alaska in January, but in cities all over America that are promoted as inviting places to spend a week or so, just serves to incite the media all the more. God help the politician who gives the impression to a reporter he or she might be enjoying the trip. Suffice it to say, we all had a good time and returned home safely. An article or two appeared, listing the members who attended, and that seemed to be the end of it. So I thought.

I got a call early in October at my school from Tim Lewis, who I will characterize as a "wannabe" anchor man on Channel 3. Lewis never got my nomination for the *"Walter Cronkite Broadcaster of the Year Award",* but he was not someone with whom, up until then, I had any cause to be at odds about. He explained he talked his boss into allowing him to "follow the foliage south" *(his words)* and he'd like to come to Bennington and do a little blip for the 6 P.M. news specifically, and only, about budget matters.

Totally unsuspicious, though I was to learn whom I could and couldn't trust, I told him to come down as long as he timed it for an after-school interview.

He showed up at the pre-arranged time and we went into an empty classroom and began the interview. Things went fine right up until the point he thrust the mike closer to me and demanded, "Why don't you tell the Channel 3 viewers about your wife Catherine's train ticket?" Totally forgetting the camera was still rolling; I shot back, "What is this, Lewis? I can't believe you're pulling this shit."

I demanded he shut off the microphone and camera. He complied, as did the cameraperson, and the lights clicked off. But, the damage had been done. After a few minutes of raising my voice in protest to what I considered at best, misleading and at worst, deceitful conduct on his part, I explained in great detail the original mix-up in the purchase of tickets. I told him I was going to travel to Seattle by train with another member at first, but when my wife agreed to join me, we tried to switch tickets or at least the names of the people on the tickets. The tickets had been pre-purchased months earlier and I had personally purchased Cathy's fare. Although we could use a member's ticket, it belonged to Leigh Tofferi, the Legislative Counsel who, having prepaid for the ticket, would be reimbursed. I did exactly that, but Lewis never bothered to track my reimbursement. I challenged him to come to the travel agent's office and look at the records himself. No cameras. I could just imagine the great shot it would make with me coming out of Tony's Travel Agency. He agreed, and we rode separately down the street to Tony's. It seemed to go fine, although I thought Tony talked way too fast, and we exited the agency and chatted on the steps for a moment. Tony still was carrying on about what a terrible mistake this all was and how he could explain it, his arms flailing this way and that. Suddenly, out of the corner of my eye, I caught some movement to my left. I began moving in that direction when a camera woman stood up from her hidden position behind a car. I was so angry, I walked away in disgust. Lewis himself, seemed embarrassed by his second act of deceit in one day. It was all so preposterous I would have bet a million dollars they had wasted a trip to Bennington. Certainly they wouldn't play that tape.

I recall sitting with my 80-year-old mother on the porch watching the evening news that warm Indian Summer evening. Suddenly, there I was, bigger than life. We were in the classroom and Lewis had just dropped the bomb. I thought the whole neighborhood must have heard my not so classy response: "I can't believe you're pulling this shit."

My mother could barely hear a normal voice, but she looked up from her knitting and said, "Did I just hear right? Did you say what I think you said?" Forced to look away from the son of a bitch Lewis in front of me, I reassured my mother that, "Of course I didn't swear, Ma. This is a family news program, so they don't play that stuff. Turn up your hearing aid."

"Never mind my hearing aid." Long pause. "Your father had a foul mouth, but I tried to teach you kids better." If I could have gotten my hands on Lewis...

I don't know how the tape came to be played, and I'll probably never know. It is hard for me to believe Marselis Parsons, the highly respected Channel 3 anchor for over 20 years, would have allowed it had he known Lewis knew the facts. All I can surmise was that Lewis, trying to justify a wasted trip, never told Marselis the truth. It isn't just politicians who have trouble staying within certain moral guidelines.

This wasn't the only time a Channel 3 reporter acted in a less-than-distinguished manner. Paul Poirier and I noticed a shadow through the smoked glassed panel on the closed Speaker's door. Signaling to Paul to keep talking, I got up quietly from behind the desk and grabbed the doorknob, yanking it open. In stumbled Mike Gilhooly, a Channel 3 reporter. He was red-faced, as Paul and I roared at his much deserved embarrassment. We never carried out our threat to tell his boss, Marselis Parsons, as he soon left to become Dick Snelling's Campaign Press Secretary.

❖ ❖ ❖ ❖ ❖

I have an immense amount of respect for what the Press do and I am convinced that without them to keep a constant watch over the political world's shoulder, we might be the scoundrels people now think we are.

However, the Press is not without human traits, characteristics and faults. They are always suspicious of anything we say or do. Too often, they assume we are outright lying to them. There is a deep and ingrained suspicion there is always more to the story than revealed. Most of the time they're correct as politicians spend all their time trying to present themselves in the best possible light.

But it's disconcerting to be met day after day with a tone implying we're only telling half the story, or worse still, we're lying. This is not exactly conducive to a warm or lasting relationship. On the other hand, they'd be quick to tell you, "It's the truth we're after, not a relationship."

Reporters come in all shapes and forms and it is difficult to categorize them. I've known reporters who are fair and accurate, and I've known the other kind. Most are decent and hard working and feel genuinely out of sorts when they nail us in a story, but I've never known one to fail to write the worst of stories if they got the opportunity. There are also those who opt to take the easiest route to meeting a deadline. They're not especially enamored of hard work, and consequently end up running things that are not in tune with all the facts, or represent the whole story. These "short-cutters" represent a minority, but they exist and have administered a lot of damage on the innocent. These, too, can be tolerated as long as it isn't a lifestyle, but just a bad day, or perhaps a poor human connection with the "victim." If they're consistent with their unwillingness to do their homework or their obsession with a "gotcha" style of journalism, they can be dangerous to both the individual victim and the reading public as a whole.

One of the most shocking of revelations for those who find themselves in a seat of power is how different their world has become. This is very obvious to me now that I have the luxury of time and introspection, but I didn't have a clue when the mantle of power was dropped on me. I also didn't have the time or the insight to realize that a Speaker, as far as the Press is concerned, is no more than a lightning rod high atop the tallest building in town during a thunderstorm.

Most of their time is spent with eyes on the towering thunderclouds looming on the far horizon. The title of "Mr. Speaker" may get doors opened and telephones answered, but these perks aren't accompanied by a sudden rise in the IQ. I struggled constantly, day after day, never getting the hang of it all. Once my public image was defined by the Press, I had to live with it. Of course, I supplied all the ingredients for the molding of that image. But, what was acceptable private conduct with people who knew and loved me, was something else with a public that was getting their first glimpse of this new public power holder.

For those who didn't especially like me, it simply served as cannon fodder. In this respect, my critics soon learned the "hot button" quotes.

Within each reporter, you can find the best and worst. It all depends on the situation. Here's an example: Barbara Snelling had just been sworn in as Vermont's new Lt. Governor. Mrs. Snelling, the widow of the recently deceased Gov. Richard Snelling, arrived at the State House among much acclaim and glowing press reviews. Within days, the members of the legislature attended one of many open house receptions put on by the various special interest groups in the Capital. In this case, it happened to be the Vermont State Employees Association (VSEA). A group of us left the State House shortly after 6 P.M. and headed to the VSEA headquarters for the reception. I had barely entered the door, when I was approached by our new Lt. Governor. She started in on me over an incident that had occurred that day.

Her secretary, on her orders, had come into my office and in a less-than-humble manner requested I see to it the Lt. Governor be given the same opportunity Howard Dean, the previous Lt. Governor, had been afforded as it related to a list of weekly committee agendas in the House. In the first place, the former Lt. Governor had rustled up this information on his own and never asked my office to assist him in compiling it. Secondly, as I related to Snelling's secretary, "I'm not here to do the administrative chores, or in this case the political tricks, for your boss. If she wants this weekly compilation, she'll have to dig it out on her own." The secretary left in a huff and stomped downstairs to relay to her boss I was a no-good kind of guy. Of course, I moved throughout my 14 different committees and assured them they had better things to do than waste their time enhancing the Lt. Governor's political career by providing material I considered to be nothing more than a Monday morning political advertisement.

All the effort managed to do was allow radio stations throughout Vermont to play a short recording of our Lt. Governor providing the groggy early morning listening audience with a very abbreviated schedule of the upcoming week's public hearings. I didn't think hearing "the General and Military Committee in the House would be taking up the Firecracker bill at 1:30 P.M., Tuesday afternoon in Room 14" was the stuff that enlightens or excites an electorate. But it got her voice over the airwaves each and every Monday morning, which was the sole political intent. I wasn't going to waste any of my time on that type of bologna. And I thought it was important to let the new "Prima Dona" know that.

Her confrontation with me was more a show to serve notice she was not going to be cowered or intimidated by the big, bad Speaker. Actually she was over-exaggerating the Lt. Governor's small and insignificant place in the world of state politics. Under normal conditions, I probably would have gone on about my business as Speaker for years without ever finding a need for any conversation with the Lt. Governor's office, as the Founding Fathers had done more than an adequate job of burying it in obscurity. It was with some amazement I now found myself being challenged by this newly, self-promoted "super star."

I cut it short by turning toward her and exclaiming in my best tone of wonder, "You're a pretty aggressive woman, aren't you?" It wasn't exactly a statement that calls for a slap to the chops, but it wasn't a response that would have pleased my mother. That was the end of that confrontation, or so I thought.

The next afternoon Betsy Liley, the *Burlington Free Press* State House reporter, came bouncing into my office with the air of a reporter onto a juicy story. I had grown proficient enough to recognize the *"I gotta story, I gotta story"* look when I saw it.

"I understand you and the Lt. Governor had a little run-in yesterday at the VSEA reception." It was more an indictment than a question.

"Yeah! We had a few words. No big deal."

And now, the point of the blade was thrust deep into my back. "Well, she says you sexually harassed her."

There are moments that terrify the most arrogant of political veterans. An "eternity" that amounts to no more than a few seconds as the mind spins into damage control. Sweat dribbles across the rib cage and the inside of the mouth feels like cotton. A whole political career rolls across a fast moving screen. What do I say? Where can I hide? It is at these times that our most basic instincts take over. In war, it is the moment of truth that makes some men heroes, and others cowards.

I did what came naturally. I went for the groin. Out of nowhere, I could hear myself saying, "That's crazy, Betsy. If she said that she must have been tipsy." Liley never even bothered to say good-bye before she was out the door and on her way to the Lt. Governor's office.

As luck would have it, Mrs. Snelling was just getting ready to appear live on the 6 P.M. news to address the subject "how the Speaker sexually harassed her the evening before." At this point I was certain, and my suspicion was later confirmed to me by someone who was in a position to know, this was all planned with the help of one of my old nemesis from when she was in the House.

Of course Liley piped in, "Well, Lt. Governor, I just left the Speaker's office and when I asked him about your charges, he denied having sexually harassed you and accused you of being "tipsy." She quickly denied this.

"Well, how many drinks did you have prior to talking with the Speaker?" Liley followed up. "I had one wine Spritzer. So, he's misleading you on that."

Quickly Liley came back, "One?" and now came the same moment of terror for the Lt. Governor I had been through just minutes before.

She searched frantically for the right answer, and then, "Well, as I think, perhaps it was two. But I certainly wasn't 'tipsy'."

Welcome, Mrs. Snelling, to Politics 101. You've been in the political world under three weeks and you're on television denying you're a drunk. Not a great start.

Neither of us distinguished ourselves in this little spat and I came off worse in the ensuing fallout. The reports characterized me as a "chauvinist bully", and there was a run on lapel buttons within days that read, "Hi! I'm another aggressive woman." What little satisfaction I got out of the whole sad event was the knowledge our Lt. Governor never went to another cocktail party without being cognizant of the number of drinks she was consuming. As for Liley, I guess she had the envy of her fellow reporters in the State House.

There was one other incident with Liley to relate. I always made it a practice to keep my office door wide open as I wanted all to know that they were welcome to just walk in. Only a stranger to the Vermont State House would approach my assistant and attempt to make an appointment. That's the way things worked in our Citizen's Legislature and I welcomed the great majority of the people who took advantage of the open door policy. But there were times when I could read bad news coming from a distance and this time Liley's entrance spelled trouble as she walked in and closed the door. I had known Liley since she first appeared at the State House a year or so earlier and found her to be much more open to small talk and gossip than the other reporters. She was quick to smile and seemed gregarious. We had a standing joke where I would tease her about showing more partiality to Doug Racine, President Pro Tem of the Senate. He was an especially bright and serious fellow who I often described to others as our "tall, dark, and handsome preppy." I could get her going with a sarcastic remark or two and especially enjoyed referring to him as Dougie in front of her. I didn't think she ever took umbrage at my teasing as it was never intended as anything but humor. It was a complete surprise when she announced she was angry about an earlier conversation between us with the normal parrying back and forth. We both got serious in our remarks over the next few minutes when she cut in, "You don't have to yell at me."

"I'm not talking to you in any louder a voice than you are to me," I shot back, raising my voice even higher. I was trying to get to the door without being obvious.

And then she started crying.

It dawned on me I had to recognize there were occasions when I had to force myself to stop treating someone like they belonged to a single social and human strata. Not everyone was a Marine.

But, it was too late for that and I started for the door and got it half open when she, sobbing uncontrollably now, pushed it shut again. "Oh, Boy!" I thought, "You've done it now." Failing to find a handy tissue, I reached for the door to go into the outer office where I knew my assistant kept the tissues. It dawned on me that, with my luck, I'd open the door and find the lights glaring and I'd be back on the 6 P.M. news as the big, bad bully again. I shut the door fast and rushed to the bathroom at the far end of the office to get a paper towel.

I came out, not knowing how to console Betsy, but determined not to go near her. I shuddered to think we might touch. That imagined scene on video tape made all my blood rush to my head. Finally, I told her I didn't wish to continue this conversation any longer and she could go wash her face or something, but I was going to leave. She could stay as long as she wanted. And I left, driven from my own office.

The next day Liley came by to tell me she had talked to her editor about the previous day's events and she was told they were ready to bring sexual harassment charges against me. All they were waiting for was her to give the "go" sign. I wish I could tell you I challenged her to go right ahead and do just that, but I crumbled in a state of ineptness. Never in my life did I feel as trapped as I did now. I mumbled I thought she was wrong, but I was truly sorry for hurting her in this manner. I didn't dare say anymore and she left. I turned and went into the office not having any idea what trouble lie ahead of me. Here I was, the powerful Speaker, the guy with the gavel and control over things that meant so much to a lot of people's lives, but I couldn't, for the life of me, grasp or comprehend the situation in which I found myself. I felt helpless, like the world's biggest wimp.

I never heard another word about it, as Liley went on about her business as if nothing had happened. I made sure our relationship was totally formal and void of any teasing over the next year or so. I got a call one day from Judy Diebolt, the same editor Liley told me wanted to bring charges against me. It was one of those calls that editors infrequently make to gather information. I had never spoken to Diebolt before, but she seemed friendly and only interested in obtaining background information on a specific issue. I gave her what she wanted and she seemed so pleased and the conversation so friendly that I took the chance and explained I was having some very serious problems with one of her reporters. She seemed genuinely interested, so I pushed it further and brought up the incident with Liley in my office a year earlier. She appeared not to have any idea about what I was talking.

"You mean you never threatened to bring charges against me?" I was incredulous.

"Look," she responded, "Betsy never came to me with any such complaint. Nor did she go to her immediate boss, as our rules are very clear at the *Free Press* that we not only want to know stuff like that, but they have to let us know. If Betsy had said anything to anybody at all around here, I would most certainly have known. I've worked for big city papers and I know our reporters are a lot tougher than you think. If what she accused you of had really happened, it wouldn't have been up to her to do something about it. You would have heard from me. It never happened."

Wow! It was all becoming clear. Liley had used me. No, more appropriately, she had "abused" me. Why? I can only guess. Perhaps by putting the fear of God in me, she could extort a favoritism from me that others couldn't. Perhaps others had taken up the teasing over the Dougie thing and this was her way of laying it on me. Or perhaps it was just the inner Betsy Liley deriving some sort of sadistic pleasure out of my rush to feel guilt where none was called for. She told me a few days later I had gotten her in trouble with her boss. For the remainder of my days in the State House, she took on the same careful air of formality that I had taken on. *Yes, all politics is personal.*

❖ ❖ ❖ ❖ ❖

Members of the Press are no different than any other group of working people, but you have to look beyond the exterior posture to uncover all the normal traits the rest of us have. Reporters are notoriously underpaid and their normal day can last 10 to 12 hours, but the persistent strain of deadline is probably the least rewarding aspect of their daily existence. They get to deal in a highly emotional and often volatile atmosphere that seldom places their names or reputation on the line. Couple this with the constant need for recognition that permeates the core of the vast majority of politicians, and there are unlimited opportunities for even the run-of-the-mill reporter to go to work every morning with an air of excitement and enthusiasm that more than compensates for the piddling pay and the killer hours.

The old Mae West line "I don't care what you say about me as long as you spell my name right" is not only a damned lie when it comes to politics, it borders on sick. I immensely cared what the Press was saying about me and no one ever heard me running my mouth with such a self-callousness. What kind of perverted creature would take joy or pleasure being called vile names? Politicians resented and were hurt by such name calling. The reporters who participated in this type of charade were just as guilty as the "starved for affection" politician, as they knew a lot of what they printed was acceptable only in the political arena and only for a select group that was protected by the first amendment.

If they had practiced the name calling they so freely enticed political enemies to use against each other on their own families or personal lives, they would have been cut off at the knees by a moral code their mothers taught them. I can't believe they didn't hear the same laments from their mothers that you and I heard from ours: "If you haven't got anything nice to say, don't say anything at all"; "Stop picking on Billy"; "Be kind"; "How would you like it if Joanne did that to you?", and "Don't hurt him." These were childhood admonishments that had little meaning to a reporter whose entire professional existence was to beat the opposition and get the juicy quote. Sometimes it ended up less than attractive, and certainly short of professional. I often wondered how some of them found solace or refuge in being greeted by their little ones at home each night, "Daddy, daddy, how'd ja day go?" "Great son, I demeaned and embarrassed a public figure."

But, most reporters are fair and honest. There are a few exceptions who prove the rule. On a national level, this group is no longer considered a small pack of misfits who fail to hold on to an identifiable set of professionally accepted scruples. Walter Cronkite is very much alive, but he's all but dead as the guiding light of what our national Press should be exemplifying to the everyday viewer of the news and reader of the morning paper.

It all started with Watergate they say, and the cub reporter's ambition to grab for fame and fortune by becoming an investigative reporter. There may be a modicum of truth to that, but it isn't the whole story. I've read enough history that goes back a lot further than 1973, and the musings of historians are filled with the turmoil and worry of the Washingtons, Jeffersons, Lincolns, and other national heroes that awoke every morning, not worrying what luck their Secretary of State had in a far-off world while they slept fitfully, but rather what type of slander or libel was cast upon their bowed shoulders during the night.

President Bill Clinton may attempt to make the case he is the most castigated of all our previous executive leaders, but he's engaging in self-pity and acting as if he never read any of Lincoln's press clippings. The measure of greatness was not the level of castigation a person of power received, but how able they were to get on with the program, in *spite* of it. Lincoln, Jefferson, Washington, Wilson, and the Roosevelts were probably the targets of the greatest venom during their times of any renown American players in our history, but they outlived their critics as the archives rounded into the shape of truth in the writing of history.

Vermont had a couple of these "bad apples" and we all suffered the consequences. These were people masquerading as professionals who would have displayed the same personal attitude in the everyday world. "I'm out to getcha, and I'll use whatever means available I can get away with. I buy ink by the barrel and it's just a matter of time; so run and dodge all that your little heart desires, but, in the end, you'll end up as just another notch on my gun."

And into my life walked Nancy Wright (no relation).

She was a Speaker's worst nightmare. She was bright, tenacious, and it appeared to me totally lacking in the feelings of others. Nancy never believed anyone could hurt as she hurt. She was a female Rush Limbaugh. No novice at "I gotcha" journalism, she set out to bring me down. And, she damn near did. I was aware on a moment-to-moment basis I was being stalked by her over a period of weeks and months.

I was my own worst enemy as I constantly provided her with the ammunition to keep reloading her elephant gun. First there was a hockey game a bunch of us ran off to in Boston. Tickets were provided by an old friend who happened to be a lobbyist for a major insurance company in Boston, which did no business in Vermont. So much of what happens in politics is the impression, rather than the reality. Scathing article after scathing article appeared in the *Rutland Herald* as Nancy pursued this like it was a second breaking and entering at the Watergate.

It's easy to look back and recognize the wisdom in the advice you so often hear around a State House that once a story breaks, the embarrassed politician is almost always better off to rush immediately into "damage control." Simply stated, get the whole story out as soon as possible, take the hit and, assuming there's no more to be written, that's the end. It's a one day story. But this advice was mere words to me and I shuddered to think of reading that we had not only gone to Boston with seven free ducats to a Bruins game, but we had a meal on somebody else's tab. It didn't matter we had broken no laws, went on our own time after the session had ended and arrived back early in the morning, thereby missing no legislative time. It was still something we knew the reading public would look upon as conduct unbecoming to a dedicated public servant. To make matters worse, we committed the highest of sins: We really had a good time.

Nancy tracked that like she was on the trail of a deadbeat dad. She couldn't get one of us to answer the simplest of inquiries from her without it ringing with contradiction. That only made matters worse. She was quickly becoming the star of the Montpelier Press Bureau.

The second instance occurred on another infamous NCSL junket. This time, it was held in Nashville, Tennessee. Because it was such a big event, a national convention with 5,000 delegates in attendance, the conference rules were rigid in the way room reservations were made, and they were quick to levy a late fee if we missed the deadline for submitting the proper information. I was required to let them know as early as February as to the number of rooms the Vermont delegation would want to hold for the July event.

By March or April, I would have to supply the actual names of members who were planning to attend. Members, often being caught up with the session's agenda, would not be willing to commit that far in advance. Others would want to hold out in order to measure what the fallout might be if they were reported to be on another "junket." If the session went well and the public maintained a high opinion of its legislature, or if we were in an "up" economical period and weren't spending time cutting people's programs, it might be it wouldn't raise the public's eyebrows.

Others simply used attrition as the criteria to wait until the last minute, as the later your name went on the list of "junketeers," the fewer times it would appear in a news story.

None of this helped my predicament. I had to have the list of 15, 20, or whatever number we were going to send by April. I hadn't planned on going, so I did not put my name down. I did put down the names of those members who asked to go and, in keeping with tradition, I put the names of the House leaders on both sides of the aisle. Come June, I changed my mind and when the Republican leader Sara Gear made it known she didn't want to go, I informed the Council since it was too late to reserve a room under a new name, assume I would utilize the room reserved for Gear. We never canceled her room knowing someone would make a last minute decision to attend and would need it.

I checked in, but not without a hassle, as the desk clerk insisted I could not occupy the room that was not going to be utilized by Sara Gear. I pulled rank as Speaker and, after some heated words with the desk manager, I got my way.

Back home, Gear saw an opportunity to make some hay out of all this and ran to the Press claiming I tried to make her look like a common junketeer. She was tired of traveling as she had just returned from dancing on the Rhine, compliments of Pfizer Pharmaceutical. Not only had I put her name on the list without her knowledge (the practice as it concerned leadership, plus I never guessed Gear would pass up an opportunity to travel at taxpayer's expense). Now she claimed I had made it appear that she actually attended the conference by leaving her name on the reserved room and checking into it. It probably never occurred to Sara, all she had to do when asked if she had attended, was to tell the truth and answer no. That would have been the end of it I certainly made a lame disguise as Sara Gear, especially since I had checked in as Ralph Wright. The normally motivated reporter would have raised an eyebrow to the complaining call from Gear. But Nancy Wright wasn't a typical reporter. She jumped at this like it was a winning lottery ticket.

She made calls into rooms of members from the Vermont delegation inquiring as to my whereabouts. During each call, she wouldn't say who she was and consequently got little of what she was looking for. Finally on the third day, I had enough of Nashville and made arrangements to come home early. By then, the rumors had spread throughout the delegation I'd probably be arrested as I left the plane upon my arrival in Vermont.

Nancy hadn't lost any of her tenaciousness as she kept up a daily attack against my conduct. And once again, I didn't know how to respond and fell back on my long standing defense that if I remained silent the story would be a "one-day" wonder and soon fade. I underestimated Nancy once again. She kept at it and with each story managed to raise the false indignation of Sara Gear. And, could Sara do the indignation thing!

Then, I got lucky.

Nancy and Sara were trying to make the case that somehow I had managed to check in without ever revealing I was anyone other than Sara (quite a physical leap of imagination). I made the case to Nancy that was remote, as I would not have used my own credit card if I had done such a thing. Even the dumbest of desk clerks would have perceived I was not a Sara.

They were making the case that the rooms were prepaid by the State of Vermont and therefore no exchange of money or credit cards was possible. To confirm this, they got Senator Dick Mazza from Grand Isle County to make a statement he most certainly had been allowed to check in without showing a credit card and to make it worse for me, to claim his room was, in fact, prepaid by the Legislative Council.

Once again, my guardian angel fell from the sky and landed in my lap. His name was Paul Teetor, a rather notorious figure in the Vermont Press for his style and ad libbing methodology in digging after a story. I don't know why Teetor entered the fray, but one can assume he saw a juicy story. Somehow he got a quote from Mazza angrily refuting the Nancy Wright story. He never told her that which she so willingly printed. His room wasn't prepaid, nor was he allowed to check in without putting up his own credit card. A call to the Council revealed that it was true none of the rooms for attending members had been prepaid. In addition, Nancy assured her editors, that in keeping with good journalistic practices, she made the effort to contact me with the opportunity to defend myself. Her problem was she had been pretty specific as to the exact time she had claimed she called me at my home, but I could produce a telephone tape that had phone messages just prior to, and shortly after that, to me. There was no call from Nancy or anyone else during that block of time. I headed for the *Herald's* editorial office in Rutland.

I might as well have been Richard Nixon pleading, "I am not a crook."

I got the steely-eyed stares as I laboriously went through my story, and it was obvious from the beginning they weren't going to abandon one of their own and take up with the likes of me, another learning from the dark side of the world of journalism. Only minutes into my plea for understanding, and realizing I wasn't getting very far, I asked to confront Nancy with the difference in our stories. A call was made to Montpelier where she was stationed and we got into an argument of some intensity and duration. A few minutes into this debate, I sensed someone else was in Nancy's company, on a separate telephone. I was more than a little upset when political columnist Jack Hoffman came on and admitted he had been listening. The editor, John VanHousen, showed no embarrassment at what I construed as eavesdropping. I left feeling I only made matters worse by attempting to explain.

They pulled Nancy off the story. Teetor had done what came natural to him. In addition, Sara, milking and pushing her dagger of indignation to the hilt, held a press conference to go through methodically, one more time, the tangled web of my scandalous conduct. By then, the Press, in its magical way, had decided there was no more to this escapade and it was Stu Seidel, another *Free Press* reporter, who declared an end to this war by asking her to explain how she could justify dancing on the Rhine on Pfizer Pharmaceutical's tab, while she was pretending not to be in conflict with the health care issues presently in front of the Vermont legislature.

There seemed to be an unfairness to the notoriety that would be given to me, as Speaker, when, at the same time, members could wander around the country at will without the Press noticing or seemingly not caring.

Nancy went on to continue her "cause" to plague me as her resilience to my most obnoxious retorts ran right off her back like water off a duck. And, it got rough. She once had her editors threaten to bring me up on charges by having a law firm notify me in writing of their intentions, claiming I assaulted her one evening by closing her out of the legislative lounge that served as a refuge from non-members. I did try to guide her out by taking hold, not firmly, of her elbow and closing the door to the lounge after her, but that hardly measured up to anything resembling assault. But that's how far relations had deteriorated between us. The tragedy was she didn't seem to care.

I called and, in desperation, talked to Kendall Wild, the long-time, street-smart editor of the *Rutland Herald*. Wild is one of those newspaper people about which movies are made. He's seen it all or at least enough to know when somebody's trying to con him. And he was not the easiest person, at least for me, to approach.

I called and said, "I give. Tell me how to get this on track. I've tried everything and things just continue to get worse." I wasn't trying any con game. I was serious and at wit's end. He arranged for me to have what I hoped would be a civil chat with Nancy, the beginning of a new relationship. I anticipated it with the anxiety of a teenager on his first date, expecting the worst, but hoping for the best. As it turned out, it was a disaster.

The day came for us to sit down and have a civilized conversation, and it was a strained and trepidation-filled encounter right from the beginning.

To my surprise, things mellowed a bit as the conversation delved into how we both were raised not two miles from each other and we noted the coincidence for the first time that we both carried the surname Wright.

And then, reaching for a higher level of familiarity, I asked "Are you married, Nancy?"

"No."

I don't know why I said what I did and the best excuse I can give is it was just the "wise-guy" in me. But, failing to harness something inside me, I heard myself utter in a tone of "gotcha", and I responded.

"Well, Nancy, I can understand that."

Boy, did she blow. I got called things I hadn't heard since Camp Le Jeune.

Way to go, Ralphie, you ass.

Nancy went on to win the prestigious Nieman Fellowship awarded to the outstanding journalists from throughout the United States. The word throughout the State House was all she did to qualify and win was submit the dozens of scathing and crucifying articles she wrote about me. I was happy for her, but even happier for myself. She was going to be 150 miles away for the next year or two.

The epilogue to this story is that Nancy Wright took on one of her own just before she departed for Harvard. She wrote a very disparaging article about a former reporter at the *Herald* accusing her of using her influence while a reporter covering a Congressional campaign, to land herself a job with the winner, in this case, Press Secretary to Bernie Sanders. After completing her stint at Harvard with all the future "Edward R. Murrows", she did not return to the *Rutland Herald*. Apparently, it's one thing to do a rogue like Ralph Wright in, but quite another thing to do in one of your own.

❖ ❖ ❖ ❖ ❖

On a professional and governmental level, our democratic doctrines wouldn't be worth the paper they're written on without the members of the Fourth Estate. There should be no doubt about that. I am convinced that not only does "power corrupt and absolute power corrupts absolutely", but without the vigilance of the Press, turning over every rock to enable the citizenry to see what crawls out, it would simply afford us the opportunity to dive to the depths of the scoundrels. Our history is chock full of examples of the Press riding to the rescue of the American people and I'm not without a slew of examples that go beyond Watergate or the Teapot Dome Scandals to prove what I am attempting to argue here.

If you forced me to save but one of the amendments that make up the Bill of Rights, without hesitation, it would be the first amendment.

When people asked me why I didn't respond to the multitude of bad press I got, I always answered that if I responded to "bad" press, then I had some sort of obligation to respond to "good" press. Beyond that, I would be hard pressed to think of too many examples of awful stories that didn't have some iota of truth to them. They might have been slanted in my disfavor, but there was still the truth holding the story together. I didn't believe I got to pick and choose the parts that pleased me. Either did the reporter. I usually let it ride knowing there would be something different for them to be chasing the next day.

I regretted not being able to gain admittance to the inner circle of reporters so that I might get to know them better. Almost without exception, they avoided this level of socialization with members. The old days of partying or hoisting a tall one with your friendly knight of the round table were long gone, at least in Montpelier.

13. HOME SWEET 'HOME'

It wasn't always that way in Montpelier. When I first arrived in 1979, Montpelier had a reputation as a party town, at least when the legislature was in session. The three or four nights legislators spent in town each week were filled with lots of different events, or if nothing was scheduled, it was not uncommon for rather large groups to gather in one of the two watering holes to gab and gossip about the day's events. At the very least, one could always find some self important person to carry on at great length as to what was wrong with Vermont, or for that matter, America. I stayed at the old Tavern, just across from the State House, during my first few years in the legislature and I must say it was as good a classroom as you could find for Politics 101. I chose the Tavern because it was convenient and had as cozy a "taproom" as I had ever frequented. The crowd would be sure to gather each day we were in session as early as 5 P.M., but one wouldn't have to drink alone anytime of the day. There were many nights I sat up with my friends Harold Weidman or Ray Poor, shooting the bull until 1 or 2 in the morning.

I learned a lot about all the business that went on in the State House during the day, and in particular, about the Senate, as Senators tended to migrate to the Tavern. The location was convenient for the generally older Senators and it attracted primarily Republicans.

That time spent with these rather conservative keepers of the public trust was to prove valuable to me in later years. I didn't win many arguments as the young holder of the liberal flame during those long winter nights in the lobby by the warmth of the fireplace, but I stored away their modus operandi.

There are two sections in the Tavern, new and old; the old section was just that: old. It long since shut down its guest rooms in the older wing, and probably not a minute before the Safety Board did the closing for them. It was a humble place to lay one's head. The rooms were small and sparsely furnished, but the biggest problem was the room temperature couldn't be controlled. Old cast iron radiators kept spewing forth heat, summer or winter, and the only defense was to open the windows. This worked best if the hall door was open and allowed a breeze to blow through. It was a giant leap in humility to lay on the bed in underwear.

Tim Corcoran and I were not in a position to move into the high rent district of the hotel, so we took a room on the fourth floor in the old section. Rent was $24 per night for the two of us. Most evenings passed without incident, so it was with a feeling of "oh, what else is new" that we fell asleep for the night in our underwear, with the window and door wide open. Before too long, we were surprised to find we had been awakened by a dog's howl. It seemed every time somebody got off the elevator to return in either direction to their rooms, the dog would begin howling. We were at the head of the wing near the elevator, so the noise came through loud and clear.

At first we tried to ignore it and fall back to sleep after the dog had calmed down. But with each new arrival to the fourth floor, our irritation grew in direct proportion to the dog's misery. Eventually, I heard Corcoran get out of bed, and leave the room mumbling to himself. Upon returning, he called down to the front desk and complained that the lonesome dog was keeping us awake. The desk clerk told him there was little he could do, as he got no answer after calling the dog owner's room. The occupant was obviously not yet in. "I'm sure the dog will quiet down once his master gets in, sir."

"Terrific," I heard Corc mumble, "we might as well be in the local kennel."

I fell back to sleep but was awakened by a door closing down the hall, followed by the hysterical happiness of a dog whose master has returned. Quiet quickly ensued as everybody, having returned home safely, fell off in that wonderful world of deep slumber. I was awakened once again, for the umpteenth time, this time by Corcoran dialing the desk clerk.

"Hello, Front Desk?"

"Could you please connect me to 401."

"One moment, please."

I could hear the phone ringing in the telephone right next to me and also down the hall in room 401.

"Hello," said someone in a sleep induced mutter.

"Yes. Is this room 401?" Corcoran asked politely.

"Yes," a women answered suspiciously.

"Do you have a dog in the room?"

"Yes," she answered in a surprisingly straight forward manner.

"May I speak to him, please?" Corcoran asked, totally under control.

"I beg your pardon?" she answered in a confused voice.

"I asked if I might speak to the dog," repeated Corcoran.

There was just the slightest hesitation before the innocent response, "The dog's sound asleep."

"Well, wake the son of a bitch; he's kept us up all night long." And he hung up, rolled over and went to sleep. The rest of the night continued without incident.

Corcoran has a heart as big as gold. And he doesn't mind mixing his need to help people with his sometimes warped sense of humor. He got a chance to practice both late one night as we sat in the lobby of the hotel shooting the breeze. It was one of those cold, wintry nights that characterizes Vermont in February.

The streets were empty of traffic and people, and except for a few hangers-on in the lobby and bar, there were no signs of the normal comings and goings of the usual crowd that passes through the hotel lobby. We were surprised when a lone straggler pushed hesitantly through the door and slid off quietly to the far side of the lobby. He did not go unnoticed by the desk clerk and within minutes, having determined that the poor soul was a transient passing through, he asked the man to leave.

He got up without an argument, and went out the door back into the cold wintry evening. Or, so we thought. I had a moment of remorse that I hadn't done anything to assist the young man, but this passed quickly and I returned to the conversation around me. Corcoran, as was his custom, got up for the tenth time, and wandered off.

Fifteen minutes or so passed, when I noticed out of the corner of my eye that Corc had gone to the front desk and gotten the key to our room. I didn't know it then, but the homeless gent had found a good Samaritan, and he was my roommate. A couple of hours had passed and it was close to midnight when the group still sitting in the lobby saw another legislator (I'll call him Alvin, since it really doesn't matter) come down from his room, and approached the front desk in a state of great agitation. Corcoran, who had just rejoined us, watched the conversation at the front desk with interest.

Now Alvin was generally known as somewhat of a nerdy fellow and he and Corc were never the best of friends. Alvin also aggravated me, but I stayed away from him. The ruckus at the desk began to reach a crescendo that made us all turn and watch with curiosity. Corc sat like a fascinated kid watching the lion act at the circus.

"I want to know what the hell some stranger is doing in my room, sound asleep on the bed next to me," Alvin bellowed at the clerk.

"Sir," the desk clerk answered while calling on all his reserve, "I have no idea what you're talking about. What room are you in?"

"Whattya mean what room am I in? I'm in my own God damned room, that's what room I'm in. I'm asking you why is there a total stranger in the bed next to me? What's he doing there?"

"Again, sir, I don't know what you're talking about. Perhaps you're in the wrong room." This was said with just the slightest hint that perhaps Alvin had consumed a few too many, and had gone to the wrong room.

"Now just you hold a minute," Alvin said, now indignant. "Are you insinuating I don't know where my own room is? I went up there, showered, and brushed my teeth, with my own toothbrush by the way, and I know my own God damned toothbrush when I see it, and when I come out there he was, sound asleep in the bed next to me."

"You mean it isn't your roommate in the bed next to you?" The clerk now grasping at the last possible explanation available to him.

"Look, I've about had it, I don't have a roommate. In all the years I've stayed here, I've never had a roommate. I didn't have one when I checked in this week and I don't have one now. Am I getting through to you?"

"Er, yes. Yes, sir! It's just that I don't have an explanation. Perhaps we could go up and see what's going on." He turned and reached for the extra key that was no longer in the box behind him, but was resting in Corc's front pocket. "Do you have the extra key, sir? We don't seem to have it here at the desk."

"I left *my* key up in my room. I can't believe this," Alvin said, totally exasperated.

"Well, no problem, I'll ask your roommate if he'll let us in," and he reached for the phone.

That was it. "Don't you dare call that room, ya hear. And I've already told you I don't have any God damned roommate, now or never," Alvin exploded. "Whatta mean 'you're gonna call him and ask if he'll let me back in my own room' It's my room. I don't have to ask permission to get back into it. Now get another key and get me back in my God damned room, ya hear?"

"Yes, sir. You don't have to raise your voice. I'm right here and I don't have a hearing problem. I'll have to get the security guard who's somewhere in the building. It'll take a few minutes." He left Alvin standing there in his pajamas and bathrobe as the rest of us just stared.

Corcoran casually got up and left us and I didn't see him until long after he had gone to bed. All he said when I came into the room was, "Boy, it's a miserable night out there. Not fit for anyone to be outside."

And then with a smile in his voice, "Alvin sure was hot at something tonight, wasn't he?"

❖ ❖ ❖ ❖ ❖

The party place to be was the old Brown Derby Supper Club. It was here the younger Democrats gathered for, should it appeal, some serious drinking. Speaker O'Connor stayed here and, as I was to find out, this was where the action was. The Derby had none of the Tavern's charm as it was in its last days, but if one wanted to drink beer out of the bottle and rent a room for $50 a week, this was the place.

Not many wives stayed here and for those who liked to dance, the night was always young. I could drink beer out of a bottle just fine, but I wasn't much of a dancer. Consequently I missed out on a lot of extra curricular happenings those first few years.

I attempted to remain at the Tavern after I became Speaker, but I soon learned that being a member and being Speaker, put different strains on my time. As a member I could go to my room and not be disturbed until I emerged in the morning. The same wasn't true as Speaker. Just like my office door was always open, so was my room door, at least as far as the members were concerned. It wasn't unusual to get a knock on the door, all hours of the night, from a member who had some important matter that couldn't wait until morning to discuss with me. Less frequent, but not unusual, were the constant pranks and general horsing around by members who by mid-evening had reinforced themselves downstairs in the Justin Morgan Room to the point of declaring it "party time." I was no wallflower and I liked a good time as well as the next person, but after a few months I gave up trying to let the phone ring or ignore the pounding on the door, and moved out.

It was Corcoran who barged into the Sergeant-at-Arms office and, with a straight face, asked if he knew the protocol as it concerned the Speaker's allowance for room expense.

"Well," Reide Payne, the Sergeant-at-Arms, patiently answered, "there aren't any apartments still available this far into the session. There's a couple here still listed as available, but I don't think you're going to find something suitable. The nice places have all been taken."

"Well," said Corcoran, "why don't we buy a place?"

"Buy a place?" Reide looked up, mystified. "You can't buy a place. That'll require a mortgage."

"We'll get a two year mortgage, unless..." and he turned to me. "How long are you going to be Speaker? Can you do thirty years?"

"Why don't you guys just rent a place for the first ten years or so." Reide sarcastically suggested.

And that's exactly what Corcoran, Harold Weidman and I did. We rented a place for ten years, or so.

We were an odd trio to say the least and the next eight years was interesting, indeed. I don't believe you could have found three people with less in common. Harold was a conservative Republican, although I always teased him that he was becoming a flaming liberal with each passing act of ostracizing his friends unloaded on him. He kept strange hours as he was a napper and a night person. I don't believe he ever slept for more than an hour or two at a time. Corcoran was in his own world of pranks and teasing and, in general, forcing one and all to keep him in view whenever he entered the room. He was born dialing the phone and he didn't need the phone book to find your number. He had hundreds stored in his head.

Corc and I slept in the same bedroom as we quickly labeled Weidman a snorer and put him by himself in the other bedroom. The fact was, we were all snorers, it was just that two of us were in denial.

Corc was a good roommate. He was considerate, and no matter how obnoxious he might be during his waking hours, he went out of his way to accommodate me in that little 10 x 14 bedroom. I got the whole closet, as I had 15 or 20 suits and Corc would generally have just a change of shirt or two. His entire wardrobe fit on the kitchen chair next to his bed. Because I would be up and out in the morning earlier than both my roommates, I got to shower before Harold, who slept in, or Corc.

The kitchen was simply a place to store the wake-up juice and once or twice a week cook popcorn. As I was the only one of the three who drank, there was never more than a beer in the refrigerator. I don't believe we ever ate a meal there.

Corc was great in one other way as he would roll in for the night, usually after I had already climbed in, and bring me up to date on what he had learned during the day. And he learned enough in any given day to keep ten people from being curious. I often went to sleep with my sides hurting from laughter when he was through. As was his custom, he would fall asleep in the middle of a sentence, and wake up in the morning and pick up exactly where he left off the night before.

We soon developed a routine. I would wake up to the clock radio at 5 A.M. and listen to the Bob Bannon Show on WSKI until it was time to get up to shower and shave. Bannon has been a Montpelier radio personality for many years, a one-man band and the only one in the station that early in the morning. To many, he was known as a nutty sort of guy who evolved into a folk hero. He'd frequently get up to visit the bathroom or walk to the other side of the studio to read the temperature, a fetish with him, and leave the airwaves in silence for however long it took him to accomplish what he set out to do. Truckers entering his broadcast area while driving the interstate that circled Montpelier for half a dozen miles, could enter and leave without ever being aware the Bob Bannon Show was on the air.

He must have been in his seventies, perhaps older, and he was a very conservative guy who didn't mind tearing into whomever displeased him at that given moment. No one was spared his embarrassing tirades. Amy Davenport, the Representative from Montpelier and presently a judge, having committed a traffic violation years earlier, was often the victim of his venom. He saved his special specimens for politicians and public figures, but his real enemies were the cops.

Bannon was convinced no matter what time of day or night, if you needed a cop, the worst thing you could do was dial 911. He would insist the only number to call for police assistance was the nearest Dunkin' Donuts. He felt that's where they lay in prey for an innocent citizen with a heavy foot. He also hated kids or parents who, on stormy mornings, would call in asking for the school closings just after he finished reading them.

I always listened with a degree of fear and trepidation that I might have made the overnight wire service and consequently would get lashed.

But he never seemed to bother Corc, who took a special joy in aggravating him with a daily call. Corc didn't awaken with anything resembling a "good morning", but I would hear the punch of the phone being dialed in the dark of the bedroom. Not only would I be listening to the voice in the other bed, but I could hear it simultaneously over the radio.

"Hello," Bannon answered in a guarded tone.

"Can you tell me the correct time, please?" said a mellow Corc.

"I just read the time two minutes ago. Listen up."

"Well, I couldn't hear you. Perhaps you can speak up."

"What's the matter with you? Whattya mean I should speak up? Why don't you just turn up your volume?" Bannon's voice rose.

"You got the time?"

"It's the same time I announced a minute ago."

"Can't be. That was a minute ago. I'm asking now. What time is it, now?"

"It's time to hang up." And down would come the slam of the receiver over the radio.

Bannon took special pleasure in embarrassing members of the legislature who broke traffic laws. Occasionally, during his daytime travels, he would observe, or worse be told about a Senator or Rep speeding on the interstate. Because they had legislative plates, he would be able to identify them, as long as he took the time to call the Sergeant-at-Arms and inquire.

He might forget, of course, but by then he would have received an "anonymous" tip about who the culprit was. Then we could be sure Bannon's world would soon know.

Fortunately, Bannon's world was a narrow one and he didn't get around that much, but he did manage to have his anonymous caller do his daily civic duty and report one or two scofflaws each morning. Representative Herbie O'Brien got his name read over the air three mornings in a row, apparently suffering from a bad case of "heavy foot", on his way to and from his home in Stowe. Herb, being way outside the broadcast bounds of the station, was totally unaware he was being labeled "Public Enemy #1."

I heard the punch of the phone and I sensed what was coming.

"Hello," answered Bannon.

"Bannon, this is Herbie O'Brien," said the voice on the radio and from the other bed.

"Uh, ah! It's Barney Oldfield himself, is it?"

"Bannon, you mention my name one more God damned time and I'm going to come down there and blister you right in the mouth."

"Well, a tough guy, huh, O'Brien. Why don't you just c'mon down here and we'll see who punches whom in the mouth."

I don't think Bannon ever caught on to who was serving as his deputy in his quest to rid the world of deadbeats and undesirables, but he had one character for whom he truly showed affection: Sheriff Bo Maloney, fighter of crime.

The sheriff called only once or twice a week, but when he did, Bannon would give him two or three minutes of air time, as he obviously enjoyed having the sheriff with him.

The sheriff spoke in a deep southern accent and carried a tone of a man on a mission.

"Good mornin', Bob, this is your sheriff calling from way down here in Plains, Georgia. I just had to make a run in my gun ship helicopter to visit with my 82-year-old mamma and have her serve me up some of her world famous fried hammocks. I don't believe that you've ever had a real taste delight until you've tried my mamma's home cookin', Bob. I wish you could join me right at this very minute, Bob, as we feed the prisoners their last meal. You know, Bob, this is confidential, but I had one of those boys whisper to me just this morning, and it is a truly fine morning down here in the heart of Dixie. Well, he whispered to me that he was almost happy to go to his death. Bob, as you know, down here in the land of truth and swift justice, we use a twin electric chair that works as fine as a well-tuned Chevy pickup. A course it's a little more expensive than hangin', but we find that since we did away with juries we have a few extra dollars to carry out justice in a real expedient manner. Well this boy, his name's Billy Bob, he says to me it's almost a pleasure to go to the electric chair if the last meal is goin' to be cooked by my little ole mamma. Now that's an honor that gits your day off right. Eh, Bob? Of course we are real thankful that the Honorable Judge Vincent Ialousa, the 'hangin' judge', so graciously took time from his busy schedule to fly on down here with me and bang that there gavel, BOOM-BOOM-BOOM. YOU'S GUILTY-YOU'S GUILTY. Well we got a regular little ole assembly line goin' here, me and Judge Ialousa. Fine American, that boy, fine American."

"Well, Sheriff Maloney, it's so nice to hear from you. Traveled way down there to rid us of some of the scum and vermin, did you? You hurry home as there's plenty to be done right here in the great metropolis of Burlington."

"Well I'll be not bothering you anymore, Bob, but I just want to call in and let you know there are still places here in this great country of ours where our mommas and sisters can walk the streets in safety; knowing that their guns are theirs forever, and the children can play in the yards without their mommas worrying half to death about their little souls. God bless them, and God bless you, Bob. And Bob."

"Yes, Sheriff Maloney?"

"And Bob, God Bless America."

And Bob Harris, alias Sheriff Bo Maloney, hung up.

❖ ❖ ❖ ❖ ❖

I often made light of the fact I had spent as much time with Harold and Corc as I had my wife. The first eight years we rented a condominium from a couple who went to Florida for the winter and, being satisfied with the care we took to maintain their home, we were invited to return each year. We never met them personally, so it came as a surprise when we heard the husband had passed away suddenly and the widow had decided against going to Florida another year.

I found myself back in the Tavern after all this time. The three of us arranged to rent adjoining rooms on the fifth floor.

One of the rooms was a corner room, big and spacious, and as I was smoking cigars at the time, Harold and Corc paid deference to me and didn't argue over the arrangement. Besides, I argued, I bunked with the Corc all these years, it was now Harold's turn. Corc was not into this domestic stuff and consequently never gave a sign of caring where he slept. There was a door connecting the two rooms, and though I locked it upon going to bed each night, it was left open at all other times.

The phone startled me awake and I looked at my clock radio. It was nearly 3 A.M.. Who the hell could be calling at this hour? I hoped it wasn't Harris, or Corc, screwing around.

"Hello."

" Ralph, open the door."

"Who is this?"

"It's me, Timmy. Open the door. You've got to come over. Something's wrong with Harold. I told him to go home, but he's acting weird."

"Corcoran, he is home. I'll be right over, but you better not be screwing around." I got up, threw on my khakis and opened the door. The light was on and I thought I'd burst out laughing at the scene. There was Harold, lying on the bed, white legs sticking out from his heavy overcoat, with a towel wrapped around his head like he was the Sheik of Araby. To his right, one level lower, lay Corcoran on his cot, his eyes closed in an effort to fall back to sleep.

Now you have to understand how Corcoran's mind works in a situation like this to realize he felt great discomfort and fright and, having made the call, served to provide the excuse he needed to turn the problem over to me. In his mind, he had done his job, and it was no longer something with which he had to concern himself.

"Corcoran, what's goin' on?" I asked, not knowing what to think with the scene now in front of me.

"Harold, tell Ralph, what you've been doin'. Go ahead. I told you, if you didn't go to bed I was goin' to call Ralph." Harold didn't move. "He's actin' weird," he repeated. "He keeps getting up and going in the bathroom and standing under the sun lamp. He says he's freezing and puts on his coat and gets into bed. He keeps talking to himself. I don't know what he's saying. Just mumblin'. I told him he just oughta go home."

I knew Harold was sick, real sick. I didn't know what it was, but he felt all clammy when I felt his forehead and I told him to get his shoes on, that we were going to go to the hospital. I went back to my room to jump into my clothes. When I returned, Harold was sitting on the bed, but still with no shoes on. Corcoran had fallen fast asleep.

"God damn you, Corcoran. What the hell you doin'? We gotta get Harold to the hospital. Now get up and get downstairs and get the car warmed up and be by the back door when I get him dressed and down there." Corc jumped up, threw on his clothes and went out the door.

 I got Harold up, put his shoes on, and brought him downstairs, where Corc was waiting with the car running. It was a bitter cold, wintry night and, as we pulled out of the lot in the back of the Tavern, it crossed my mind that Harold was probably having a heart attack. Maybe I should have just called the Rescue Squad. Well, it was too late for that now, and I tried to console myself that ordering Harold up might not have been the smartest move, but it beat Corc's suggestion that Harold go home to Wallingford.

We got to the end of State Street and instead of Corcoran taking a right and heading for the hospital, he swung left heading for the Canadian border. It didn't take long for me to shout at him, "Where the hell you goin', Corcoran? The hospital's the opposite way."

"I've never been to the hospital." He made a U turn.

"You've spent half your life in this God damn place, and you don't know where the hospital is. If it was a poker game, you'd know two shortcuts. Just step on it. Harold's really not feeling too well."

I kept talking to Harold as he was moaning and I wondered if he knew that he was having a heart attack. I finally quieted him as we were going up Berlin Street, when Corcoran, who hadn't said a word, suddenly burst forth with this observation:

"It was right here, somewhere."

"Right here, what?" I inquired.

"You know. Where what's his name croaked." He was referring to a former member who had passed away suddenly in a nearby apartment on this road. This got a response from poor Harold and he moaned anew.

"Corcoran, will you shut the hell up, and just drive."

We got Harold to the hospital and checked him in. We went back and tried to grab a couple of hours sleep. We stopped at the hospital the next day before leaving town to see how Harold was doing. Even though he was in Intensive Care and we were not family, we managed to talk our way past the Nurse's Station and entered Harold's room. It was a world of tubes and wires, all intricately hooked up in an effort to keep poor Harold on this planet. He didn't look too well, but at least he was alive. I talked small talk and Harold had all he could do to show a polite recognition that he cared what I was saying. Corc was just sitting, looking left and right at the maze of wires and tubes.

"Harold where's your check?" Corc said suddenly.

"It's in my coat, in the closest over there," Harold answered feebly. Corcoran got up and went to the closet. After a moment he stuck his head out.

"Harold, I can't find it. You come get it." Like a robot, and to my horror, Harold got up, and headed across the room toward the closet. Following him was all the different apparatus to which he was hooked up. Out in the Nurse's Station, I guessed the buzzers and lights were going off like a Fourth of July fireworks display. In rushed nurses and doctors, and we caught hell. They didn't lay their hands on us, but they made it clear we weren't wanted there any longer. Corcoran, moving fast, did manage to find the check and get Harold to endorse it before we left. Once we got on Route 89 and headed south, my curiosity got the best of me.

"Corcoran, ya mind telling me just why the hell it was so important that you got Harold's check back there?" His response was casual.

"Yeah! If Harold croaks before we get this check, then it goes into his estate and Probate holds it up for a year, maybe longer. This way in an hour, we stop in Wallingford, and Helen's got $1,500 and she gets to buy the groceries." Amazing.

There were times when the State House took on the appearance of a M.A.S.H. unit. I'm happy to say Harold recovered, though he had a quartriple by-pass several months later. He was just one of many who succumbed to the crushing pace a lot of members try to maintain. Many were older and not in the best of physical condition. Coupled with the hectic nature of the entire process that envelops a legislature, it put many of them at great risk. I've never seen anything like the pace of a State House, unless it's the news footage on TV from Wall Street. This place literally killed people. I've seen them pass away in the bathrooms, and in their rooms back at the Tavern. One even expired on the dance floor at the Brown Derby while doing the Twist. Some of the lucky ones came in on crutches, or in wheelchairs. It seemed there was always somebody in a cast.

Members take their jobs very seriously, and if they didn't know when to break away and grab some relaxation, or better still, learn to laugh at a lot of the goings on, it was bound to catch up with them. That's why I was always grateful when we managed to recruit a medical doctor and comforted with his presence while we were in session. I went so far as to set up a mini emergency room in my office. It wasn't stocked with much more than a bottle of oxygen, couch, and a stethoscope, but it served as a semi-private harbor for Dr. Jim Shea to administer the sick and wounded. I would vacate the space each morning as soon as Doc arrived and the line, inevitably, started forming. It seemed to me there were an awful lot of chest pains, and this worried all of us. On the other hand, I often thought it was a convenient opportunity to get medical care. There were no health care benefits, or any other types of benefits, with this job, nor free prescriptions. Doc Shea was terrific, as he seemed to enjoy the opportunity to be useful, but more than once he complained half-heartedly that he was busier now, in retirement, than he was in all his years of practice I felt more than grateful to be able to recruit a Democratic M.D. from Shaftsbury. He was never happier than when he provided medical attention for members.

Playing the political game is a dangerous participation sport.

14. THE GOVERNOR IS A LADY

1985 was an historic year. It was also the most productive legislative year in recent memory.

The Democrats, taking advantage of their new position at the helm of both the legislative and the Executive Branch of government, pushed through a multitude of legislation that was to send a clear signal to all who would listen that we had power and were not afraid to use it. The fact that our Chief Executive was one of only two female governors in the country, and the first woman to ever hold that high office in the state of Vermont, only added to the pride we felt as bill after bill was passed into legislation.

It was also the longest running session in 20 years. That didn't mean anything to me then, but it was the first of a decade of sessions that were labeled overtime sessions, and I was to realize it would become a weapon in my critics' arsenal that would prove politically aggravating to me. The length of a session was never my criteria as to how I judged the success of a legislative session. It seemed like an odd measure to apply to government. There was a small group that had a big stake in doing nothing. The Republicans did not have passing environmental legislation or additional educational funding in mind. Within a month or so, we noticed the opposition was content to complain and whine about personalities, instead of preparing to present a competing agenda. Consequently, we went about our business and paid little heed to them. We had the votes.

Madeleine Kunin rode into office a nose ahead of John Easton. She managed to win by less than 3,700 votes and even this thin margin could be credited to her labeling an "Easton government", merely a "caretaker government." She painted a status quo picture if Easton was to succeed Richard Snelling.

If the people of Vermont wanted a government that would push to protect Vermont's environment, an overhaul of how we funded education, or simply a government that would deal with the common person's concerns, then she was the only choice. It worked and she took her oath of office to great excitement and acclaim. And, she was successful.

My relationship with Madeleine Kunin, as with any of the three governors I worked with, was based on respect, if not always for the person, most certainly for the office. I had a clear sense of the

Founding Fathers intent regarding the separation of power between the three branches of government, and I paid careful attention to any endeavor on a governor's part to weaken or abridge the legislative prerogative to make the law. I was careful in return not to cross into the governor's domain. Some interpreted this as an effort by me to control all that went on in the State House. It was true, but I didn't pursue this philosophy for any reason of self-aggrandizement. I believed, in fact, all that went on in the State House was a matter for the legislature, and the legislature only. It was the Executive Branch's job to enforce what we did; it wasn't their job to tell us what to do. The governors were never in agreement with this type of thinking, as 200 years of history had afforded them entrance into the process to exert great pressures on us. Their State of the State Address was more than an address of where we were; it had evolved into a call to arms. It had become an address of intent as to where we were going, whether we liked it or not. We didn't disagree often, but when we did, I was not about to roll over.

Kunin, like me, was brand new, and we both embarked on a period of learning by doing. It was not without its tense moments, but anytime we disagreed, I tried to keep our spats confidential. I looked at these disagreements as family squabbles, that could be settled without all the neighbors listening. It was no different to me than having an argument at home in the kitchen. You could let it all unwind or explode, but keep your voices down as the kids were sleeping upstairs. This way, a restraint was placed on the level of nastiness from either party. I knew the strangeness of politics set a limit as to how long a grudge or hate could be held. I had analyzed, more than once, the old political adage "don't get mad, get even", and I totally disagreed with it. I felt it was always easier on both parties to get angry, blow up if the cause called for it, but then forgive the supposed transgression. It was a "don't forget it, but forgive it" attitude. It seemed odd to me people didn't understand this. Countless times I got into the worst of fights and got so angry, I would be at my wits end psychologically, and often physically. It took a lot of years, but eventually I realized the sooner I put the confrontation behind me, the better I felt about myself and the world. I didn't believe any religion worth its stock had vindictiveness as part of its foundation. My weak grasp at being a religious person certainly didn't have room for such hatefulness. Most important, it wasn't smart politics.

It didn't take long for the governor and me to cross swords and it was over an issue about which we both felt strongly. The flagship of my agenda, actually the only boat in my fleet, was property tax relief. Like every governor who saw her job as keeper of the purse, Kunin spent most of her waking moments worrying about balancing revenues. This never precluded governors from spending every available nickel, and some unavailable ones, but this spending was only justified if it was on their programs.

If a projected revenue forecast said we could expect a six percent increase in revenue in the next fiscal year from the 33 tax sources available, that simply meant to a governor they could fund all their favorite little programs up to six percent. Woe be to anyone who felt sharing should enter the process. When you read about the constant Congressional squabbles, whether it's between the different parties, or between the Congress and the President, the fight is over who gets the bag of money, not whether it's going to get spent or not.

If there was unlimited money—no deficit, or a money making machine that could pump out coins without any need to raise taxes to give it value—then you would find the old art of compromise clicking in and both sides would find a way to satisfy the other. Both sides would get what they want in the way of programs. This is the American way.

I made it very public I intended to increase the funds available to our property tax rebate program early in the session. This was a program that was not only extremely effective in providing relief to the beleaguered home owner and renter, but because it did its job so well it was, by far, the most popular relief program the state government offered. Originally an idea put forth by Gov. Tom Salmon in the early 1970s, it was credited with his come-from-behind win that catapulted him into office. Both sides of the aisle now laid claim to its ownership, thus my proposing an enormous increase in its funding did not come with any political risk.

It was for that reason the governor set out to kill my suggestion in a behind-the-scenes assault. If this meant she had to work closely with the Republicans, then so be it, that's what she set out to do.

I had real trouble with this thinking as I looked upon the Republicans as the enemy. Besides, it flew in the face of all I had been taught since I was a kid. It was a political form of treason to me for her to simply analyze the situation, and decide I was wrong and that she now had a license to leave me on this issue and consort with the enemy. I couldn't get the cliché, "Dance with the guy who brung ya", out of my mind. This was how it was going to be: "If I agree with you, we'll work together. If I don't, we'll work with the

Republicans." I took her on.

She enlisted the loyal efforts of Appropriations Committee Chair John Hise.*

John was a respected member of the Assembly and his committee members, whether Democrat or Republican, liked him to the point of reverence, as he truly worked for popular consensus and almost never went behind his committee's back to play political games. I say almost never, because in this instance, that's exactly what he set out to do and he did it. If it was not in conjunction with the governor, it was certainly with her blessing and support. I had a seven to four Democratic majority in the committee and it was clear to those seven members my goal to put a couple of million dollars extra into the rebate program was a goal shared by the Democratic caucus.

But their love for John kept them from serving him notice they were eventually going to use their strength in raw numbers and push the bill out. I didn't know what to do. Every time I inquired about how my rebate bill was coming in committee, my buddies would simply shuffle their feet and dust as fast as they could. I tried everything to wedge the bill out, but to no avail. John was telling the press he wasn't the culprit, as he made a habit of never interfering with the will of the majority in the committee. He argued, "We simply haven't found the time to deal with it." What was there to deal with? Simply allocate two million into the fund.

I felt the time to confront John had come finally and though I didn't look forward to having this conversation with a man whom everybody considered equal to their lovable old Grandpa, it was something I had to do if I was ever going to get my bill out.

"John," I started, "I think you're well aware I want the rebate bill taken up and voted on in your committee. I've got the votes and you know it. I also want you to know I think what you're pulling is shitty. You're out telling the world I'm the big bad guy as I'm threatening to commit some sort of ethical violation by usurping the committee process and forcing the bill out. My Democrats believe I'm the bully here and though I haven't said anything to them, they think I'm a wretch for doing this to their beloved chairman. What they don't know, but I know as sure as I'm standing here, is you're playing politics by

---

* The reader may wonder why a Speaker would appoint a member of the opposite party chair of an important committee like Appropriations. In this case, he was the best available person for the job, he had experience in the role, it perpetuated the Vermont myth that we did things "differently here", and there was little risk in appointing someone as respected and qualified as John Hise.

intentionally killing my bill. It's not fair for me to do that, and it's not fair for you to do that. The difference is the whole world would believe I would do something as sleazy as that, but no one believes you're doing the very same thing. I guess I could understand and even tolerate the sleaze ingredient here, but I'm really finding it impossible to climb over your unfairness by not telling the truth.

"Do you deny, John, that you're simply trying to kill my bill and that you're misleading people who think you're above all this?" He stood tall, silent and uncomfortable.

"No," he replied. "I am trying to kill your bill, however, as I don't think the state can afford it."

"We'll let the members decide that," I said.

I asked Vice-Chair Walter Moore to make the motion to move the bill. He didn't want to do it, but Walter was a good man in a thousand ways, none more so than in his sense of loyalty. He trudged back upstairs like a man going to his own hanging and made the motion to move the bill. It passed out of committee without testimony and several of the members broke down in tears at doing in "Grandpa" Hise. It was a testimony to how deep the affection members can have for their chairman and how far an honest man will go to win a political battle.

We passed the bill on the very last day of the session by a margin of three votes. It taught me a lot about the lengths people would go to in order to derail somebody else's program. I also learned I better be prepared to take the heat, because no matter how right I feel I am, it isn't necessarily how it's going to play. I took a lot of heat from my governor, from the Republicans, and even from financial gurus who talk to Wall Street and tell them big lies. All I knew when all the bullshit was cast aside months later, we had increased the funding to the rebate program by nearly 35 percent. This enabled nearly 7,000 additional people to become eligible for help. And, by the way, our fiscal house did not collapse. Kunin never failed to "dance with the guy who brung her" again.

We worked very well together, at least 99 percent of the time. She was bright and committed to doing the best she knew how, but she never quite got over being the first woman in a "man's world." Politics did not come easy to her and it took her the longest time to come to grips with the wheeling and dealing that is part of everyday life in the State House. I never thought this inability to cope with the underbelly of political give and take was because she was a woman, as the females of the world can more than hold their own with the roughest of rogues. I simply thought it was merely a matter of her unwillingness to engage herself in the mundane day-to-day in-fighting that was normal in the world of politics.

Madeleine Kunin was a visionary, whose talent was in laying out the future, and if the task was enacting Act 200, the far reaching environmental planning law, she could totally enmesh herself and do first class work. If the problem was getting someone like Frank DaPrato to vote for Act 200, she didn't have a clue, even if his vote was the one to put us over the top. Whenever we had to work a deal, I had to go to Liz Bankowski, her most trusted friend and aide.

Bankowski was from Dorchester, Massachusetts and grew up on the same streets that I did. A former assistant to Father Drinan, the Congressman Priest from Boston, she knew her way around and could make comfortable talk with pauper or prince. It helped she was Kunin's best friend as well as trusted aide. She was that key person every governor and President surround themselves with, and if you wanted the governor's ear, Bankowski was the one you would have to talk to in order to get it.

We were in an immense struggle to pass one of the half-dozen environmental bills that found their way into law that first year. We went over all our lists, which we counted some ten times, but still couldn't find the one vote we needed to bring about passage. Out of desperation, we went through the list one last time trying to find that reluctant soul whose mind might be changed. This time we went into great detail having somebody who knew the person explain why they wouldn't vote with us. We heard all the sound reasons until we got to Frank DaPrato.

"Why isn't DaPrato coming around for us, Brooksie?" I asked Francis Brooks, the Democratic Whip from Montpelier..

"He's mad at the governor," Brooksie said matter of factly.

"What the hell do ya mean he's mad at the governor? Everybody's mad at the governor. What kind of cockamamie reason is that?"

"I don't know. He just says he's mad at her and isn't going to vote for the bill. He didn't lead me to believe it's anything philosophic."

"There's more crazy people in this building than in 'One Flew Over the Cuckoos Nest'," I said, and bolted out the door to find DaPrato.

I searched high and low until I finally tracked him in the cafeteria.

"Frank, I gotta talk to you about a problem I understand you have with the governor. What is it?"

"I don't have the problem. She does," he answered. "She can go to hell, and if you're here to get me to change my mind, just forget about it. I ain't going to do it."

"Now wait a minute, Frank." I pleaded. "Tell me. What's the problem?"

Frank took five minutes, non-stop. The governor seemingly had snubbed him several months earlier and he had not forgotten it. Of course, Kunin had no idea of the affront, thus she had gone on about life in the State House without ever being aware that DaPrato was angry at her or that the anger had grown to giant proportions.

"I won't forget it. What goes around comes around. Let her cook, I don't want her God damned four number license plate," he spouted out, getting angrier all the time. I was only sitting and listening, letting him unload, when "four number license plate" crashed inside my head.

"What about the license plate?" I asked nonchalantly.

"She can stick that, too. I'm never gonna ask her for another thing."

I broke away with the parting I'd be back to him and headed for Bankowski's cubbyhole, just off the governor's office. "Liz, can I see ya a minute?" and she immediately got up and huddled with me in the corner. "Look, Liz, I think I can get the vote we need, but it's gonna take a conversation with one of the members and the governor. She's going to have to apologize to DaPrato," I said hurriedly.

"Apologize for what?" Bankowski was willing, but wondering.

"Well, I'm not sure exactly what she did to him, but just have her apologize, ya know, sort of generically." Listening to my own conversation, I was beginning to realize how stupid this was all sounding.

"Where is he? Can we get him in to see her?"

"I'll get him, but you gotta brief the governor. Oh, by the way, can you see to it he gets a four number license plate? Apparently somebody's given him a hard time over it." I was genuinely confused as to why DaPrato hadn't been able to get his own plate, as they were available to even the most naive of freshmen, and no special "OK" from the governor's office was necessary. Hell, Corcoran had most of Bennington riding around with four number license plates. You would have thought driving into the Bennington Town Municipal parking lot, you were in the United Nations garage.

Liz mulled over what I had described as the problem. She thought she knew the solution.

"Mr. Speaker, that's what he wants? The plates, not an apology. How am I going to tell a governor she has to apologize for some unknown infraction to a Rep from up on the Canadian border? We'll do it. I'll find a way, and I'm sure she'll do it as we've got to have this bill, but let's try the number plate first, and then we'll get them together and she can apologize for whatever."*

It worked. He got his plates and an audience with the governor. Though she didn't have to apologize, she was forced to schmooze with someone whom she obviously didn't have a helluva lot in common, and we got our bill, by a margin of victory that totaled one.

This legislature is an interesting place.

❖ ❖ ❖ ❖ ❖

Madeleine Kunin did not look at politics as a science, but rather as an opportunity to express her vision as to the purpose of government. This, in itself, would have been enough to guarantee her a place in Vermont history, as she accomplished a great deal, especially in the areas of education and the environment. The fact she left office under siege and an ever-growing cloud of criticism is testimony, not to her giant efforts, but to the constant attack that came from the opposition. A certain amount of this was unavoidable, and I'm not sure there was anything that could have been done to keep it from happening.

The fact she was the first female governor in Vermont's history brought out the worst in a large group that hadn't rid itself of chauvinist hang-ups. But, this was never her real problem, as that type of garbage could and should have been used against the perpetuators; the problem was simply a matter of her failure to understand the more she accomplishes, the more fire she's going to come under. Kunin thought the marriage was supposed to be a lifelong honeymoon.

A look back makes it extremely clear the governor's first year in office was more than fruitful. Major bills on the environment became law. And, they were not insignificant. Legislation was signed into law dealing with important steps to protect our ground water, underground storage tanks, special funds for the clean-up of hazardous wastes, and a "right to know" bill concerning toxic wastes within our borders. These were initiatives pushed for the most part by Kunin and her talented staff. There was a good deal more to come in the ensuing years, but this served notice she intended to be a hands-on catalyst in the environmental field.

---

* There is a certain prestige that accompanies a four number plate as there are only 9,000 available-1,000-8,999-and generally any Representative or Senator can pry one loose from the Motor Vehicle Department. Since there are only 900 three number plates, only the governor can give the OK.

In addition, we had passed huge increases in state aid to education (11 percent), and nearly doubled the property tax rebate program's funding, increasing both eligibility and benefits. This was less her doing than it was ours and I wore some public scars from the resistance she put up against my determination to adequately fund both of these programs.

The battles over minimum wage, from which we emerged victorious in the end, and the fight to make sure equal wages were paid to Vermonters on the construction of the interstate construction project at Rouse's point, (a bridge connecting Vermont and New York) were fights Poirier and I fought without her help. Like other governors, she picked and chose the issues she would become totally enmeshed in, and if they weren't her original ideas, or she was dragged into the fight reluctantly, we were never certain who she was helping behind the scenes.

On the surface, Kunin might appear to be involved, while in the privacy of her office things could be initiated to hinder our efforts up on the floor. I know that this occurred to my efforts during the property tax squabble, as I had words with her Secretary of Administration when I learned he was consorting with the House Republican leadership in an effort to thwart our expanding the program. Months later, she admitted as much when she visited Wall Street and boasted "she had taken on her own Democratic Speaker in her Herculean effort to show fiscal restraint."

Well, it wasn't quite the whole story and she knew it, but public relations discretion often becomes the better part of valor in the political world. I let her get away with that because she was my governor. The Press had a good time running an article with the headline, *Wright Doesn't Mind Being Governor's Whipping Boy.* Another read, *Wright Accepts Blame From Kunin.* I kept my real feelings to myself.

There was more, as the governor signed legislation into law making auto insurance mandatory and we pushed through the first bill that established alcoholism as an illness rather than a crime.

I recall the great level of exasperation that came over me after standing at the podium for several hours while "law and order" members stood to attack the idea "drunks" shouldn't be thrown in the slammer. Their resistance to accepting the fact alcohol problems might be connected to something other than a desire to be a menace and misfit to society, made me feel progress in human understanding was a hopeless cause. I reflected how my Irish mother taught me

40 years earlier what apparently was a mystery to these great statesmen now sounding off in front of me.

My mother worked every day of her life as a waitress, earning dime tips in order to keep us in clean underwear, and not once did I hear her complain about her lot in life nor speak ill of anyone. She played the hand that was dealt her, and I would later come to appreciate just how much she had sacrificed for us. I was "no walk in the park" when it came to keeping me on the right path. We had an elderly aunt who got us up in the morning, made sure we got some food in our stomachs, and tried her best to get us off to school. By the time I was in fifth or sixth grade, school was fast becoming just a place to carry my basketball or glove, and I wasn't the easiest to get up and out each school morning.

My mother, God love her, was always willing to take in a relative or a friend who had no place to go. As a single, working mother she found, in exchange for room and board, that the extended member of the family could prove helpful in overseeing the domestic responsibilities for which she simply did not have time or energy. Thus, it was left to Aunt Kate to perform this unpleasant chore and she proved to be more than a match for my obstinance. She was relentless in her early morning nagging. One day, I pushed even poor ole Aunt Kate too far and she had to report my back talk to my mother. Mom lit into me and finally, in desperation, that only a snotty little kid would stoop to, I blatted out everyone knew the "ole bat" liked her sauce and I wasn't going to take any more nagging or bullying from a common drunk. I can never recall my mother laying a hand on me, but before I could get to my feet, she reached up, grabbed me by the ear and twisted it. "I don't ever want to hear such words from you as long as I live. Your aunt has a sickness and there, but for the grace of God, go I." It made me cry and I never forgot her words.

And now here I was, 40 years later, listening to ignorant arguments from people entrusted with public responsibility.

Ignorance, or at least what I felt was ignorance, was not confined to elected officials. We had to fight to pass the first law making kindergarten mandatory for all school districts in Vermont. We actually had to take on some school superintendents to pull it off. They argued "local control." We argued "local control" was not a supervisory power over anyone's right to keep a child from going to school. We won, and for the first time in Vermont's 200-year history every five-year-old in the state would have the opportunity to go to school at the same age.

We didn't adjourn until the second week in May, and the fact we had held the longest session in 20 years didn't go unnoticed by the Press. Regardless, we had spoken for the children, the elderly, the sick, the working person, and the environment, and I left Montpelier tired, but with the feeling I did all I had set out to do, and more.

I admired Madeleine Kunin and respect her to this day. Yet, it seemed to me she never got over the apprehension of being "the first."

If Kunin had just accepted the fact she was the Governor of Vermont, rather than the first female Governor of Vermont, the rest of her world would have slid into that mode, and life in the corner office wouldn't have presented itself as the "us against them" adventure it became. I was made aware of this during one of the early years of our joint venture in the sphere of power politics, when she asked me to visit her in her office in the Pavillon Building next to the State House. Upon entering, she laid out a proposal that would assist the City of Burlington in bringing an end to a major problem with the city sewer plant. They were in desperate need of building a secondary plant to handle the overflow of sewerage that was an emergency. On numerous occasions, after a heavy rainfall, the entire sewerage system in the city would simply unload into beautiful Lake Champlain. The city fathers had missed the boat in taking advantage of federal monies available to them in the 70s and early 80s and were now faced with the dilemma of having to provide the funding for the plant with local taxes.

That is, unless they could wrangle the bulk of the enormous expense out of the state of Vermont, where our newfound windfall saw us sitting on a surplus that was to grow to 60 million dollars. Kunin lived in Burlington and was well aware that 30 percent of her constituency voted out of the lake's neighbor, Chittenden County.

"So you understand, Mr. Speaker, this is very important to the entire state that we help out and give them some assistance from our surplus," she explained.

"Just how much are you proposing we help out, governor?"

"Sixteen million should do it."

"Sixteen million? I can't do that," I answered. "What makes them so special?"

"Well, the lake is a state jewel. It belongs to us all. We have a responsibility to protect it for all of Vermont. I must say your attitude surprises me." Now she sounded like a governor.

"I've never so much as stuck my toe in that lake, Governor, and I'd have a helluva time explaining to the people of Bennington why I was partner to loaning 16 million dollars to the people of Burlington to do what we in Bennington did 15 years ago."

"They got federal funds that are no longer available, and it's not a loan, it's a gift!" she said.

"A gift? You're kidding. We're just going to give them $16 million? That's crazy! I'm not going to be a part of that. Let them do what we had to do and pay their own way."

Now she came forward in her chair and she startled me by slapping her hand on her desk. I jumped what seemed like a foot out of my chair.

"See here, I can be just as tough as you are. Don't think I can't."

At this point I didn't know what to do or say as I'm sure I must have looked fairly stupid by jumping when she banged the desk. On top of that, I couldn't find a way to assure her I was certain we could work something out and I was just playing political games by making her plead her case. It was too late for that now. I followed my heart.

"Look Madeleine," invoking the personal," I don't love you because you're tough. If I want tough, I can go down to Charley O's. I love you because you're warm and sensitive. You can have your $16 million, just don't do the 'tough' thing with me."

Her eyes began to moisten, and panic rushed through me as I thought, "Oh, no, please don't do it, Madeleine. But it was too late. She cried. And, I thought, Jesus Christ, there you go again, now you did it, there's something wrong with you, Wright."

That story never came out either with the Press or in Kunin's book. But, it's a story that should be told because it helps to explain how perilous a road it is for someone who attempts to be somebody they're not. As for me, it just served to further verify if I was going to survive, I was going to have to learn that what you see isn't necessarily what it is.

History will record Madeleine Kunin was a pretty good governor. It probably won't record she had other insurmountable obstacles. Some were political, like being a liberal Democrat fighting to hold back the tide of domestic neglect washing the shores of the Reagan/ Bush era; some were more personal in the sense she was forever intimidated by her role as a woman in a so-called man's world. Hell, it was bad enough to be a man in a man's world.

She'll eventually get the credit she deserves, especially as it applies to her breaking down doors and admitting women into the higher echelons of state government. She did this with such a commitment,

I once joked upon walking into her office and finding myself the only male surrounded by a half dozen women who were part of her inner circle, "Christ, I feel like I'm at a Tupper Ware party."

This time I made her laugh.

15. KING RICHARD

Richard Snelling, a Republican, was the governor whom I admired most. The ripping noise you are about to hear is the sound of my Democratic Membership card being torn in half.

I admired and respected very much the person he was and the politician he was. I know you can hear all the horror stories you want from hundreds, perhaps thousands, of people who are all too willing to tell you about his bad temper or his arrogance, but there was a whole lot more to the man than that.

If my only experience with Gov. Snelling had been during the two years I served with him during my tenure as Democratic Minority leader, I would have little more to tell than what I have already told, but as Speaker, I had an additional eight-month window with him when he returned to the governor's office in 1991. Once again, this was proved to be a very difficult time in Vermont's financial history. We were in the throes of a deficit again, and this time it was of even bigger proportion than in 1983-84. We were $91 million in the red.

Our fiscal house was literally in shambles. Snelling was going to get little or no help from his own party, and as usual, we Democrats were going to be asked to ride to the rescue.

There was a different twist here, as the 1983-84 deficit belonged to the Republicans and this one was the sole responsibility of the Democrats. Because of our devil-may-care spending, no matter how deserving the cause, we not only spent the surplus, but placed ourselves in a helpless position with the downturn of the economy and a new recession on our hands. Snelling was the unfortunate inheritor.

There was never the slightest question whether or not we were going to cooperate. We would and that was a foregone conclusion. The question that most concerned me was how was the deficit to be paid? What taxes were we going to raise? Was there going to be the rush to make monstrous cuts? I was no tax or budget expert. Far from it, as I was often frightened by how little I knew in these highly complex areas.

The Press never wrote much about these inadequacies that were all to obvious to me. The impression with many was the Speaker knew a lot more than was the case. I never even served on a financial committee and that remains an amazing sidebar to my rise up the ladder. I never served on a conference committee either.

The ladder I climbed had most of its rungs missing. So now I had to rely on the Executive branch to put together the package that would bail out the state, both from the tax side and the expenditure side. This took a giant leap of faith as we were at the mercy of the governor's staff to be precise as to what a tax would raise in revenues, how it would be spent, and most important, a guarantee that any raising and spending would not make matters worse. Did it fit? Could it be done without collapsing the economy of the state? This was the distinct and obvious disadvantage that the citizen legislature labored under, as we are part-timers, without staff, and we simply didn't have the resources or know how to put together anything resembling a comprehensive plan. Only the governor's office had this level of expertise.* We simply had to put our trust in a single political force, Dick Snelling, and trust him not to play politics with it. He never let me down, and that was a good measure of his greatness.

He must have had the same thoughts running through his mind as I had racing through mine, as he did an extraordinary thing in that it was an act that was least expected from him. It was an act of humility.

It was our opening day of the 1991 legislative session and we had just finished with the Speaker's election and I had returned to my office to begin my fourth term as Speaker. I was going through the myriad of chores I would have to complete to assign the members to their new committees and prepare for three or four days of ceremony that would take place in the well of the House prior to all the members heading off in their own worlds of making legislation. It was a time of idleness for all but me, but an air of excitement permeated the building.

My office was filled with all my "Lieutenants" milling around, making phone calls, or simply basking in the afterglow of having another two years in power. They were just sitting around, their feet propped up on desks and conference tables, shooting the bull. It was too early to crack open a Budweiser, but we were all aware of the high my re-election to a fourth term generated. I looked up through the glass separations and saw the governor sitting in the far waiting room, thumbing through one of the old magazines. Jesus, nobody ever sat out there waiting for an appointment with me. He could have been a Fuller brush salesman for all appearances.

"Nance, is that the governor sitting out there?" I called to Nancy Mason.

* *Since the governor is "boss" of each department and all 7,000 state employees, he receives the tax revenue information direction which he can choose to share with the legislature at his will. The Legislative Council (or Joint Fiscal Office) is overseen by the legislature and, while qualified to analyze these things, the governor's staff has more expertise and information.*

"Yes," she answered. "I told him, Mr. Speaker, he could come right in and you would see him right away." With that she looked around with disgust at the gang who occupied the Speaker's office. It was one of those looks our mothers gave us, telling us she loved us, but, perhaps, not our friends. "But, he said it was no problem," she said, "he'd wait until you had finished with your guests." She finished with another hostile glance at my friends.

"Geez, Nanc, we can't have the governor sitting out there. Let me get rid of these guys and then ask him to come right in." I turned, and in my best 'I'm not fooling around voice' said, "OK, you guys, let's go. Out."

You would have thought I had just cut them out of my will. I got more than one look of indignation, and feeling a little sheepish at my air of disloyalty, tried to explain I had a governor waiting to see me. They got up slowly and began to shuffle out, grumbling under their collective breaths, "Hummmph! Big deal!"

Well, it was a big deal. No governor yet had gone to this extreme to visit with me in this manner while I had been Speaker. Sure, I had had such visits in the past, but they were always announced, and I always made sure I was standing at the ready when the governor and entourage entered in a fashion that had everything but music playing "Hail to the Chief." This time the governor looked like a forlorn figure, sitting patiently, all alone, in the vacant outer entryway. He hardly looked like a head of state.

I rushed out, embarrassed, and invited him in, making sure to pull together two chairs in front of my desk. Even that seemed inadequate in my effort to indulge him with what I felt was his proper stature. I sat across from this larger-than-life figure, nervously trying to remain in whatever conversation that he had in mind. It wasn't easy, as Dick Snelling loomed over all in his presence, a personality who turned everybody's head when he entered a room. After taking a moment to offer his congratulations on my being re-elected, he got right to the point.

"Mr. Speaker, I didn't want to break in on your meeting with your friends, but it's important we have this meeting as early as possible so we can work together and get this extremely dangerous deficit behind us. It's beyond just our political well-being, the future viability of the State of Vermont is at stake. I know what my role is going to be, and it's going to take all my energy and good will to bring about the solution. But, I can't do it without you. That's not rhetoric, I mean that."

I shifted nervously in my chair, realizing I must have looked like a very small figurine sitting not two feet from this man.

"I've been reading the papers like you probably have been," he continued, "and all this bull about 'finally, the clashing of the titans, Wright vs. Snelling.' Well, that simply isn't going to happen. I guarantee there isn't anything that's going to make us start fighting with each other; nothing you say or do is going to make me angry. Nothing. You'll see. We've, and I emphasize we, have a job to do. It can't come about without us working together, perhaps against everybody, whom in the past we might have relied on individually. Somehow, we've got to bring them together to bail us out of this awful dilemma." And then he leaned forward. "I hope you can help me."

Help you? Christ, I'd slay a dragon for you.

I didn't know it then, but it was going to be even more dramatic than anyone could possibly have realized, as three months later, after the most heated and bitter of events as the Governor and I pushed and prodded the solution through the process, the final passage vote on the largest tax increase in the entire history of the state, was tied up 72-all at the end of the roll call. I would be forced to vote and break the tie.

Corcoran screwed me that time and I ended up throwing him out of the apartment. I should have handled my need to get his vote better, but I assumed he'd be there when I needed him and I let it go. He simply watched quietly over the next few months, as I exhausted all my reservoir of debts and 'I owe you's' to get to the point I felt I was going to win by a very small margin. Corcoran, being Corcoran, never spoke about things that made him uncomfortable, and increasing taxes made him extremely uncomfortable. On the other hand, I always found it unpleasant to get into these types of discussions with him as it would end with me blowing my top at his intransigence. So, we never really talked about how he would vote, but I assumed (stupidly) Corc would eventually see my predicament, and throw me his vote.

When they called "the member from Bennington, Mr. Corcoran", he voted, without looking up at the podium, and in an obvious sheepish voice, "No." I was surprised and upset, but roll calls don't offer time to reflect or ponder things. I had to maintain a level of "cool", while checking off and maintaining my count on the roll call sheet in front of me at the podium. This sheet was my bible as I never failed to have predetermined how every member was going to vote and have it in front of me as the clerk methodically went through the roll.

A well-trained Speaker could track the votes, including surprising switches either way, and still feel a level of security as to the final count. This switching by members could occur from A to Z, so I'd have to make the correction in mid-stream, and be quick to maintain a pace that coincided with the speed of the clerk's call. If I knew I was going to win by 30 or so votes, then I could stand back from the podium with an air of confidence and simply listen for the occasional surprise. If the list of surprises grew larger and larger, it would draw me closer to the podium and my list. I knew how close this vote was going to be and nobody had to push me to that damned podium that day. What I didn't know was Corcoran's "no" vote was going to be the only surprise, and it meant I was forced to break the tie on the largest tax increase in history.

There is that moment when a vote is so close members sense something momentous is about to happen, and this stirring is evident from the podium as the roll call gets well down into the alphabet. The count goes back and forth. By the time we get to the Ws, it feels like an electric current is circulating from seat to seat. Lots of members go through the exercise of keeping track by dashing off groups of five in what is usually a feeble effort at keeping an accurate count, but as Speaker, I had an advantage. I trained the clerks sitting in front of me to move their hand after logging each vote. In that way I could track their roll call sheet with mine and, unless I got careless, both sheets would coincide.

I never got careless, thus as the clerk was running through the names of the five previously absent members, I knew I had a tie vote on my hands. I never hesitated, for though I would be faced with breaking the tie, perhaps only once a session, I made it a practice to always be prepared to cast my vote. There was a small window of time that Corc, knowing I was on the spot and knowing it was all tied up, could have jumped up and requested to change his vote. I glared at him, waiting for the life preserver. He merely sat there, head down, staring at his cluttered desk. The clerk handed me the official tally and I read it to a very attentive body. The Republicans all had smirks on their faces; the Democrats were fascinated with the irony of the situation. "Those in favor of passage, 72. Those opposed, 72 . Your vote is a tie, consequently the Chair votes 'yes.' The bill passes."

I went back to the apartment with Harold Weidman who was pleading for mercy on Corc's behalf. After about a month, the "c'mon home" call went out to Corc and the incident was never mentioned again.

Making law isn't like making sausage, as the making of sausage has a beginning and an end. Making law is constant. The failure rate far exceeds the rate of success. It is difficult enough if what one is trying to accomplish is the right thing to do, and everybody knows it, but even then, the opposition isn't going to roll over and simply let it happen. Imagine taking millions from not just a small group, but from the vast majority of the population. That's what the governor and I set out to do the day he came in to recruit my cooperation in meeting the emergency.

The plan Snelling had put together was well laid out, and more important, it was fair. The corporate interests didn't escape their share of the tax levies he proposed, but the bulk of the money raised was through a flat income tax across the board. I didn't say anything at the time, but my secret desire was to create a sliding scale income tax that taxed the rich at a higher rate than it did the poor or middle class. If we could accomplish this, we would be the only state in the nation that had a progressive state income tax.

I nearly fell out of my chair when several weeks into our effort to bring this all to fruition, Dick Snelling once again came to my office and asked if we could talk in private. A private talk in the legislature isn't any different than a letter from a friendly IRS agent asking you to come on down and have a cozy little "one on one." It's the harbinger of bad news. With some degree of trepidation, I led the Governor out onto the floor of the empty house and sat in the red seats. Strange as it seems, such a public gathering served as a signal to others in this body, that a private conversation was taking place, and they would leave you alone.

"Mr. Speaker, I know you haven't brought this up and I appreciate your not doing so, but I just want to tell you how great it's been working with you, and how much I appreciate your efforts. I also am very aware of all the heat you've taken from different sources, some within your own party, for doing what you're doing. I, too, have had them screaming and hollering at me, but that's OK, they don't bother me. I hope they don't you."

"I'll be all right," I interjected. He went on, leaning closer to me.

"I've thought about all this so please don't respond until I've finished. I'm here to offer you a progressive income tax. One that puts 28 percent on the lowest rung, 31 percent on the middle group, and 34 percent on the richest Vermonters. The one caveat is you've got to promise me we sunset* it all back down to the present flat rate of 25 percent when the deficit is paid. I know that's more than two years out and a different legislature can do anything it damned well pleases, but I'm just asking we put in the bill that it is our intention to sunset back to 25 percent at that time. I think it's the fairest way we can go and it's a small thank you for helping me on this."

Life never ceases to surprise me for here was the governor, my partner, but still my political opponent in the eyes of the world, offering to do what I had only dreamed of doing. *I coulda kissed him!*

---

* *"Sunset" simply means a date or time to set in law for it all reverting back to what existed before the law is passed.*

I tried to stay calm and responded, "And?"

"That's it. Let me know." He got up and left.

What the governor didn't go into was he was taking a terrific amount of heat from members of his own party and especially from the business community who never publicly let up their cries of anguish at the tax increase. Privately, I later learned, he actually had an audience with a small group of them in an effort to convince them this was the only solution to bailing out the state. Of course, they had little interest in such "drivel", and they actually went to the extreme of accusing him of being manipulated by the evil Speaker.

They made a mistake going too far, as God love him, Snelling threw them the hell out of his office. Years later, after the deficit was well on its way to retirement, I had to fight to abide by the promise I had made to the governor. By then, he had fallen dead of a massive heart attack by his swimming pool not six months after we passed the tax increase. I lost a comrade in arms, one I had respected greatly, and now as the deficit had been paid, the state was again in the black. I was being beseeched to renege on my word and not allow the sunset of the progressive income tax to click in. I tried to explain I had given a man my word, but this explanation met with more than one raised eyebrow as they argued, "Christ, Ralph, he's dead." I didn't know how to answer this without getting angry so I made a joke out of it all and answered, "Yeah, I know. But I'm hoping I end up in the same place as the governor, and if I ever do after going back on my word, I don't want to spend the shortest moment with him, let alone eternity. He'll tear my ass apart." Everyone knew there was a finality to my answer. We sunseted the taxes, as promised.

That one was for you, Dick Snelling.

16. Just Another Day In Paradise

I never had a day in the legislature the same as any other. Making law, no matter where, is a fascinating experience. I don't believe there's a similar setting, or a more unique group of people to be surrounded by. They make up the very best of what America has to offer and, in fairness, the very worst. I loved nearly every minute of my stay, and though I had moments I thought would never end or couldn't get any worse, I never ceased to be surprised that both emotions were possible.

Even the worst moments eventually ended. It is this latter capacity that makes the legislative process different from any other process. Members have to succumb to the inevitable certainty today's most pressing problem will be tomorrow's fading memory. Things happen fast and issues line up so incessantly, one soon learns to move from one to the other with a fluidity that often looked to be callous to an outsider. It's working in a big city emergency room without the benefit of miracle medicine. These were situations that demanded attention and didn't leave much time for anyone to dwell too long on any previous setback. Putting the past behind you and getting on with what was in front of you at any given moment not only made life bearable, but pushed the sound and sane to always look forward to the task at hand.

It could be hard on the sensitive and more reflective members, but once this operational mode was understood and mastered, it made for an exciting way to live. I marveled at the way alliances came and went among the members, and how easily each of us adjusted to victory and defeat. Woe be to those that never got it.

There was one negative, that in fact did get worse and never ended. It was the constant erosion of my credibility. It began almost from the day I was sworn in as Speaker, and picked up considerable speed by the end of my first year. Looking back, I have no one to blame but myself.

My sin was not so much what I was trying to do, it was how I attempted to do it. I truly believe I was part of a massive evolutionary change in Vermont and it wouldn't have mattered who the Speaker was as he or she would have been caught up in it and gone with the flow.

Another personality with a different philosophy might have slowed the juggernaut, but couldn't have stopped it. Times were changing and all for the better.

The ten-year period was as exciting a decade as one could possibly hope for. Issues were important and they were the right issues: education and the environment. If America was going to be overwhelmed with the massive economic and social changes that crept out of the fifties and exploded on the scene in the sixties, it was going to have to deal with the results of all this in the eighties. Vermont did, but, I'm sad to say, America didn't.

To be sure, we didn't have the same complexity to our challenge that the nation as a whole had. They were faced with foreign affairs and urban problems which, obviously, we were not. Our largest city, with about 35,000 people, hardly made up a neighborhood in the major cities. Still, there were problems we held in common with our brethren in Washington that had reached crisis proportions.

We took them head on and dealt successfully with the environment, while laying the ground work for education and the funding of our schools. Kunin can take a very large measure of the credit for both, but she didn't do it alone. Had she found herself with a Republican-controlled House or Senate, had she been strapped with a shortage of revenues (the money poured in during our second term reaching embarrassing proportions of riches), or had she been forced to deal with less talented people, both on her staff and in the Assembly; she would have faced a much different six-year tenure than she did.

History will stand her, and the people who worked by her side, in a bright light. The 20 or so pieces of environmental legislation pushed through during those years not only better prepared us to protect our treasured land and waterways, but it forced everyone into a consciousness and awareness these were issues that had to be protected and further developed.

I've felt these laws and even the action I took on the Interstate Banking bill served us in good stead when we were forced to deal with the recession that hit in 1989.

New Hampshire, for example, suffered untold damage due to the overdevelopment that was in full and reckless force during the boom days. People who bought condominiums and second homes with no more concern than if they had filled their gas tanks to the brim, were now forced to purchase plywood and board up the places. The banks who lent the money now sat with debts that were uncollectible. That didn't happen in Vermont anywhere near the degree it did in other states. The reason was plain and simple: We made it difficult for the banks and developers to hold free reign over our future.

My killing of the banking bill didn't stop the "big guys" from Boston and New York from doing business in Vermont very long, as we passed a narrower version of the same bill the very next year. But we also passed the environmental bill that had been the other half of that contentious bone, and added to the reality Vermont was not the nirvana other states were when it came to a blank check for development. Our reputation as an environmentally conscious state was matched only by Oregon. Woe be to politicians who wanted to undo it all. They might survive back in their district, but they met with almost certain failure in their efforts in the legislature.

I'm very proud of whatever part I managed to play in that scenario, but it didn't come without its price, both for Madeleine Kunin and myself. People can't be forced from their envisioned profits without a huge outcry and, consequently, great resistance. Money may not make the world go round, but it is a vital part of the engine. Groups formed and battles ensued. We stuck by our guns, and at times felt besieged by the outcry. The bottom line was inevitable. We made a ton of enemies.

This war was one that occurred over a greater time span and was not something that pre-occupied us every waking moment of the day. The day-to-day operation in the State House more closely resembled a series of fire fights than a war. A Speaker is always in the middle of it.

The kind of day I was going to have could seldom be predicted. It would depend what year we were in, what month we were in, what day of the week it was, or even what time of day it was. These things mattered, as there were "seasons" in the legislature: planting seasons (early January and February) when the seeds of ideas took the form of bills being worked on in committees and harvesting seasons (when the seed came to full bloom in March and April). There were moods that were recognizable. Early in the session, people would be upbeat and friendly. Mid-way through, they would be connected to their work in committee. Then would come a period where the contents of the issues worked on so long and hard would be connected with the politics of getting it through to final passage. These were thoughts of renewing acquaintances with "step brothers and sisters" in other committees and the Senate (where coincidentally your treasured work would have to pass through, and the first faint thoughts of finding hostages to hold for old enemies who couldn't be schmoozed into your way of thinking began to appear). The final days were when tempers grew short and fierce battles would begin.

If it was early in the session, my days would be consumed with housekeeping, or management rituals. Committees were assigned, bills sent to the committees, and small details to attend to. These were casual times and I often found myself wandering the halls looking to shoot the breeze.

I would sit and chat with lobbyists on occasion who, knowing it was too early in the session for any bill they were concerned with to be moving, would spend countless hours of their time milling around and drinking coffee. I enjoyed sitting with them for reasons other than they were bright and interesting folks.

The lobbyists contained a wealth of information, as next to the press corps, nobody worked harder at making it their business to know what was going on under the Golden Dome. I was at a disadvantage because of who I was, though I wasn't aware of this until years later, because I tended to intimidate them just with my presence. Unless I had the knack of asking the right questions, I wasn't going to get much pertinent information out of them. I never could shake the feeling I had just interrupted, thus I never stayed very long.

As the session progressed and committees began popping bills out onto the daily calendar, we would be forced onto the floor for ever-increasing durations. Floor time increased and committee time decreased by direct proportion. It was much like the slow and gradual increase in daylight that comes with the onset of spring.

I enjoyed my time at the podium more than any other responsibility entrusted to me. This was where I got to be the conductor and I flourished in the role. Speakers rarely, actually never, get to make a speech. We chant little paraphrases from Mason's or Robert's Rules, and though we don't have to master all of them, we do have to take care to be familiar with the two dozen or so motions used each day. When the occasional divergence from the memorized rules demanded, I could call on my clerks, seated directly in front of the podium. They were the experts and I usually heeded their advice. They might tell you I drove them crazy with my occasional divergences, however.

Like all Speakers, I had my own style, and no matter how big a critic we might have among the membership, they all got used to the chant and ways of whomever was at the podium for any length of time. Though it was within the prerogative of the Speaker to leave the podium and take the floor, I never did it.

I believed it was like putting one's name on a secret ballot. I followed my own advice religiously. If I wanted to rally the troops with my presence or oratory, I would simply go to Caucus and give it my best shot. I never went to the enemies' den, the Republican caucus. My presence there would simply serve to forewarn my agenda and was certain to rally them against me. My taking the floor would only incite the same reaction and I equated it with visiting one's mother-in-law unnecessarily.

I also believed the advice I repeatedly gave to the freshmen members: If you can override your own self-serving inner urges and stay in your seat, you won't have to wait too long to find someone who will rise and say exactly what you were going to say, and probably better.

That's not very good for the ego, but it was pretty good advice. I believed if the bright and well informed people who sat in front of me couldn't provide what was needed to deliver quality legislation, I certainly wasn't going to add to the solution with my two cents.

If I had to compare a single location that equaled the hubbub of the podium, the closest I could come would be the "out of town" newsstand in Harvard Square in Cambridge, Massachusetts. If you wait long enough, you'll see and hear all you ever wanted and maybe more. There just was no end to the visiting entourage that constantly passed by me as I stood at the podium. It was invaluable. In any given hour, 50 or 60 people might come by. Some to say hello and let me know they were in the building; some to discuss a wide range of concerns that would run from important to frivolous. I tried never to turn my back on the members on the floor and to make sure I listened attentively to whomever was with me. I remembered the advice John Murphy offered years earlier that this was the center of the state government's universe.

It was here at the podium I constantly gathered my stockpile of information I could draw on to make decisions down the road. Members, deprived of this access that a Speaker received unsolicited, were always at a disadvantage since they did not know all I knew. Murphy had been right. It was another example of the position of Speaker carrying a built in "edge" others didn't have. An edge made all the difference.

The later into the session it became, the longer we would be on the floor, until we would arrive at a time when committees would all be shut down, their bills having incubated and sent to the floor. Then, if well formulated and adroitly presented, they passed and were sent to the Senate. When this action occurred, it signified we had reached the beginning of the end, with just weeks remaining before adjournment. It was not unusual for us to be on the floor all day, and sometimes into the evening. Night sessions were something I swore I would do everything within my power to avoid. I remembered the embarrassment I felt when Speaker O'Connor, who held frequent evening sessions, had to deal with members who had broken for supper and drinks, and came back not qualified to legally drive. I saw one member, sensitized with cheap liquor, weep on the floor when he got carried away with his own cause in a slurred address. I also saw debates come close to fist fights without blows actually being struck.

There were things that occurred every day no matter what the day or month. I always arrived at the State House just before 7 A.M. and I seldom left before 6 P.M. I used to joke with members who would chide me over my late hours that I once left the State House before the last

Republican and got beat the next day on a tough issue. Neither part of that story is true, but it always seemed to be an effective response. The fact of the matter was these were simply my hours. It's the hours I felt comfortable with and I just maintained the routine.

No matter how early I got into the building, I never beat Mike "Obie" Obuchowski, the long-time Rep from Bellows Falls. This may go farther than you think in explaining why he's Vermont's current Speaker of the House. It was the best time of day as nobody was around, the oatmeal was still hot in the cafeteria, and Obie's morning newspapers would still be in one piece. It was also a time for me to have the only relaxed conversation of the day, with the second most powerful person in the House, Obie, who was Appropriations Committee Chair. It didn't hurt in my effort to maintain a semi-literacy on money matters.

Murphy often would be there, or returning from his committee room after making his morning call to his wife, Flora Belle, and the three of us would spend the half hour chatting. I could always tell what Murphy had for breakfast as the remnants would decorate his tie. On the other hand, he would always profess to be satisfied with his progress in maintaining his diet. This in spite of the fact that with each new session and renewed commitment to his new diet, he would always manage to put on weight between January and our adjournment. By 8 a.m., the cafeteria would begin to fill. People came, ate, and went off to begin their day. Whoever sat with us could expect a lot of teasing and general bantering that seldom got very heavy. Members who wanted to discuss serious matters inevitably would ask if they could "have a minute of my time", and this meant in private, and was always more than a "minute." I would get up from the "Lieutenants' Table", so labeled by the more serious dedicated servants who sat by themselves, reading the *Wall Street Journal* or *New York Times*. I never trusted any "man" who didn't turn to the Sports section first. I felt my life would have to be considered moderately successful if I could get through it by never playing golf, learning algebra, or reading the Journal. So far, so good.

Once the session was over and I returned to my office, I would go through the mail placed on my desk by my staff. I would either dictate, or write out a note in longhand for the items requiring an answer. Much of what I had to answer could be done by Barb or Nancy as they knew what I would want to say. I would dictate the more personal stuff. Answering my mail was never very time consuming as I didn't believe in putting anything in writing I could deliver verbally. No historic vanity for me, but U.S. Senator Packwood might have heeded this method.

I would also get my schedule for the day, as Barb and Nancy spent more time than they wanted seeing to it I got pushed in the right direction to my next appointment. I was terrible about keeping a schedule. I was not a disciplined enough person to keep a routine. It wasn't any different in my personal life.

By 8 A.M., Doc Shea's patients would begin to line up outside the Speaker's office, and this would be my signal to gather up whatever I was doing or whomever I was talking to and go into the outer reception room. This outer office really belonged more to the rest of the people in the building, as it was the easiest access to the outside for those who smoked. Members, lobbyists or visitors would happily puff away, rain or shine. This never bothered us, as the leadership could concentrate on going over the new day's gossip and calamity.

This was the closest we ever seemed to come to what could be called a leadership meeting. We never scheduled one as we didn't have any need to. We would be in constant contact over the next ten or so hours. It was really one of the most convenient spots, as we could see through the glass dividers out into the cafeteria where all the discussions were taking place between the members. If we had a list of people we wanted to get to, then this provided the opportunity to go and "run into them." It also afforded us the chance to see who was plotting with whom.

One day we were sitting leisurely in the two chairs when we heard the downstairs door open and somebody struggle to get in and up the stairs. By the time this person was halfway up the stairs, I knew it was Corcoran. I also knew with what he was struggling.

This was the morning his turkeys had to be hefted up the two flights of stairs from my car trunk out in the parking lot. They were frozen turkeys, ones he purchased from one of the super markets in Bennington. For one reason or another, my regular assistant was out that day and the Legislative Council, as was its custom, would send up a replacement from the Council's staff pool. I didn't recognize this young woman and I surmised she just joined the Council's staff. I paid no heed to the footsteps struggling up the stairs as I was trying to make certain my temporary aide overcame her trauma at having been drafted to work in the Speaker's office that day.

Corcoran finally emerged at the top of the second floor steps and made his way down the hall, past the clerk's office and turned left, pushing the glass door leading into the cafeteria with his shoulder. His struggle was evident. Sweat ran off his forehead. Under each arm, he carried what must have been a 25 pound frozen turkey. Corc was too busy to see me sitting off to the side, but I could see both him and my new assistant. Her eyes were bulging. Suddenly, just as Corc was about to get himself through the door, the pressure of pushing with the turkey under one of his arms forced the grim creature to "squirt" out. It hit the floor like it was a large stone, bounced once or twice, and then slid somewhat ungraciously across the marble, finally coming to rest at the feet on the dumbfounded young woman. She moved ever so slightly in an automatic gesture to help the near- exhausted Corcoran. He paid absolutely no heed to a soul as he fumbled to get the turkey tucked up under his arm once again. Corc was focused on his frozen friend. She was frozen in her chair.

Corc, once he had the meal for 30 or so youngsters precariously balanced under his arm, simply continued on his way. I didn't say a word, nor did I let on that I had just witnessed something the least bit unusual. She tried to busy herself, attempting to rectify this scene with some degree of decorum. Finally, she brought it up and in a polite way mentioned the architects might have done a better job designing a more convenient way to the kitchen for delivery men.

"Oh! You mean Representative Corcoran and the turkeys. He's not a delivery guy, he's a member of Appropriations."

I never saw her again.

Once the sick and wounded left our little "M.A.S.H." unit, the office was mine again. I would take 15 minutes to go over the day's work with my clerk. If it was during a period that bills were flooding the floor, I would go through the ones up for second or third reading, noting in the calendar who was reporting the bill, the complexity or impact it might have with the members (fight or easy passage), and the vote in committee. This last simply gave an additional hint as to the level of argument that I could expect. If it came out of committee with an 11-0, or 10-1 vote, then I could conclude at least the committee was in agreement with the contents of the bill. An 8-3, or 7-4 vote sent warning signals. A 6-5 vote might be a signal to get everybody off the beach.

If it was early in the session, the extent of my task would be to assign bills to the proper committee. The clerks were most helpful in this, especially when I was new at my job, as they had guidelines they followed to help decide where a bill would go. I soon got to the point where I could play a little game with Bob Picher, the long time Chief Clerk and a whiz at what he did, as I would dare him to let me assign bills without reading his prepared written list. I got fairly efficient at it, but every once-in-a-while, I would choose his second or third choice. On rare occasions, I might even choose to send it to a committee he hadn't recommended. We would joke good-naturedly about how I wasn't tracking it properly, but he knew I had a member who wanted the bill sent off to their committee and I was being accommodating. That would be the end of it, as Bob used to say, "there's Mason's rules, and there's Ralph's rules."

When the minister of the day showed up, I would get ready to go on the floor, unless there was a last minute conversation with someone or a call that had to be taken. I was less than diligent about keeping to a schedule and it caused a lot of petty grumbling over the years. I wish I could have shown better discipline, but it was generally a matter of dealing with somebody else's problem. It was never a case of my reading the sport page while I left members cooling their heels, waiting for the morning's prayer.

I've often been asked why we even have morning religious exercises that always end with the Lord's Prayer (unless we have our rare appearance by a Rabbi). I didn't have a good answer for them then, and I don't have one now. It was odd, because on the one hand liberals would complain about saying prayers in a legislature, when the Supreme Court wouldn't let them be said in classrooms all over the state. The conservatives would jump me for not saluting the flag. I thought we had everything backend, too.

Personally, I didn't care if the prayers were ever said, and more important, I sympathized with the non-Christians who, if they chose to attend morning services, had to listen to our prayer. Whenever we were without a priest or minister and I had to lead the services, I would ask the members to rise and be with their own thoughts for a moment. Everybody would join in and stand, as they appeared to find this unobjectionable. I had even less objection to saluting the flag, but as this was something that wasn't done when I became Speaker, I felt no need to raise the anxiety level of those who objected to, as they claimed, "rising every morning to reaffirm their patriotism."

Over the years the pressure kept growing to salute the flag than to cease the prayers, until I found myself spending more time that I thought was advisable, trying to find a way to get beyond these two "side items." and get back to the real issues I felt better deserved our attention. There were others who saw things differently and they persisted in making this their cause célèbre. I put the "saluting the flag issue" to rest temporarily by surprising the members on the second day of the 1993 session. Being in the "warm and cuddly period" this early in the session, and knowing that opening ceremonies would not be well attended, I simply waited until the clergy had finished the prayer service and stepped to the podium and announced, "If you would all be kind enough to remain standing, I would ask you to join me in a salute to our flag." I nonchalantly turned around and led them in the Pledge of Allegiance. I don't know if anyone refused to participate as I had my back to them, but it all happened so quickly I believe those members on the floor simply went along. As there was no press in the gallery that early, nobody made a big deal out of the whole event.

But the issue of patriotism attracts zealots on both sides and I was finally forced to meet it head on as it cropped back up in the form of a Constitutional Amendment over burning the flag. The national head-quarters of the American Legion placed a resolution calling for a "Flag Burning" amendment* on the 50 states dockets, and a number of my members were more than happy to volunteer to sponsor it. Pressure built with each passing day to bring it out on the floor and force a roll call. I'm in great sympathy with those who have deep feelings for the stars and stripes and its symbolic meaning. In fact, my mother's sacri-fice of war took my dad. For those left behind, symbols are all that's left. But I also see the Constitution and all it stands for. Our freedoms tenuously hang on our commitment to protect the right to be wrong. I was convinced it was this steadfast determination of toleration of the ugliest side of our nature as a people that separated us from the "Banana Republics." I often thought, "Where else in the world do you get to be a jerk, but in America? And, if you're a big enough jerk, you get to be Speaker."

It was a tough question, that's for sure, but I always came down on the side of it's a person's right to be wrong. It is the true difference of a compassionate and free nation. The problem only got beyond reason when politicians got their hands on it. That's when "grandstanding" controlled the issue. It pushed emotion ahead of reason and dema-gogues rushed in to fill a vacuum. That's where we stood in January, 1994, the second year of my fifth term as Speaker.

The legion's resolution had been hastily introduced, and in order to protect the committee that it would normally be sent to, I opted to refer it to the House Rules Committee which I chaired. I hoped to sit on it until I figured a way out of the dilemma. My more liberal colleagues (mostly Democrats), if forced to vote yes or no, would have followed their conscience and voted no. These same Democrats, voting from conscience, were going to take tremendous heat back home from vet-erans groups in retaliation for their perceived lack of patriotism. Republicans licked their chops in anticipation of forcing the liberals'

---

* *The flag resolution ultimately failed and Vermont was the only state in the nation that did not pass it.*

hand. It had become a political issue, and some of the more conservative members reminded me of that daily, as they inquired when I was going to let the resolution out of the Rules Committee. The question was often accompanied by a gleam in their eye.

I knew the answer. I simply had to find a way to pass the damned thing without forcing anyone to go on record. I would wait until the right time came along. Resolutions come before the Orders of the Day, which means if I was going to pull anything together to get this problem behind us, I would have to do it first thing in the morning. There are few members on the floor then, so I could go through a litany of mundane matters without anyone paying much heed, as they busied themselves with their housekeeping chores while seated leisurely at their desks. But this was an issue the Republican leadership knew I would eventually be forced to bring to the floor and they were alert enough to make sure that a small cadre of their lieutenants would always be in their seats when I brought down the gavel. My task was to find the brief window of opportunity that might present itself if everything fell into place. This "edge" I needed wasn't going to happen without a little help from my friends.

The morning came when the super patriots were all off tending to other business. Some were called to the phone. Some were beckoned to private conversations beyond the floor of the House. I saw the window open and I rushed to read the wording of the resolution as fast I could, hoping the 15 or so members who were in their seats would not be able to distinguish what I was reading from any other monotone-like housekeeping chore that had to be sent out of the way in order to get to the more serious business of the day. It didn't take more than 30 seconds or so to deal with the whole matter, but it seemed a lot longer to me as I nervously rushed through reading it. I actually shifted into a higher gear when I noticed the stirring of the two Progressives to my left. They seemed to be catching the gist of the content of the resolution that was being read to them. I didn't doubt their political courage in such matters as these. But, before they could react, I had finished and immediately called the question.

"You have heard the reading of the resolution," and without the slightest pause or hesitation, "All those in favor, please say aye." There was a weak response.

"All those opposed?" I heard two barely audible voices from the progressives to my left. "The resolution passes." And it was off to the Senate. I pulled it off.

Hell broke loose within minutes. The watchdogs came rushing back into the well of the House, scurrying from one colleague to another asking if it was true what they heard had happened. I got more than one hateful glare. Several confronted me later in the day, and I gave it right back to them.

"You people don't give any more of a damn about the flag and what it stands for than the chair you're sitting in," I said. "The whole purpose of this exercise was to embarrass those who will vote their conscience and differently than you. It's political grandstanding at its worst, and does more to desecrate all that you profess to stand for than some half-crazed college kid torching a dollar flag. If this weren't the truth, you'd be happy the resolution has passed the House and is now half-way toward passage into law. That should be all that was needed to satisfy your professed love for this country. But, no, what you really wanted was to make political hay out of an issue that means a lot more to most Americans. Well, you'll have to find some other time or place."

I didn't, but I should have left them with Samuel Johnson's line: "Patriotism is the last refuge of the demagogue."

In spite of this single act, I tried to maintain the reputation of being fair on the floor of the House. I took great pains to run the House without providing fodder for even my biggest critic. This often was to the detriment of the Democrats. If two members stood at the same time to be recognized, I would always call on the Republican first. If there was some question as to whether a question was germane to the issue under discussion, I would give great latitude to the member speaking, and usually let him or her continue, perhaps with a warning to try to get back on course. The very first time a point of order arose in my Speakership happened in a debate between Republican and Democratic leaders. I ruled for Mike Bernhardt, the Republican Whip. I caught hell from Paul Poirier, as he knew I could just as easily have ruled in his favor.

I was especially critical of members who would get carried away with the heat of battle and venture into the personal zone of disparagement of one of the other members. Granted, all politics is personal but I didn't think meanness had a place in it. I only brought down the gavel once in anger at a member who I felt was being out of bounds in my entire ten years at the podium. There were other occasions a gentle tapping of the gavel handle was all that was needed to bring the member back to civility.

Things were different behind the curtain. I don't want to leave the impression politics is anything but a "noble" profession. I truly believe that, and I take great pride in being allowed to participate in it for as long as I did. But it also is a game where both sides spend nearly every moment searching for that elusive "edge." An edge often pushes the borders of what is fair and what is right. People come to the realization being right isn't enough. If that's all it took, we could just decide on the most righteous among us and send that ordained soul off to make all our decisions in private. It would be a way of ruling that would be quick and cheap. Things aren't that easy in the legislatures of this country, or in our lives. Life itself isn't fair and we have to play the cards that are dealt us, so to speak. I didn't invent the system, but I never hesitated to play the system as I inherited it. Perhaps I took it to a higher (or lower) level, but I didn't ever create a new way of doing things.

The system was so entrenched through its 200-year history, I felt helpless in recreating it. On the other hand, I am not so creative I could have thought of a new "idea" on my best days. If I wandered from the pack of previous Speakers as it related to exerting power, it was perhaps only to the degree of better understanding the powers inherent in the process, and having the nerve to use them.

It was no secret I tried to take advantage of any large or small blessing we might come across. We were just barely in majority by my second term in 1987, and we obviously had the advantage of numbers, at least on paper. This proved to be nice for bragging rights, but still the best guarantee of winning the vote of a majority was tied to the issues. We had an agenda and the Republicans didn't. It wasn't just an agenda for agenda's sake, but one we agreed with and were willing to fight for. We always thought we were right, and that separated us from our opposition.

I don't believe we read five percent of the bills that came to be part of our agenda. We didn't feel that was leadership's job. Very few bills could work their way toward passage without even the most naive bystanders knowing more than they ever wanted to know about any given issue. If a bill was going to have any impact on the normal order of things, it most certainly was going to gore somebody else's ox. They'd let us know the specifics of the bill in no uncertain terms. It was knowledge that couldn't be avoided, even if we tried. One didn't have to read every word. That doesn't mean we didn't talk about the agenda. We did this incessantly. But the talk always surrounded the mode of operation we were going to take politically to get it passed. This took place mostly in the Speaker's office, but it might just as likely have taken shape over coffee in the cafeteria.

Once off the floor, I might spend the rest of the day visiting committees (though I felt as awkward as a school principal visiting teachers in their classrooms,) meeting with different members, strolling over to the governor's office, or walking the hallways looking for people with whom to talk. The days never seemed to have enough time to get done all that I wanted to do. As the ten years went by, I began to feel my age. During my last term, I would feel so drained by dinner time, all I wanted to do was to go back to the apartment and sleep. I wasn't much company at supper, but I couldn't imagine how early I'd be getting up if, at least, I didn't go out to dinner. I was home and fast asleep long before 10 P.M. awaiting the clatter and chatter of the radio the next morning at 5 A.M.

17. Coming Back For More

My first term ended in less than a harmonious atmosphere. We had our way with a dozen major causes and had served notice not only could the Democrats run a government, but we were going to run it in a different way, not necessarily to the liking of the defenders of the status quo.

The Republicans left the capital grumbling about Boston Irish politics, arm-twisting, and whining about everything in general. They had accomplished little in the way of bringing their party together, and nothing in the way of passing anything in which they believed. They did manage to throw Gordie Stafford of Brighton out of his own caucus when he made the mistake of informing them he was going up on the floor and do what he thought was best for his constituents back home, and not necessarily what was the sentiment of the Republican caucus.

I finally got to vote when I decided the issue of divestiture from racist South Africa. I also had my number plates stolen at the annual St. Patrick's day party. Former Speaker Morse was in attendance as my special guest. They found one of the plates on another member's car the next day. Murphy, being the man of honor that he is, gave it back to me.

We actually picked up a couple of seats during the November elections and drew even closer to obtaining the majority. One always worries about fate when your name's on a ballot, and I spent a lot of my time doing just that. I had the advantage of incumbency, but I had also managed to so totally alienate my colleagues on the other side of the aisle, their entire agenda incorporated nothing more than a call to arms to get me. Our response to their bully-like charge was simply to dodge and once again work harder and smarter than they did.

My opponent this time was Ed Zuccaro, a lawyer and former lieutenant of Speaker Steve Morse. He was, of all my potential opponents, the one I feared the most. My fear proved to be unfounded as I beat him by the comfortable margin of 87-63. I did have to go through a lot of hassle. Though the Republicans weren't getting any better at counting, they were developing a vein of meanness. It wasn't their repetitive cries that "Wright is destroying the Citizen's Legislature" or "the Speaker has squashed the members individual freedom" that got to me, as there might have been some small point of truth to these recriminations.

It was their willingness to throw out the most bizarre accusations that had me wondering if they had any limitations to their shamelessness.

They came up with a new twist that accused me of subverting the democratic process by claiming I masterminded a ballot system that intimidated the members into voting for me. I felt this said more about the lack of character of members who would let me threaten them into voting against their will, than it did about me. There wasn't a speck of truth to the charge and I would be the last person one would want to threaten in an attempt to get my vote. Why would I be so unprincipled to place others in this position?

They kept running to the Press making the claim, and the Press kept printing the garbage. They never could tell anyone who they had heard it from, but insisted "they exist." Who? Where? And, most important, *why?*

Finally, they got Jim Douglas, their trusted Secretary of State, to play the game. He announced that in order to insure the integrity of the vote for Speaker, he was going to wheel voting machines on to the floor of the House. As presiding officer of the election, he had constitutional authority to oversee the process. But I had the authority to decide what came in the well of the House and what didn't. I let him know I'd utilize my power of arrest as Speaker if he dared to roll in voting machines. The Vermont House had managed to elect their Speakers without Douglas' innovations for 200 years, and I was determined we would do it by secret written ballot.

The accusations kept flying and although I knew it was motivated by their knowledge that Zuccaro was running way behind, it bothered me they could get away with it. Not only were they seriously damaging my reputation and character in the eyes of the public, but they were doing an untold amount of damage to all the members of the legislature, including themselves. I guess it no longer seems unusual anymore, as America has seen more than it deserves of shameless politicians and "dirty tricks." Little can surprise us anymore, but this was nearly ten years ago and we were closer to home. And, it was happening to me. I was furious.

When Douglas was asked about the validity of his implied cries of corruption, he said things like, "No, I haven't spoken personally to anyone who complained", and "I've heard from several different sources there is a move afoot to require members to show their ballots to other members before they deposit it in the box."

And, what on earth would possess someone who was voting for me to run to Douglas 'friends and squeal on, not just me, but themselves. If I had been the recipient of the tattletale's story, I'd follow up with a question of my own and ask them what the hell they were doing getting that cozy with me to begin with. If they told me they would vote for me, and were now blowing the whistle, what does that say about their character? If they refused to vote for me, why would I want someone to see their ballot since I already knew? One way or another, they were liars. I felt Douglas knew that and so did everyone else.

But it played in "Peoria." On top of all this, it was more than a coincidence all this rancor came after a *Free Press* secret poll had me winning 82-57 with 11 members undecided. This was published on the Sunday before the election. I emphasize this was a secret poll conducted by the staff at the *Free Press,* and it had Zuccaro in a hopeless position, unless the members polled were being clandestinely intimidated by the pollster. Besides, how come the *Free Press* reporter could know, as they certainly knew who they were calling while marching through their poll, but somehow it was a felony if anyone else did?

Douglas did ask the members to allow voting machines into the House, but he was overruled 88-62, one vote better than my 87-63 victory. He eventually got Gordon Booth, a Republican from Barre Town to come forth and claim, "he had been pressured to vote for Wright." Booth said he was "told to vote for the incumbent Speaker if he hopes to gain a committee chairmanship."

There was no mention of "show your vote to your neighbor, Gordie." And it certainly wasn't a first that a Speaker would promise a committee assignment in return for someone's vote. That's called "smart politics" and I was just a bit smarter, it appeared, than Zuccaro. I would challenge any candidate for Speaker to look somebody in the eye and say he had never made this type of commitment. Every Speaker I knew did it. I noticed in my first years that Republican Speaker Morse had placed a number of Democrats on the prestigious Appropriations Committee. Maybe they got there on ability, but if that's the case, it must have been an easy exam. I never talked to Booth, nor would I have, as he really wasn't one I thought might cross over and throw me a vote.

❖ ❖ ❖ ❖ ❖

I was re-elected for a second term and by a bigger margin than anyone had anticipated, except for Paul Poirier and me. We still knew how to count and we had both predicted the final result within one. The fact the opposition was so far off was more a case of their failure to recruit winning candidates and an attitude that I was an aberration who had been lucky in 1985. They assumed my re-election in 1987 was no more than a continuation of their string of bad luck. It was a lot more than that, and we seemed to be the only ones who recognized it. Madeleine Kunin was being re-elected by the same people as the legislature, and the Senate remained Democratic.

It was obvious to others something else was going on that escaped the Republican party, and it had to do with agenda. The people of Vermont hadn't taken issue with our agenda, while the Republicans continued to refuse to place any coherent plan for Vermont's future on the table. While we were passing bills protecting the environment, the opposition was fighting a back-up battle to keep us from equalizing wages on an inter-state bridge in the northwest corner of the state between New York and Vermont workers. While we were pushing increases in the minimum wage, they were fighting to kill a resolution condemning President Reagan placement of flowers on the graves of Nazi S.S. troopers at Bitburg. To even the untrained eye, they were coming off as cheap and mean, people with no agenda, more interested in protecting the special interests and preserving a past that did little to focus on our needs for the future. Kunin kept sending her visions to us for the next century and they kept reminiscing about the past. We kept ramming her bills through the House and Senate, while they continued their mean spirited attacks.

In 1987 alone, we paid witness to an increase in state aid to education of better than 25 percent. We jumped from $86 million to $112 million. And that was on top of an increase in the previous session of nearly an equal amount. We passed a "rivers" bill, an underground storage tank bill, a solid waste bill, a lot sub-division bill and the controversial rapid growth bill that died the previous year as part of the interstate banking massacre. We had begun to deal with what was becoming evident to all as the most ominous issue facing the state when we passed a new, State Aid to Education "foundation formula." This was an effort that spoke to a solution to the disparity of rich and poor towns and their struggle to finance education.

It was a colossal problem that still remains unresolved as I write this, but we put it on the table and made it clear we weren't going to run from the issue any longer. The Senate, for the first time, took the effort to create a system of sharing between rich and poor towns seriously, and though I was convinced people ought to be responsible for supporting education, not towns, the problem was there for all to see. The opposition reacted as expected and successfully fought the visionary measure, but its resounding defeat in the Senate in 1987 only sounded the call for continual effort at fairness in supporting our schools. The battle still rages, and it may eventually be settled by Court injunction, but change is coming.

Personally, I wasn't doing as well as the numbers might indicate. It was clear I was the Republican target, superseding any other agenda. If they could just get rid of the "ogre of the citizen legislature, that

Boston Irish pol", life would settle back into what they defined as a zone of comfort.

I never believed any of that malarkey, and I often thought how ineffective they made themselves by failing to concentrate on the issues while pursuing my demise. It bothered me to be called some pretty disparaging names and I wouldn't be telling the truth if I said otherwise, but I only looked at these attacks as something that went with being a successful Speaker. *All politics is personal.*

People can forgive almost anything except the success of a rival. God help those who emerge the winner in the political world. The more you become involved in politics, the more toes you're going to step on. A lot of pushing and shoving ensues. And sometimes it can get pretty rough. The prettiest girl at the dance braces for the backlash of envy and jealousy. This isn't a phenomenon unique to politics; it's a common guideline in life.

In spite of this, it wasn't in me to throw a fight here and there just to gain a measure of acceptance or love. But it was within my capabilities to deal with our success in a more humble manner. Unfortunately, I just didn't get it. I made matters worse because of this lack of humility. It's something I would try harder at in retrospect, but I wasn't aware my image was the problem at the time. I was just being myself.

As time passed, it became more obvious I would have been better off laying back and not forcing myself into the multitude of fights that I did, but that would have changed dramatically who I was perceived to be. I believed in personal growth and being a better person tomorrow than today, but I had no guidelines that spelled out such a route, and I reasoned I couldn't be doing everything the wrong way as we were passing our agenda, were getting public acceptance for our efforts, were now a marginal majority and I was serving a second term. We must, I believed, be doing something right.

I also realized the legislature was a place of confrontation, in spite of the Pollyanna diatribe spewed by those who, when confronted, handed over their lunch money. I wasn't against compromise as I did more of that than I cared to, but once the gauntlet was thrown down, I thought it was always best to have my hands out of my pockets. I think the willingness to fight for what we believed in, even if it meant we risked everything, was what made us the formidable force we became. At times we skirted the edge of propriety and acted in a Machiavellian manner, but to do otherwise would have ignored the fact we knew the other side was boning up on their own version of chicanery. My copy of *The Prince* wasn't the only one.

We had a job to do and if it meant we risked a public beating to accomplish our ends, so be it. That was just how life in the political arena was.

Early into my second term, Francis Brooks, our Democratic Whip, came face-to-face with the dilemma of doing what it takes to get the job done. I don't recall what the issue was, but it was important enough that Poirier and I were spending a lot of effort trying to line up enough votes to go to the floor and engage the issue. We had been counting and recounting our votes as we always did, but had reached that point where we were still a vote or two short and were down to our last short list of hopeful converts.

This list inevitably was made up of members who, for the most part, were simply holding out, looking for a deal. I was never bothered by such mercenary attitudes, but rather by the frustration of not knowing what it would take to get them to come around. Everybody had a price, and we just had to know what it was. We were well aware it didn't take much of an effort to get 40 or so of the 74 (I could vote in case of a tie) votes technically needed. Even the next 20 or so votes that would get us into the 60s and within striking distance, usually encompassed no more than some time spent with the members to explain the merits of what we were trying to accomplish. Some of these could be accrued simply by calling on their team loyalty; that is, if they weren't going to dig in on principle.

A legislature without loyalty is like a family without love. It made up a significant base from which we methodically plodded to a hoped-for majority vote on any given issue.

Whatever the issue, there was always a large group that were committed for and against and we left them with their conscience. We made it a point not to infringe on their right to vote for those things about which they felt strongly. But, there would always be a group that either hadn't made up their minds and were waiting to hear all sides, or they were waiting to make a deal. It was the last small number that made up the short list that drew our concentration in the final drive to the magic number. This is where we were when Brooks got his baptism under fire as a new assistant leader.

"Brooksie, why don't you go see Kevin and see if he won't give us some support on this? Poirier will take his list and I'll work mine." I instructed, as we anticipated Brooksie's newness to the job of "whip" would necessitate taking what we thought was the easiest prey of the eight or so possibilities that were on the roll call list in front of me. Kevin, we felt, would eventually come around, and it might only take a team pep talk by one of his leaders to have him cooperate. If Kevin was in need of something, it never amounted to a demand beyond reason. The trick was to recognize it would have to be negotiated. Kevin, no novice pol, knew opportunity when it knocked. We reasoned.

It wasn't long before Brooksie was back. "Kevin won't do it."

"Whatta ya mean he won't do it?" Poirier asked impatiently.

"He says he won't. That's it."

"What's he want?"

"I don't know, I didn't ask. I don't think he wants anything," the minister's son answered naively.

"That's baloney," I answered coldly. "Everybody in this place wants something. Brooksie, why don't you go back out there and make him tell you what the hell it is that's he holding out for."

Brooksie, having spent his life respecting people's right to differ, hesitated, but then, in an effort to prove he was part of the leadership trio, begrudgingly pulled himself off the couch and left to chase Kevin down once again. It wasn't long before he was back and said he was right the first time: Kevin wasn't going to come around.

"How'd ya make out?" Paul glanced at me like "I think you're wasting your time."

"Well, he still says no deal, but I did find out what he wants. And we can't do it."

"Whatta ya mean, we can't do it? What does he want?" I asked getting angry.

"He says he isn't going with us guys anymore, as we didn't help him with his bill in the Ed Committee."

"What bill has he got in the Ed committee?" Paul countered.

"Oh, it's some little thing his school people want, but it's a bad idea and the committee agreed not to even take it up. It's tacked back up on the bulletin board in the committee room. A dead issue."

"Well, that's easy enough," I said in a relieved tone. "Just tell him we'll get it out for him."

"You don't understand, Mr. Speaker," Brooksie answered. "Remember, you put me on that committee. That's such a bad bill, the committee unanimously voted not to take it up. It's dead, dead."

Paying no attention, I gave Brooksie further matter of fact instructions, "Look Francis, you go back to Kevin and tell him you've talked to the Speaker, explained his problem to me, and that I immediately got up to go see the chair of the Ed Committee and the Speaker will get it moving."

"Ralph, it's a bad bill. You won't, I don't believe, like it either. I don't think you should lift a finger on behalf of that bill, Mr. Speaker. Really, I don't."

"Don't worry, Brooksie, I'll take care of everything. You just go promise Kevin it will be taken care of and come back with his vote." Off he went for the third time with Paul rolling his eyes impatiently.

This time, Brooksie came back with the look of a man that had accomplished his mission. "He says OK. He's gonna go with us, but I promised him, actually I gave my word that we would move his bill. Have you talked to my Chair? Is he gonna actually move that bill?"

"No," I responded, turning my attention to the roll call list and putting a "yes" check next to Kevin's name. "Good work, Francis."

"No, you haven't spoken to the Chair, or no, he's not gonna move it?"

"Both," I answered, without bothering to look up.

Brooksie fell silent, as Paul and I worked out our final strategy for the upcoming floor fight. When we finished and were heading out to corner a last reluctant member or two, Brooksie finally got the courage to ask, "How often do you guys have to do that?"

"Do what?" I asked.

"Lie!" He was barely able to say the word.

"Oh, not that often, Francis. Don't worry about it. Ya gotta do what ya gotta do." And then, in an effort to relieve the pain of sin that had taken over his face, "Look, Brooksie, I don't know where you're going in the after-life, but I suspect you'll fare a lot better than the rest of us. If it's any consolation, you're not going to run into me."

I'm happy to report we won on the floor of the House the next day, and I went to confession the day after that.

18. COMMITTED TO COMMITTEES

The real work is done in committee, the heartbeat of the legislature. People often gave the Speaker unwarranted credit or blame for whatever happens in a session, but it was never one person that decided the fate of a piece of legislation. It was the committee, led by its chairperson.

There are no simple bills, often referred to as "little housekeeping" bills. When a member gets an idea of his or her own, or a suggestion from someone back home, it always seems like a simple matter of having the Legislative Council put it in the proper legalize and, before you can say, "Mr. Speaker, I have a problem with the member from 'our town's' proposal", it's on the governor's desk awaiting his or her signature. But it's not that simple. Bills, or ideas, have to have a purpose, and not one that can necessarily be seen clearly, but that a majority of both houses, and a governor, sees clearly. I don't ever recall a bill that didn't change something in the way people were accustomed to having things done. People resist change. So if a bill is going to alter how government operates, or how people do things, it has to be done correctly. That's the committee's job, and the chairperson is responsible for seeing to it things are done right or, as is so often the case, not done at all.

The easiest thing to do in a legislative process is to kill a bill at its lowest common denominator. That's why lobbyists make the big money. They'd be making minimum wage if they had to pass bills, but they don't; more often than not, their focus is on making sure things don't happen. And they're damned good at it, too. They conserve what is and tend to break out in a rash at the thought of change. Why would they want to change a system that guarantees they come out on top? If it were 1912 and you were Vanderbilt, or Rockefeller, would you sent your lobbyists into the halls of Congress to push through the creation of an income tax? If you were a health provider, and you had the license to charge whatever the market would bare, would you advocate or lobby for Medicare or Medicaid that has limits set by others as to what they'll pay? I trust you wouldn't, and the record shows they didn't. Conservatives are aptly named as they want to conserve that which is now in existence, though they would consider going back to what was.

I remember all too clearly during my first year in the legislature of being confronted with this fact of life. I had become involved with a piece of environmental legislation that would have raised the handling charge on our bottle deposits from one to two cents a container. It was an extremely important increase for the small grocer. I didn't introduce the bill, but I had more than a passing interest as my alternative school in Bennington had opened the first non-profit Redemption Center in town as a training center to teach kids how to work. An extra penny for our efforts was extremely vital to our ability to make a go at keeping the student-run business open, to say nothing of how crucial a role it played in making the visionary law operative. The other side of the coin was the cost to the two dozen soda and beer distributors who would have to pay the extra penny to the retailers for handling all those containers. They weren't going to let this pass without a fight.

We got it through the House, but not without a great deal of anguish and resistance. I followed the bill from its introduction in the House and, being a naive freshman, assumed it would get a fair hearing. After all, the bill had everything. It was fair and it was the right thing to do.

It had worked its way to the mid-station of its long journey through the House to Peter Giuliani's Ways and means Committee, where it seemed to have run out of gas. I had, with great humility, approached Chairman Giuliani and asked if I might inquire when the committee would find time to schedule testimony on the bill. He couldn't have been more receptive or cordial.

"Well, member from Bennington (he didn't seem to know my name), it's a coincidence that you should ask. I believe I can put it on the calendar the day after tomorrow. What time would be convenient for you, as I assume you want to testify on behalf of its passage?"

I hesitated, taken back at how easy this seemed to be.

"Could you be in the committee room at, say, 11:15 A.M., Thursday?"

"Ah! Yeah! Sure!" I quickly responded.

"Great. See you then."

This passing law stuff was a piece of cake.

Thursday came and with my best suit on, I showed up early for my big moment. I was alone in the committee room, except for one committee member.

"Can I help you?" he asked cordially. He was obviously another member who hadn't the foggiest idea who I was, nor did he care.

"Ah, yes. I'm here to testify on the bottle bill," I answered.

He looked confused, but maintained his facade of friendliness, "Um! The bottle bill." He rose from his seat and went to the bulletin board that had all the bills sent to the committee on 3x5 file cards.

"Do you know the bill number?" he asked.

I gave it to him. His search remained futile.

"The Chairman asked me to be here at 11:15 to testify. I'm a little early, but I can wait."

This time he turned and faced me, like a man that had heard something slightly amusing. "Well, you're certainly welcome to sit and wait for as long as you would like, but the committee is through for the morning. Peter's gone home to lunch. I don't know where everybody else disappeared. I guess it's just you and me."

My anger grew as my confusion decreased, "What the hell do you mean, gone to lunch? It's barely 11 o'clock. What time's the committee coming back into session after lunch?"

"Tomorrow morning, after we adjourn on the floor. At least, that's the usual schedule." He maintained his effort to be helpful. "There must have been a little mixup. Actually the Chairman had to go home to prepare lunch for his daughter. Peter's a great guy. Must have been a little mix-up."

I accepted this plausible excuse, thanked the member, and headed back to my committee on the top floor. No sooner had I turned the corner headed for the stairs when I ran into David Shaffe, also from Bennington, and a member of the committee whose room I had just left.

"How's it goin', Ralph?"

"Not so hot. I just came from your committee where I was supposed to testify at 11:15, but Mr. Giuliani had to rush out to prepare lunch for his daughter." I said.

Shaffe seemed not the least bit surprised at my unexpected delay and answered, "Peter's gone home, that's for sure, as he leaves at this time every day." Now I felt especially bad I questioned anyone's explanation as to why I had missed my opportunity to testify, and resolved to simply make a point to set up a more convenient time for Mr. Giuliani in the morning. He turned and started off in the opposite direction, but not before adding, "Peter doesn't have a daughter."

I had been taken.

The forces against the bottle bill were at work as they knew what I had so unceremoniously just learned: delay is the unrivaled weapon of the proponents of the status quo.

I managed to convince Speaker O'Connor I wasn't being treated fairly by Chairman Giuliani and his cohorts. He did me a favor and managed to convince the Chairman to bring up the bill and I consequently watched it move through the House. It was a great exercise for a new and naive member to be forced to wrestle with all the forces the process produces, in an effort to get a bill through. None of what I learned in that excruciating experience topped what Jim Finneran had to offer.

Finneran, at that time, had the reputation of being the most effective lobbyist in Montpelier, and the best paid. He was worth every penny. It didn't hurt either that he was the owner and operator of the legislative "hang out", the Brown Derby Supper Club.

As the bill proceeded over every hurdle, and through every hoop, it became obvious to even me this thing was going to pass. It was at one of these final stages that I finally got the honor of meeting Mr. Finneran as he stoppped to talk with me. He wasn't there to offer his congratulations.

"Hey, you," he yelled, unceremoniously, across the lobby. And without waiting for any response he came charging over to where I was standing. There were no preliminaries with Finneran.

"Ya think ya got this thing won, huh? Well, let me tell ya something, kid. I've been around a lot longer than you've been on this planet, and I got a little advice for you. I learned a long time ago if ya wanna kill somethin' , then ya better kill it at its lowest common denominator. Ya kill it while it's just a germination in the mind of the nut that's building a case that the world needs it. Now you think that your win an hour ago in the House is the end of this, but it ain't. Ya can't trust all the God damned crazies in the House. But we'll kill it when it gets back to the Senate and is sent to the Conference Committee. There, saner minds will prevail. Six people will decide. And I've got the votes to get to half of that six. You'll see."

Though he was so right in a generic sense, he was wrong on this particular bill. The Senate passed the Conference Committee report by one vote. Actually it ended in a 15-15 tie, and Madeleine Kunin, then lieutenant governor, had to vote to break the deadlock. The bill went on to become law. Finneran suffered an infrequent loss, and I won a lucky fight. I learned more than Jim Finneran ever intended to teach me.

Legislators act on the premise they want to make things better, or at the very least, different. It's this need to do something that brings out those that want to keep things as they are. A battle is all but guaranteed. New legislation isn't any different than new shoes. They don't feel right, may pinch, or look too big for your feet. They're hard to get used to, but what's a person to do since the old ones have sprung a leak, and they can't take you where you want to go anymore. Still, it's tough making the transition.

Good committees become good at what they do in the sense they make change possible, if not easy. A good or effective committee has to have someone who can bring them together and lead them to their goal of moving a bill. It's a talent many Chairs have, but a few don't. The Speaker, when he or she selects the Chairs never knows. I've had

Chairs I appointed on purely political grounds who blossomed into leaders, and I've had others I appointed because of their imminent qualifications, fall on their faces. Intellect, energy, and good intentions weren't enough if they couldn't get their committee members to respect them and work with them.

Certain aspects of the committee process are considered sacred and are as old as the Republic. Foremost among these is the "unwritten" rule that no one pulls a bill out of committee unless the chairman gives the OK. To do so represents a desecration of all they know and trust. Committees reporting a bill on the floor of the House to the body, of whom 90 percent haven't any idea what the bill does, have to be trusted much as a child trusts the comfort of his mother's arms after having a bad dream.

The reporter of the bill has an obligation to tell exactly what the bill does on a paragraph by paragraph basis, and they must tell both the good and bad sides. When interrogated, the reporter's answer has to be straight forward and complete. I never assumed because 90 percent of the listeners didn't care or understand, or so it might seem, the other 10 percent weren't listening and understanding. This was especially true on highly technical issues. If they didn't get up to challenge a misrepresentation or an omission, it wasn't because they were shy.

To bypass or cast aside this trust in the committee members or the committee process was a dangerous road not often traveled. But there was one occasion this treason was practiced, and it happened to John Murphy, not by the members at large, but by his own committee members.

"Mr. Speaker, I've been here long enough that I can't deny I've seen it happen, but not to me," he said.

"In a move some condemned as an unprecedented breach of the legislative process, a House committee approved a drunken driving bill in the absence of its chief foe, the committee Chair." It was big news when this hit the front page of the morning papers in May, 1988. It wasn't because the committee process had been end run, but because the blockers had run over Johnny Murphy on their way to the end zone.

Murphy was no ordinary person, nor was he an ordinary chairman. No one who spent a day with John would ever forget him, and the end result would be a love/hate relationship. I had gone beyond that and forced myself to believe if I wanted to be accepted by John Murphy, then I would have to accept Murphy's Law. There were going to be times when I would worship the ground beneath him, and then there would be times when I could strangle him. Most Chairs earned respect from their committee colleagues by their diligence, intellect, patience, and sense of fairness. Murphy, who could display all of these talents, and usually never at the same time, was something beyond that. He was interesting, not just after lunch interesting, but always interesting.

Murphy worked through to retirement at General Electric while standing on a box at a lathe that was taller than he. He was a defender of the "little guy"and he liked the fight. Any committee member who didn't agree with his efforts for those people whom he determined in need of his help, were simply assumed either without all the facts, or elitists. He'd just get on doing what had to be done without their aid, or in spite of their resistance. Often this meant he had to resort to Murphy's Law. His colleagues found this meant bills they had been assured would never leave his committee ended up on the floor within days; others who were promised their bill was in the clerk's office would find to their dismay that it was, in fact, in John Murphy's pocket.

He once reported on the floor a bill had received a 9-2 vote in his committee "and, Mr. Speaker, this bill ought to pass." I had to remind him he only had nine members on his committee. His quick response, "You're right, Mr. Speaker, I stand corrected as the actual vote was 7-2. But, Mr. Speaker, if I may?"

Smiling, I queried, "Yes, member from Ludlow."

"If I had had 11 members on my committee, my guess is it would have been 9-2."

The Breath Test bill was one of those bills that didn't make Governor Kunin's publicized agenda, nor was it something that she addressed in January in her State of the State message, but it was important to her as it spoke to the problem of drinking and driving. The state had been witness to a number of highly charged and tragic drunk driving deaths and the public clamor to get these people off the road had been louder than normal. The bill was not an earth-shaking piece of legislation, as it merely closed a loophole that presently existed in the law. In fact, all it did was make it possible for police and prosecutors to use alcohol tests as evidence in court. Previously the tests, in order to be used as evidence, had to be done within a half hour of arrest. The bill that the governor was pushing gave the authorities up to two hours if the breath alcohol content was 0.15 percent or more.

I never quite understood why Murphy didn't see this as a good bill. My guess is his distrust of the police, the "Jim Bobs" as he called them, was enough for him to arrive at the conclusion "this little bill should just rest awhile" in his committee.

Kunin did everything that was reasonable and logical to convince Murphy the bill was right and therefore ought to be brought up in committee. She had testimony taken from a group of authorities that would support the bill. Her mistake was she assumed Murphy would do the logical thing. With every attempt to sway him, she was convinced he finally had seen the light and would act in accord with her wishes. Her first efforts were through her staff. They would run Murphy down and impress upon him how urgent this matter was with the governor. Murphy would agree and assure them he was going to get right on it. No sooner would they turn the corner to relay to their boss the mission had been accomplished, than Murphy would turn his corner and promptly forget he ever had the conversation.

Finally, after weeks of these charades, she decided she would have to take matters into her own hands. She invited Murphy to a private luncheon in her office, a special occasion for all who cherished the company of the high and mighty. Murphy was never one to miss a meal and he made a point to put on his best suit, shine his shoes, and show up on time. The "Gov and the General" broke bread together and they parted with the full understanding they both agreed with what had to be done. Kunin assured her staff she had broken the stalemate and he was going to move the bill; Murphy just assured himself the bill wasn't going anywhere.

It went on like this for weeks until the desperate governor turned to me as her last resort. It wasn't a demand, but simply a plea, "Please, Mr. Speaker, get Murphy to move the bill."

I had no better luck than in the past as I had tried, unsuccessfully, to talk reason and logic to Murphy on more than one occasion. The governor's personal plea had taken on an air of tying me to the problem. She persisted and went so far as to challenge me to use my power as Speaker, ("after all, Ralph, you appointed him") to force him to take action. It would have done no good to tell her there were limits to what I could do to pressure a chairperson into doing something he or she didn't want to do. Besides, Murphy wasn't just any Chair. I had waged war with him in the past and I wore the scars to prove it. I didn't need any more scars. But there was a way to deal with it if I got lucky and the stars all lined up. It amounted to fighting fire with fire.

The opening of the fishing season was our lucky day. Murphy, being an avid fisherman, always rose early on opening day, traveled to Ludlow to pick up his little skiff, and returned to the building before we opened the session at 9:30 A.M. This allowed him to have his boat handy for a little fishing after adjournment, and made it impossible for any hanky-panky being done to him on the floor in his absence. This is how it should have worked, except the clerk of the committee received a call from Murphy around 9 A.M. informing him he was in Ludlow picking up his boat and was running late.

Fire broke out in the minds of Harris and Poirier. The group swung into action and devised a plan to get the committee together, bring up the bill, and vote it out onto the House floor where its passage was assured, as long as John Murphy was 100 miles south of Montpelier. A diabolical plot to be sure, but if enough committee members could be rounded up, hustled into the committee room, and implanted with enough courage, they could get the bill through the House before the "General's" return. Bob Harris, Democrat from Windsor, was the Vice-Chair and had the authority to act in the Chair's absence. He was delighted to do so, as was Poirier who as leader, had been the recipient of the same type of pressure from the governor as I had, as well as being on the losing end of a committee clash with Murphy earlier in the session. From me, they got the wink of approval.

Though the members of the committee, knowing the seriousness of their deed, shuttered in fear and trepidation, they also agreed with the bill and saw the hopelessness of its passage if they didn't strike when the iron was hot. They voted the bill out 4-1, barely a quorum.

They hustled it through the clerk's office and hand-delivered it to me at the podium. After two or three rule suspensions to move the bill through the necessary stages, we were getting to the point where I would call for the final vote to message it to the Senate. We did it in record time as most of the members, because of the bill's political notoriety brought on by the clash between Murphy and the governor, were more than willing to see it finally on its way to passage. The trick was we had to get it all done before Murphy arrived back at the State House, and we feared that his presence was imminent.

We nearly made it as we were just three or four minutes from completing our much hastened exercise when, lo and behold, who did I see pushing through the glass doors, but Murphy. There must have been a deep contrast between the expressions of terror that flashed across our faces, and the look of a happy man who had visions of 10-inch trout.

Harris and Poirier had no choice but to continue on, being careful not to give the slightest hint by mentioning or referring in any way to the bill that they were trying to move on the floor. For the longest time, Murphy didn't appear to care in the least what was happening on the floor as he seemed to be talking with several people.

The final approval to send the bill to the Senate, and Murphy's blood pressure, both blew up at the same time. He, finally realizing he just sat through his own execution, jumped up and stood, red-faced, glaring across the hall at Harris and Poirier. And without waiting for me to recognize him spoke in an angry, but controlled voice.

"Mr. Speaker, I think I know the dirty deed that was just performed on the floor of this House, and there's nothing that I can do now to stop it. But I'm sure, for those whose thinking is a bit fuzzy this morning, you haven't heard the last of it."

The bill received its final vote of approval and was messaged to the Senate. All the while Murphy sat, feet swinging under his chair, a look of great hurt from eyes that never left Poirier and Harris. It wasn't long after, he came storming toward me along the ramp in front of the red seats and stopped abruptly at the podium. I shuttered knowing there was nothing in the world I could say that would bring forgiveness to his soul. I braced for the onslaught.

"Mr. Speaker, I know that you're too good a man to have had anything to do with what just happened, but you mark my words they won't find a hiding place dark enough or distant enough to escape my retribution. I'll have my pound of flesh, you can take that to the bank. And I know who masterminded this," he said. Sheepish, I stood silently.

"Perrier' (he never pronounced it Poirier), that's who!"

"Now be careful, John, you don't want to fly off the handle and accuse someone who's innocent."

"I know it's those two, and I know who's the brains behind all this. Ya know how I know, Mr. Speaker?" he asked, without a pause, "because I know Harris has the mind of a child, and isn't capable of this level of intellect. So it's Perrier. He's the smart one. He can't be trusted, and you tell him he should spend the $100 I gave him for his campaign (Poirier had announced he would run for Congress several months earlier), because I'll be working my ass off for his opponent."

If you're ever in Vermont partying and get pulled over, expect a breath test. If you're ever down Murphy's way, don't order Perrier at the bar.

All committees don't work this way. The vast majority of my Chairs ran solid and expediently. Seldom did I find members who weren't extremely loyal to their Chair and their responsibilities.

There were signs that would hint at a developing problem, and perhaps the most reliable sign of a Chair having trouble with a committee was either the lack of work coming out of it, or the unwillingness of veterans to request a return to the same committee the following session. It seldom happened members would be allowed to transfer from one committee to another during the biennium, thus once assigned, it became a two-year sentence. For those who got the committee of their choice, and had the pleasure of serving with a competent Chair, it would be a pleasant two years. Even the people who complained of being "dumped", could find solace in a good Chair, and at least a bearable hitch, that a new Speaker, more to their liking, could remedy down the road.

It was the people who served on committees who worked long and hard hours with few results who complained the loudest, and their last resort if a solution couldn't be found, was to simply refuse to request the same committee the next time around.

Republicans, who were lucky enough to find themselves Chairs without having supported my candidacy for Speaker (and there were a few), were aware it wasn't necessarily a lifetime contract. I told them so. I saw no reason to appoint people to Chairmanships who had done all they could to bring about my demise. Even in my last term or two, I stopped the practice of appointing whomever was my opponent for Speaker to a Chairmanship, as I was beginning to notice a brazenness in their willingness to take me on. I would do the same, of course, if knowing I was going to be beaten, the "benevolent" Speaker was going to pick me up, brush me off and give me a plum assignment. It simply didn't seem like a smart approach to protecting what I had worked so long and hard for. My attitude became, "deal the cards, but don't expect to lose and get your money back. We're big boys and girls." It didn't keep me from having an opponent, but in my last two races for Speaker, it made the more level-headed among them weigh the price of defeat and opt to let someone else take me on.

Upon being elected to my third term in 1989, I ran into problems I either overlooked in the past, or simply avoided because they were unpleasant. To this day, I regret firing two of my Democratic Chairs.

All the factors seemed to leave me no choice at the time, and even today I'm not sure a different approach would have achieved satisfactory results. I heard numerous complaints about the two Chairs all during the previous session and I dismissed them as just members complaining about the "boss." Yet, I couldn't help feeling uncomfortable that some of the gripes were coming from people who didn't strike me as chronic complainers. I passed it all over, hoping things would get better and resolve themselves, but when I had a crucial and complicated bill that changed the way we funded education, I knew politics was going to be a major factor in our getting it out of committee and onto the floor. I transferred Paul Poirier temporarily from the General and Military Committee he was on, to the Education Committee where I had sent the politically charged bill. He provided the necessary leadership and got the bill out with an affirmative vote. Then, I moved him back to his original committee. That wasn't the way things were supposed to work, but the manuever brought about the expected results.

In the other case, members complained about the extremely long hours without a high production count. There was no shortage of people in a "citizen legislature" who find their obligations at home prohibit them from working into the early evening. There are suppers that can't be missed too many times, kids to be picked up, rides to be caught, and just plain exhaustion, especially after months of this routine. It might all have been tolerable if the members felt the level of results equaled the hours and effort. This was not the case with this committee and they complained.

I might have been able to put it out of mind as eight months had passed since we adjourned and I first heard the sounds of griping, but when I took the committee assignment request sheets home on that first weekend of the new biennium to begin the task of assigning members, I noticed not a single veteran member of these two committees requested to return. A number of them made comments at the bottom of the request sheet.

"Please, Mr. Speaker, not again. I just can't do another two years." Or, "Don't want to go back if so-and-so is going to remain as Chair." This might not have been a problem of colossal magnitude if they had been referring to committees I didn't expect to do heavy lifting, but they were committees of middle level importance and I felt we could not get the job done with a veteran Chair and ten brand new members.

A legislature is like a family in that it's possible to have malfunctioning sibling relationships in two or three rooms of a house with 14 bedrooms, but if all 14 are engaged in small wars, the house ceases to function as it should. I don't think I ever experienced the luxury of having all 14 committees functioning cordially and productively. That was OK, as the break downs were usually temporary and as one would erupt, another would be settling into a cordial relationship. There was always a war going on in Murphy's room, for example, at least between he and Harris, but I never had a doubt as to who was in charge. And I never worried about Murphy pumping out bills.

I really disliked making committee assignments. It seemed no matter what I did, there was no way to avoid having 30 or more members furious at me because they had been "dumped" into committees on which they didn't want to serve. This wasn't my main concern, as I knew full well somebody had to be "dumped", and I made every effort to make sure it wasn't one of my friends. The indignation level from my critics was certain to reach record levels of criticism, but it was something I managed to grin and bear. The purists, as well as the opposition, argued everyone should have their first choice and be placed where their abilities (or wishes) were best served. Since all demands could not be met, it was inevitable someone would be hurt.

I had over 50 requests for the powerful Appropriations Committee one year, though I only had two vacancies. That was an impossible task, but that type of dilemma never was brought up. If it just had been my political enemies who ran to the Press to harangue about "partisanship and good ole boy politics", that would have been bad enough, but there was a lot of quiet mumbling and dissatisfaction from my own Democrats. They may have been assigned to a powerful money committee, but wanted more. It wasn't enough to be a member, they had been hoping and sometimes lobbying for a Vice-Chairmanship, or the top job, pushing their loyalty to their present friend and chairperson into the background.

To some degree, that was what was happening to my two problems with unproductive committees. People were making their moves to the top, and somebody had to either step aside, or be pushed. My head stayed clearer than the potential winners of additional power, if only because I managed to stay concerned with institutional well-being, rather than anyone's individual well-being. The institution is shored-up and better positioned to function at a higher level when incompetence is replaced. On the other hand, the bad news is that two people are personally hurt. I chose the latter and have regretted my actions ever since. I hurt two people deeply.

The people I denied Chairmanships were good and decent, not simply because they were liberal Democrats who never failed to be with me on the issues that were most important, but because they were bright, extremely hard working, and took their jobs seriously. They simply had a problem being leaders. Not everyone is born to lead and not everyone is born to be successful. Whatever the reasons these two were not successful by the standards demanded of the political process as practiced in a legislature. With one small difference, it was exactly the standards I lived, or died, by. To be sure, 149 other souls determined my fate, whereas I had to determine theirs, but if I couldn't somehow manage to keep a majority believing in me, I was out of a job. Worse, my fall from the bridge would probably end in a less choice committee than the powerful Ways and Means committee where I assigned them trying to create a soft landing. Any fall from grace I might experience was most certainly going to have me showing a sudden interest in six-inch trout.

I would take the entire committee request sheets home for the weekend and wrestle with them in anticipation of formally announcing them from the podium the following Tuesday. I would take all the advice and input that was offered while in session that first week, but once I left the building on Friday to head back to Bennington, I knew

I would receive only a handful of calls, and those would be the desperate kind from people who just couldn't walk away feeling they had done all that they could and now let the chips fall where they might. I would call Poirier a dozen times running this or that appointment by him, and he would lend his political expertise to the effort.

Upon returning to the State House late Monday afternoon, the Democratic leadership, a few trusted lieutenants and I would meet behind closed doors to hammer out last minute changes. This was all taken seriously. We were well aware we were playing with at least two years of people's political lives and it was not unusual for the five or six lieutenants to get into some heated arguments on behalf of their friends. There was at least one occasion when the room broke up in laughter and left us holding our sides.

We had gotten down to the Fish and Game Committee and much to our surprise, we found that of the eight members proposed to serve there, three of them had the same last name. Let's, for humanity's sake, call them Smiths. Well, every Smith in the legislature was on this committee, none were Democrats, and not all had it on their request sheet. They didn't have any defenders, or admirers, in the room that I could hear.

It just looked funny with eight people on a committee and three of them named Smith. We no sooner unanimously agreed they would stay right where they were, than it dawned on me I had to read these assignments aloud from the podium. It was one thing to play partisan politics, but another to make these three poor souls the butt of certain laughter. If we couldn't control ourselves in the privacy of my office, chances were a lot of the members, including myself, wouldn't handle it well on the floor the next morning. Someone suggested I try reading the committee names aloud to see if I could do it without breaking up. I tried every which way, but each try ended up with tears of laughter in my eyes, and the others in the room were practically rolling on the floor.

"OK, OK, let's be serious now," I pleaded, trying to calm them down. "I'll try it again, but this time I'll read the names fast." They broke up again, barely able to sputter, "Sure, sure, just read Smith, Smith, and Smith, that should do it."

Several moments would go by and we'd all calm down and try with all our might to be serious and then, "Well, try this: name the first five, and then just say 'and the rest of the committee is filled with Smiths.' That'll do it." This time it would take five minutes to calm them down.

We never did find a way to read those names and consequently there's a man named Smith who much to his little Republican heart's surprise ended up on the committee of his choice. Another affirmation that it's better to be lucky, than good, or at least it's better to be a Smith than a Jones.

Only Poirier knew I was going to have to make the changes in the two committees I felt had to be made more productive, and the next morning I did it. Their replacements were equally qualified, and they did an excellent job in the years ahead, but I never felt good about it and it destroyed my friendship with them. Several months later, the two joined a cabal to embarrass their new committee Chair by yanking, or attempting to yank, a bill from his committee. I took some solace in that.

"Val" Valsangiacomo, a Democrat from Barre City, was the most senior member of the House, having been first elected in 1967. He was perhaps the steadiest guy in the building. I never ever had an instance where I was frustrated or dissatisfied in the way he conducted himself. A much decorated WW II veteran with three Bronze Stars and a Purple Heart, he was highly respected and literally loved by his committee. The cabal, led by the ex-Chairs, came out of the blue, as the process to pull a bill out of a committee had to have the element of surprise. It was over within minutes, as it only took a simple motion. I stood in disbelief when one of the Ways and Means members rose and caught my attention, "Mr. Speaker, I move that the Ways And Means Committee be relieved of H-000."

Like most of the members, I didn't have the faintest idea what H-000 was, and the members voted simply on their trust it was the a committee member who was asking to be relieved of the bill. That normally meant all was OK, and the member who was making the request, wasn't someone who might be involved in chicanery. It worked, as Val was not on the floor at the time, and no one jumped up to thwart the conspirator's effort. When I heard what actually happened, it was too late to do anything about it and it was, with great sadness, I spoke to my friend and war hero, as he tried to understand what would motivate his committee members to do this to him. I had to break away from Val that day in order to fight back the same emotions that welled up in his eyes.

You might ask, "What's the difference between what was done to Murphy and what was done to Val?" The answer is the difference was that one was Murphy, and the other was Valsangiacomo, night and day personalities. Murphy was constantly playing these games on others and could actually admire Poirier or Harris who displayed a love for this type of "gunfighter " politics. That wasn't Val's style, as being a student of the rules and devoted follower of the process, he never was a participant in the "games" people played. Maybe they did it to get back at me for their demotions. It was a common practice to see whole committees, unhappy with their assignments, spend good portions of entire sessions plotting and scheming against someone or something. They knew I was especially close to Val, and I would be hurt to the same degree that Val was hurt. Maybe it was as simple as a need to lash back at anybody. I assume they knew they wounded the wrong man. I'll live with my misdeed and I trust they'll live with theirs.

19. READY, AIM, FIRE

Four years is a long time to be Speaker of the House. The record up until that time was six years, held by Tim O'Connor (1974-1980). To get elected Speaker is a feat in itself and to get re-elected, even once, is a test in tenacity, persistence, and luck. I knew my luck would run out and that eventually I would end up a portrait on the wall of the Speaker's Hall. It's hard to believe it took as long as it did.

In spite of the fact I defeated John Hise by ten votes to gain my third term in 1989, I knew my survival would demand talents that I didn't have. The Press had defined who I was, and though many of them enjoyed my style because I was a good quote, I was suffering from that very same style. Here's Kevin Goddard's view as he saw it in April, 1989 in the *Times-Argus*. We begin with the headline:

Luster May Be Fading for House Speaker Wright

The luster has faded somewhat from the glory days of the last few years, and the agenda is now far less ambitious. There's still the elevated podium he ascends every morning to oversee the workings of the Vermont House and the big, comfortable office with the stately desk (actually the desk was made by inmates in the St. Albans Correction Center at very little cost to the taxpayer) *and the large windows to retreat to when the schedule permits. But his trusty side kick, Paul Poirier, is gone. The Press, as they say, has been unfavorable. And it may be that, for the time being at least, the good fight is just not quite as much fun anymore for the silver haired school teacher who in the 1980s has emerged as one of the strongest and most compelling personalities in all of Vermont politics. Ralph Wright. His style, philosophy and Marine-like efficiency as the Speaker of the House are the stuff that political legends are made of. In an arena where weak personalities and over-inflated egos are all too common, he is a genuine character, almost a caricature: a battle-ready Irishman with a passion for the little guy and an addiction to politics. Some say that for several months of the year at least, he is more powerful than the governor. No one who enters the State House takes him lightly. He can be the most charming presence in Vermont or the most miserable SOB who ever banged a gavel or berated a reporter..."*

Goddard goes on for an additional 21 paragraphs running down a litany of escapades I managed to get myself into over the past four years, but then ends with the point I'm trying to bring out:

"Meanwhile, Wright rails and fumes, complaining that a news organization is out to get him and lamenting that even the Governor doesn't have

to sign expense vouchers. So it is a different kind of year, this year. It's a far cry from the days when the chamber was heady with self-confidence, buzzing with landmark environmental, educational, and developmental control legislation. It's that his authority to conduct business as he sees fit is being openly challenged. And in the end that may be what these controversies are all about."

It's true as some of the luster had faded, but not to any degree that my love for the process or the whole idea of public service was mitigated. It's also true Poirier was gone from the legislature, having lost his race for Congress, and I missed all his talents. It's also true I had accumulated a ton of "bad" press. But I never believed these things were anything more than attrition and inevitable events that were merely the symptoms and not the disease.

I was suffering from being around too long with all the baggage that encompassed. If I had been a "nice guy" who didn't take care of his friends while disregarding his enemies, and had been a whole lot less successful, I might have been better tolerated. In fact, if I had been more restrained in my efforts to push through legislation and avoided the fight more often, that would have gone even further to enhance my public stature. If I had been more adroit at pretending I didn't enjoy the immense power that accumulated around the office of the Speaker, I wouldn't have become as big a target as I had become. But that would have been a whole lot less than honest, as I immensely enjoyed wielding power. It's probably not considered polite to mention succumbing to these temptations of power, but I didn't feel any semblance of guilt to having people answer the phone when I called, or responding quickly to my efforts on behalf of my constituents. I felt this was what they were supposed to do. I didn't like it if they failed to do the same for others, but I wasn't going to let them do it to me, at least as long as I could wield my power club.

I never asked for any special privileges for myself; I got to the back of lines and paid my own way as the others did, but neither was I going to roll over if they insisted that, because of my position, I was fair game to be whacked at will.

Some said I raised the art of wielding power as a Speaker beyond any others. These people were not only guilty of failing to read history, but of distorting what little they knew. I wasn't the first Speaker to punish people who weren't "cooperative." I told you how Speaker Morse "dumped" me and another half-dozen Democrats in 1983, nor was I the first to use a knowledge of the rules to my advantage.

I was committed to my own liberal agenda, but I held this in joint ownership with a majority of the members, or the agenda never would have been enacted into law. No one ever questioned my belief in that agenda, and for that I'm both proud and grateful.

I believe my problem, coupled with my personality, was that I was successful. I say this only to point out I was just doing what came naturally. I could fill up a chapter with members who had higher IQs, and at least a page with members who had better political sense. If I had anything special, it was that I knew where the talent lay and I wasn't the least bit frightened to call on them. Of course, I never overlooked the fact I was only the second Democratic Speaker in the 200-year history of the state, and I had the "hammer" in my hands that the opposition would have killed for.

20. TIT FOR TAT

Maintaining any semblance of control in the House took all the personal and political skills I possessed and then some. A Speaker, no matter who it is, or which party he or she belongs to, is ultimately and fatalistically at the mercy of their membership. It was a significant enough trick to become a minority Speaker in the first place, it was a miracle of sorts to maintain that high post. There were times when it seemed everyone had a gripe, or was on a mission with, or against, the person in power.

I broke the membership into a number of categories so I could generalize as to what motivated them. I soon earned a reputation, somewhat deserving, of being able to "read" people. What I really had developed was a patience to take the time to learn all I could as to what was important to them. Then it was a matter of delivering the goods.

A large group concentrated their efforts on getting legislation passed and I accommodated them by learning to count potential votes. There may have been no better counter than me in the body, but there wasn't anybody else who spent the time going over the numbers as I was willing to do. It was nothing more than hard work that I took the time to do. Any first grader can get to 76, but it takes a doctorate in politics to know where to go to get the 76. It's a combination of reward and punishment; and being right, or wrong. I'm not sure to be consistently successful these two attributes can be separated. Because of this, I was often accused of being an " arm-twister" or a manipulator.

I could gain a giant step on the road to winning simply by explaining what the bill did to the members. This group would see things my way for no other reason than they believed it was the right thing to do. Their conscience was their guide and that sufficed. The liberals were a blessing to me, as I was into passing liberal legislation. Seldom, if ever, did I have to "tell them" how to vote. In fact, they would take it as an insult if I did approach them. Whenever we got into counting on issues that were anticipated as being a battle royal, we could merely sit down and check off the members whom we were aware of who would agree with the intent of the bill. They were like money in the bank.

I never, ever, literally twisted anyone's arm. Did I ever do what amounts to the same? You bet your life I did. I used all the cunning and charm I possessed to win. Sometimes it wasn't enough, but more often than not it did the job. I felt that was exactly what I was supposed to do. It was what they selected me do to, and I never worried a moment about it. Some couldn't resist the urge to carp and whine I was using "Boston-style politics" to accomplish my goal. The Republican leadership, however, was trying to do the very same thing, but usually with less success.

The difference can be measured in a number of ways. I was pressuring, some would say unduly, people to do what either they didn't want to do, or didn't believe in doing, for themselves, or their constituents; or they were succumbing to my wishes in spite of what was best for themselves, or their constituents.

If they acted solely on the latter motive, they wouldn't have been around very long as the voters back home would have ended their career at the next election; or they didn't deserve to be there in the first place if they became subject to my will so easily. In this case, the latter can be dismissed, as I never met, but a handful of members, who upon arriving in the legislature felt they didn't like the job and didn't care if they returned. Quite the opposite was the rule as most of them would have done anything to maintain their posts as public servants.

There were a lot of members who would force me to "make a deal", and I did my best to accommodate them, depending on the price. I drew several lines, as to how far I would go. I could dismiss making deals with a large number of people, mostly Republicans. This group, in many instances, was filled with people I never talked to. They did not like me, and I didn't like them. Talking to each other was just a waste of time. They were opposed to whatever I was trying to get passed and weren't going to change their minds, whatever the cost. In this case, I would be respectful of their commitment, no matter how misguided I felt they might be, and leave them with their "sin." I never felt it was within my rights to push or prod, beyond insisting that I get an opportunity to present my counter arguments. I might feel disappointment, but I never felt disrespect. I would have defended their right to be wrong with the same vehemence that I would have brought forth what I thought was right. In essence, that was what I concluded was the heart of this nation's greatness.

One time I failed to vote the "liberal" line. It was during my second term as a member of the Health and Welfare committee. The issue had to do with spraying some sort of chemical for the clearing of brush that flourished under power lines. The power companies were pressing to see that it got passed. I was totally unaware it was even coming on the floor, and had not read the bill. This was one of the many instances that members, who spent most of their time absorbed and tied to their committees, relied on other avenues to reach a conclusion as to how they would vote.

Often it would be as lacking in intellectual exercise as plunking one-self down while debate was raging and asking your seatmate how he or she was going to go on the issue. Sometimes it was the debate itself that helped make up one's mind. More often, it was who was speaking for, or against, the measure that determined the vote.

I had no sooner left committee to the ring of the quorum bells* when Bobby Starr, a member I liked and respected, stopped me and asked if I could give him some help on the bill. I quickly agreed, and it was a mistake I never repeated. I had committed before I knew what I was committing to, a newcomer's "boo-boo" in an effort to please. I could have changed my mind, gone to my friend, and informed him I had had a change of heart. The unwritten rule was once we gave our word we better keep it, or suffer the loss of trust within the group. Going to the person who thought I was on his or her team created a good deal of disappointment, but it maintained the vital right to "change one's mind." Having never given a second's thought to how those neat paths were maintained under the power lines that criss-cross our beautiful hills and dales, I kept my word and voted "yes."

No sooner had the roll call concluded and the results read by the Speaker than Althea Kroger, then Assistant Democratic leader, came storming up the aisle headed towards me. She was more than a little upset.

"You mind explaining why you thought that was something that you should vote for?"

This was a first to me and I rushed to make up any excuse I could find, but to no avail. I wasn't beyond telling her a lie, but I couldn't think of any as I was experiencing my first act of disapproval from my leadership. Instead, I got angry. It's not the best defense, but a common response of somebody who just screwed up. And I had screwed up.

"Well, I, uh, I think it's a pretty good bill," I responded angrily.

"Ralph Wright, I know you better than that. That bill does nothing more than allow the power companies to spray DDT, and save them-selves a whole lot of time and effort, to say nothing of a whole lot of money. You voted wrong, and I'm disappointed you weren't smart enough to see that."

"Listen here, Althea, I got elected by the same amount of people that you did and I don't have to stand here and listen to this. Furthermore, I resent you thinking I have to have your permission to

*Constant rings, continuing uninterrupted, meant members were being called from all over the building to assemble in the "well." Three consecutive rings signified a roll call had begun.

vote any damned way I please. Don't, and I mean this sincerely, *don't* you ever question one of my votes again." With that I turned and stormed back up to the committee room.

It was absolutely clear Kroger was 100 percent right. I had made a dumb vote. She knew it and so did I. She was nice enough never to bring the incident up again. I regret it to this day. But there was another lesson I wasn't going to forget: People have to maintain the inviolable right to be wrong if we are going to have a free society and a democratic government.

The latter is of much more importance than the former as it embraces more than the expediency of consensus. It is the very foundation of tolerance and community. It goes even beyond those two vital qualities to the heart of love. Ask any spouse if this isn't the linchpin to holding a marriage together. I never forgot how I felt when I had experienced this, and I never practiced this heavy handedness with anyone else. *OK, there was one exception.*

Murphy again! He was holding up some bill or other in his committee. I was getting the pressure from Governor Kunin and a number of members to get the thing out. I begged and cajoled, but with no success. Murphy knew how to handle me. Sometimes he'd tell me he'd do what he had no intention of doing. Other times he told me it had been done when it hadn't. I was at my wits end, and this time he wasn't going to leave the building. In desperation, I threatened him with his job. Still no results.

"OK, Murphy. Two can play hardball if that's the way you want it. You've pushed me as far as you're going to."

"Mr. Speaker, I didn't mean to do that. You're getting upset over a small thing." He knew he wasn't describing my angry feelings properly. "I don't think you'll like the bill if it passes."

"Murphy, damn you, don't stand there telling me whether I like the bill or not. I like it now, bottled up in your committee, and I'm going to love it once I get it on the floor. It's you, you little bastard, I don't like a lot right now. Now I'm going to get it out like I promised you I would two days ago. If necessary, I'll do it over your dead body. I don't have the power to bring that about, but I do have the power to get rid of you, and that's exactly what I'm going to do. Read what I've got and then sign it." I pushed it across the desk at him.

He looked at me with all the innocence of an unjustly accused child and then looked down at what was in front of him. He took care not to pick it up.

"Mr. Speaker, I can't sign this. It's my letter of resignation as Committee Chair. You don't really want to do this."

"Murphy, not only do I want to do this, I'm going to do this."

"Mr. Speaker, I may be stupid and I may even be guilty of a horrible crime, but I'm not so dumb that I'm going to push the on switch while I'm the one sitting in the chair." With that he casually turned and walked out of my office.

He somehow knew I was bluffing. But he took it a step further. I didn't know this then, but as soon as he walked out, he searched the building until he found the *Rutland Herald's* Jack Hoffman, a reporter especially critical of my "power politics", and told him everything that had just happened to him in the Speaker's Office. Hoffman, sensing he had the story of the year, rushed to my office, his note pad and pen at the ready.

"Murphy says you just relieved him of his Committee Chairmanship."

Looking surprised and astonished I grabbed for the ledge. "He what? C'mon, Jack. That's preposterous, I wouldn't even think of such a thing. Murphy may be the only friend I have left in this building. He's just jerking you around. Maybe one of the other members is teasing him. No truth to that at all, Jack." He gave me his "I'm a hard boiled street reporter" glare mixed with skepticism and disappointment. He left.

Murphy knew I couldn't withstand the brutal news reports my firing him would have laid on me. He was quick to fight fire with fire.

There were a lot of members who drove a hard bargain. They didn't care one way or another about a bill, so they would accommodate me by throwing me their support, or they were making me pay a price for the vote I wanted. Some just wanted to be asked and asked and thereby assume a brief mantle of importance. I could understand this, and I never hesitated to approach them in my most humble posture and do just that.

Others wanted something in return and if they didn't ask then, I knew they would find a time to come around and make their requests. This was fair, even though I knew in some of the cases the member was going to vote with us, but purposely gave the opposite impression to acquire our indebtedness. To some degree the claim could be made that they were selling their vote, but I feel that would be judging them too harshly. Tit for tat was all it amounted to and it was no different than what everybody else practiced. You cover for me and I'll cover for you.

The fact I was involved in this type interaction was more dependent on the reality that, as Speaker, I was in a better position than anyone else to do more with the power inherent in the office. The cases where an argument could be made that a member was just out and out selling his or her vote, I never chose to be judgmental. What was the difference between a member doing a favor for another, and a member of the Press offering to withhold a quote or story, in return for a later and bigger dividend? That happened often.

I recall a reporter who once gave me information only he was aware of in return for a "scoop" only I could give to him. It was a blatant "deal", and we both knew it. The only ones who got hurt were the other reporters who were beaten on the story, and me, who got punished by one of those reporters. I was careful to never do that again, not because I thought it was wrong, but because another reporter felt wronged and punished me for it. It wasn't a question of morality, but one of revenge.

21. THE JUNKET PRIZE

Junkets were not the biggest prize I could offer, but most of the members liked to travel and would accept my offer to go to a conference without much persuasion. The state belonged to a half-dozen different organizations and we paid heavy dues for the privilege. I thought we should take advantage of whatever they had to offer, and for all the same reasons that other groups justified sending their employees to similar events. The difference was I never pretended too hard that lots of the members went to have a good time. My attitude was "God bless them", but the Press, in their never ending quest to root out crime and corruption, couldn't stomach the thought of it all. It was bad enough members were wasting taxpayers money, but a "Pox on our House", if we went and actually had a good time.

The outcry got so bad I literally stopped traveling. The hit in the Press for other members wasn't half the decibel level if they weren't accompanied by the Speaker. I could send the Republican leader across the country and little note would be made of it, but if I traveled to a neighboring state, the roof would cave in. During my last two terms, I simply stayed home. There is one trip I took to New Orleans I did regret on moral grounds. I was wrong. It wasn't that I didn't have a good time. New Orleans is a fun city.

I was beginning to be known around the country with these organizations as a survivor, a Speaker who lasted longer than a summer thunder storm. I began to be invited to the "big guys" special dinners and receptions and I was asked to speak.

I received a call from one of the national tobacco corporations informing me they would like me to give a "special" address to my fellow Speakers and President Pro Tems from around the country at a VIP dinner that was being planned in our honor during the week-long conference. They suggested I prepare something on the deficit in Vermont and keep it to 15 or 20 minutes. They also mentioned there would be a "token" honorarium for my contribution. I actually spent a considerable amount of time preparing my address and somewhat nervously awaited the event.

It took place in a very fancy four-star restaurant in the Latin Quarter and I spent the cocktail hour moving from one small meaningless conversation to another. Finally it came time for the after-dinner speeches and I was horrified to see on the program they had scheduled about half the "big deal" Speakers and President Pro Tems in the country to address the group. To make matters worse, we were listed alphabetically and I was the very last speaker on the agenda. I had promised, and I had to go through with it, no matter how long the evening turned out.

We were no sooner seated at the head table when I discovered a check made out to Ralph Wright buried beneath the half-dozen forks. And it was for $1,000. I only had a 15-minute speech, on the deficit no less. At this rate of remuneration, I figured I'd have to speak for about 27 hours. So this was the honorarium game. My only hope was that by the time they got to me, about 15 speakers down on the list, everybody would have left, or died of boredom.

Any organization that got rich enough to hand out $1,000 checks to 15 or so of the likes of us isn't stupid enough to schedule about five hours of our hot air. This became obvious from the moment they introduced the first scheduled speaker. And that's all they did. They introduced him. He, in turn, stood and took a bow, waved, said a word or two about how happy he was to be a guest of such a prestigious group, and sat down again, stuffing his check in his coat pocket.

We were seated at an oval-shaped head table so I couldn't help noticing the smiles of all the rest of my colleagues as they discovered the checks.

"And now it is my honor and privilege to introduce the Speaker of the House from the most wonderful tiny and pristine state, the Honorable Ralph G. Wright, Speaker of the State of Vermont." I rose, giving notice to the polite round of applause and instead of just sitting back down again, I waited until the applause had ceased and the room became completely silent.

"I want to thank our gracious and most generous host for inviting me to come here this evening to address you." I could see the incredulous looks on the faces of my friends who were thinking "this rube actually thinks they want him to deliver a speech." "I must confess I felt a little guilt in that I have prepared a 20-minute address that our hosts requested I deliver this evening, but the hour is getting late." There was relief now on the faces of my dinner-mates. "I trust I can mail it to each of you back in your home offices and thereby let you read my thoughts at your leisure. Again thank you for having me and a special thank you for the exceedingly generous honorarium. I don't believe I have ever received $2,000 for not delivering a speech."

I sat down and watched the others with glee as they examined their own checks. Only the Master of Ceremonies, who knew the truth, found my comments funny.

The legislature is such a parochial institution, it is difficult to think of the members as single-talented individuals. I was amazed at the vast array of talent that was amassed in their little souls. We were blessed with the company of members who had been achievers in other walks of life. Certainly many of them had proven to be extremely successful in a vast number of fields. It wasn't that I was overwhelmed by those who accumulated considerable wealth through their business careers, or even that we had the company of former governors, Pulitzer Prize winners, or Rhodes scholars. It was the common everyday talents that impressed me the most.

For example, Peter Youngbaer, a stalwart on the Appropriations Committee, made his living at being a clown. That's right, a clown. Andy Christiansen, from the Agriculture Committee, was an accomplished pianist and during more tense moments, he would entertain us at the keyboard. We would have the grand piano rolled out onto the floor of the House. Julie Peterson, Helen Riehle, Sally Fox, Jane Potvin, Doris Lingelbach, Annie Seibert, and a number of other women would form a gutsy chorus, and belt out songs from material they wrote from scratch. To be entertained by these people, some of whom I had gone into battle with or against, never failed to give me a rush of camaraderie that wasn't often experienced in a setting that functioned primarily on controversy. The biggest surprise was a talent possessed by Bob Stannard, another member of the Appropriations Committee.

Stannard was another of those genuine characters in the House during my tenure. He is extremely bright, with a great sense of humor, and looked upon as a "player", except by the majority of the Republican Party, of which he was a reluctant member. Having made the mistake of voting for me for Speaker, Stannard immediately caught the full wrath of his caucus, and was ostracized to the point that he opted to change his party affiliation. His problem was not that he denounced his loyalty to the Grand Ole Party, but more the timing of his act of conscience. He did it within days of being elected as a Republican.

I never doubted Stannard's anxiety at belonging to a party that, at least, as represented by the group that made up our House's Republican caucus, was at opposite poles with his "people-oriented" idea of government's purpose. My worry at gaining an additional member into our caucus was I didn't think they'd ever forgive him for such a treasonous move. I was right. He never got re-elected.

There were no bounds to the level of meanness and contempt shown to someone like Stannard from his former party, as this was the group who never hesitated a moment to throw Gordy Stafford (a Republican from Brighton) out on his ear simply for having a different opinion than the rest of the Republicans.

I wasn't aware Stannard was going to make the drastic move of changing parties until I read it in the paper. If he had called, I would have advised him not to do so. I had strong feelings as to how far I would let anyone go in showing anger and displeasure at my right to think for myself, or to be as different from the norm as I chose to be. I never experienced the degree of animosity that Stannard had, but I have had my differences, philosophically, with the Catholic Church. On more than one occasion, the Bishop himself served notice he was upset at my "straying." I responded I would answer to my God without any guidance from the more earthly, and carried on. I wasn't excommunicated for my "anti-Catholic" views on abortion, but I wasn't recommended for a Deaconship.

The change took a great load off Stannard's shoulders, and he blossomed, finally, into one of the more effective legislators in the House. But it was in New Orleans I came to truly enjoy his company and talents.

We followed the crowd into the Latin Quarter early one night, to experience the gala atmosphere that seemed to go on almost around the clock. It was about 10 P.M. when a group of us tried to push our way into a bar where the crowd had already overflowed onto the sidewalk. Most of the bars were jammed, but this one obviously had a real show going on, and people were clamoring to get in.

Nobody had seen Stannard for a while, but this wasn't unusual as the crowds were so great, it was difficult to keep everybody in a group. The joint was rocking with the great Dixieland band playing inside. It took some effort, but we managed to squeeze into the back of the smoke-filled room. The crowd was largely made up of white tourists, but the talent on the bandstand was black, with one exception. Their star performer was a bald headed white guy. It was Bob Stannard playing the harmonica. Sweat was streaming down his face and the crowd was going wild over his performance. I couldn't believe my eyes. And, could he play!

He said he had a great time that night as he met a lot of new and admiring friends. But it was a considerably disappointed voice that greeted my wakeup call at 6 A.M. the next morning to arouse him for our previously scheduled three-mile jog though the streets of New Orleans. I took sadistic pleasure in pulling my rank and ten minutes later, we were loping through the already cruel heat of a New Orleans August morning. We passed some of the places where Stannard had enjoyed such great fun in just hours earlier, but now they represented something a lot more painful.

I enjoyed the run and when we finished, I dragged him to the top floor of one of America's fanciest and best hotels to take a dip in the swimming pool. It was still much too early for the previous night's revelers to be up and around and we had the pool on the roof all to ourselves.

Much to our horror and disgust, lying at the bottom of the pool was every table and chair from the deck. Some revelers expressing their idea of a good time had chucked it all in the night before. We could have just left, but we had worked up a heavy sweat from our exercise and the pool was just what the doctor ordered. The only thing we could do was to carefully step around the broken glass ash trays and unload what seemed to be a truck full of patio furniture from the pool. Just as we were nearly finished, the morning maid came into the pool area, spotted these two weird guys diving for metal tables at the deep end and turned and fled. We finished and got the hell out of there before we ended up on some Louisiana chain gang.

Weird didn't just come in New Orleans packages. I experienced it walking from the Tavern to the State House one cold January morning. I just started up the hill when I heard this noisy car coming down State Street and I watched it turn toward the State House. The noise was loud enough to attract my attention and it was going *backwards* up the hill. I could barely make out the bundled-up driver steering through the small peephole in the ice-covered windshield, but I got enough of a glance to recognize Will Hunter, the Senator and Rhodes Scholar, from Windsor County. Hunter was probably the most brilliant mind I ever encountered, and I admired him greatly for his willingness to fight the impossible fight and dream the impossible dream. He was tireless in his pursuit of justice, and the causes of the poor. But he could be different. By the time I got to the State House, he had disappeared into the building.

I forgot all about it in the craziness of my normal day, but the very next morning, lo and behold, the same car come zig-zagging down State Street and toward the State House. This time my curiosity was killing me and I rushed up the hill and caught him as he was emerging from the heap of junk.

"Will," I asked, "what the hell's the idea of coming up State Street backwards?"

Will, retrieving his cardboard box "briefcase" nonchalantly responded, "I'd drive the right way, but the car doesn't have any forward gears, it's only got a reverse."

OK, that was perfectly explicable.

"You asshole, Will, you mean to tell me you've driven all the way up here from your apartment down on the river *in reverse?*"

"Yeah, I told you it doesn't have any forward gears. What the hell would you do? Push it?" And, he started to go in the building with me following.

"How'd you end up with this piece of junk?" I pushed the issue, though he didn't give the appearance of feeling there was anything the least bit unusual about the whole scene.

"Some guy I went to court for." Bored with serving in the legislature, Hunter quit two years earlier, and deciding he wanted to practice law, was accepted to the Harvard School of Law, where he finished first in his class. He left Harvard Square, returned home to Vermont, set up his practice out of his cardboard box, and promptly got himself elected back into the Legislature, this time as a Senator.

"Ya mean the guy got arrested for driving around in this? What'd he do, give you the car to safekeep while he went to jail?" I asked sarcastically.

"No! No! The guy was in a jam, had a couple of kids, no place to live. I kept him out of jail, and got him and the kids into an apartment, and this is all he had to pay me with. He gave it to me in lieu of my fee. Actually, he hadn't had it running for a couple of months and I got it fixed up, so at least it goes backwards. Hey! I know people who go backwards." He disappeared once again.

22. 'Check The Closets, Mr. Speaker'

As the 1992 session drew to a close, I began to think very seriously of calling it a career. I had actually gone so far as to write a press release announcing I was not going to run again. I dropped it off at my local radio station and asked Bob Harrington not to run it until the following Friday when I knew I would be at the beach in Maine and beyond the easy reach of the Vermont Press. I didn't have any doubt it would create quite a stir among the reporters throughout the state. As for the Republicans, they would have danced in the streets at the news.

I chose Bob, as of all the reporters I had the pleasure of working with, he was perhaps the most decent of the bunch. Not that there weren't others whom I admired and respected, as I had had good relations, or at least professional relationships, with others.* In fact, when I look back I can say with all honesty there was only one reporter I felt had lost all sense of professionalism. That was Jack Hoffman of the Vermont Press Bureau. Hoffman was different. Here is a guy who lives in a glass house. He had picked up his own share of "bad" press as he had been wined and dined by power company lobbyists and the price reported would signify he knew his fine wines. This, however, never curtailed his constant attacks of self-righteous condemnation of others when he went on the air. I had resided in the glass house often enough that none of this would have been within my prerogative to take to the soap box preaching about the sin in the world, but Hoffman seems to have the capacity to never look in the mirror. His fellow reporters reflected often enough on their ill feelings towards him, no matter how subtle. I'd like to have a penny for every time his own colleagues agreed with my opinion, but of course I could never get any one of them to speak on the record. The Press is an incestuous group and they have their own 11th commandment to speak no evil of fellow journalists.

Anyway, Harrington was a neighbor and friend and his need to get a story didn't force him to forget we were all just trying to do our best..

I had reached the point where I felt I was both physically and mentally tired, and perhaps it was time to go. The problem was I had usurped so much of the authority to get things done, I worried there

---

* Peter Freyne, Chris Graff, Diane Derby, Dave Karvelas, Debbie Sline, Meg Dennison, Sam Hemingway, Candace Page, Sue Allen, Ross Sneyd, David Gram, and Bryan Pfeiffer come to mind.

was no one in the wings to pick up the baton and do what had to be done to maintain Democratic control of the House.

I wasn't worried about carrying on the Democratic agenda, for the House was filled with talented people who were at least as committed to those causes as I was. I never doubted there were scores of members who could replace me as Speaker. I had seen too many "irreplaceable" members leave or get defeated and never be mentioned ever again to worry about "replacability."

I recall sitting up in the Appropriations Committee in 1985 observing the group at work, when Bob Graf blew in the door. Bob was a 20-year veteran who had been defeated the previous November in what many considered the surprise result of the election. He waited a respectable two months and was now returning to the old arena where he had been the *"man."* It didn't matter what your cause, Graf was the guy to go to. Some called him Santa Claus.

He politely took a seat and waited while Chairman Hise and the rest of the committee finished grilling some poor Commissioner who sat in the witness chair trying to defend his budget recommendations. Actually, I was surprised Hise didn't stop everything and recognize this long-serving veteran, but nothing of the sort happened. Some of the members never even looked up.

Finally, they finished with the witness and Hise immediately called the next person sitting in anticipation to testify. Another ten minutes or so went by and it became embarrassingly obvious that poor Bob might sit through the day awaiting the faintest recognition. He eventually got up and left, probably wondering what happened to all his friends. But that's the way this place is. The process goes on, and few look back.

I never had trouble distinguishing between friends and acquaintances, so leaving wasn't going to be that traumatic for me. What I was concerned with was who would do the recruiting of Democratic members, how much damage would the fight in caucus nominating a new Speaker candidate do to the unity of the party, and could I transfer the loyalty and friendship of those Republicans who had supported me to the new Democratic candidate.

Candidate recruitment was not something that was to be done in their spare time. We had to be dedicated to the purpose, willing to make and spend full time on it, and have the mountain of data that amounted to contacts in almost every district in the state. I had done that in conjunction with others, first Poirier, and then Micque Glitman. They were both gone now, busy doing other things. I was convinced only the Speaker candidate would have enough political fear in his or her heart to be motivated to go all out. If I left, we wouldn't even know who the Speaker candidate would be until the December caucus, after the election.

I was also coming to the conclusion I made my own bed and was forever going to be forced to sleep in it. That was not a bright vision. My negatives were sky rocketing with each passing session. As I became labeled "the most powerful politician in Vermont", my negative ratings kept pace. The more I accomplished, the more I raised the hackles of those who opposed the legislation we were passing. I had become a lightning rod and I was beginning to notice the frequent response was not to the issue I was trying to promote or push, but to me. I was becoming bigger than the issue, at least, in the minds of those who were my counterparts. This went beyond expected Republican foes, but had come to encompass Democrats, too.

It seemed all to evident to me it was time to go. The thing that finally stopped me from doing what would have been best for me and my family was this question: "What if we lost the Speakership?" What would happen to all those who had stuck their necks out for me and got me elected, if suddenly there was a Republican Speaker? No punishment would have been too severe to lay on my friends who would now be the focus of the biggest "payback" in memory. Heads would roll. I owed them better notice I wouldn't be returning so that they could reflect on whether they would want to run another time. I hadn't said anything to anyone with the exception of Tim Corcoran and he had not revealed it to anybody .

It was almost July. The election was four months away; registering to run was three weeks away. No! I couldn't do it. And besides, I didn't really want to do it. I called Harrington and told him to tear up the press release. I had decided to run again.

But there were other things happening in my personal life that had a profound impact on my priorities.

My two oldest daughters, Cathy Marie and Sheila had recently returned from a two-year stay in Hawaii and the once "empty nest" had begun to fill up again. This delighted Cathy and me as we truly enjoyed having the children close to us. Things seemed very much like the old days and though the girls had matured into fine, beautiful women, they were appalled Cathy and I had never replaced the pets that had passed on. Sheila, in particular, kept hounding me quietly to come with her to get a puppy.

I resisted, as Cathy had made it clear we finally had cleaned up the mess a pet can leave around the house and had absolutely forbidden even the thought. But Sheila's determination knew no bounds.

The week before Thanksgiving she approached me with a newspaper ad she clipped for Golden Retriever pups. O'Callahan, named after my grandmother, didn't know it, but he was about to enter the best of all possible worlds.

I picked up Sheila after work and we snuck down to Massachusetts to pick out our new friend. I warned Sheila she was going to have to defend me against the wrath of her mother. My manly defense was going to be "Sheila made me do it."

We arrived home about 5:30 P.M., just in time for supper and I was both relieved and concerned that Cathy wasn't home yet. Half an hour or so passed and I began to wonder where she was. She had called me at school during the day and told me she had a doctor's appointment.

Finally, we heard the car in the driveway and I grabbed the puppy and pulled him under the kitchen table. Here it comes, I thought. She entered, apologizing for being late and just as she finished, O'Callahan broke free from under the table, raced across the kitchen to greet his new found friend and promptly peed from joy all over the kitchen floor.

I braced for the storm and standing tall, as any red-blooded decent American male would do, blurted out, "It was Sheila's idea. She made me do it."

"That's OK," Cathy said. "Whatever Sheila wants. The house hasn't felt right without a dog. Isn't he cute?" And she busied herself petting an overjoyed O'Callahan.

"I better get you people something to eat." She started to prepare supper. Something was wrong and I wasn't sure what, but this wasn't a normal reaction. The facade came to an end when after a few minutes of small talk I finally said, "There's something wrong, Cathy. What is it?" She looked at me as if measuring my ability to stand up under what she was about to tell me.

"Sit down."

Whoa! It's a "sit down" problem. I hadn't ever gone through a "sit down" problem before.

"Sheila. Suzanne. Come out here, I want to talk to you." They came into the kitchen unknowingly. The three of us were now sitting around the table.

"I've got a problem. I've got *cancer.*" I responded with all the understanding of a New York cab driver.

"What the hell ya mean 'you got cancer'?" She flashed me that look that said "not now, jerk, the girls are going to be taking their cue from you."

"I'm going to be all right, so don't worry. It's breast cancer and I'm in the last stage of the second level. Oakly thinks we caught it in time." Oakly Frost, an old family friend, is a surgeon.

I didn't hear the second stage stuff, or if I did, I couldn't get by the question of what Oakly was doing giving his opinion, as he was a surgeon.

"Whatta mean, Oakly? What's he got to do with all this? He's a surgeon."

"Because he's going to do the surgery the day after tomorrow. He's worried if I wait too long."

Holy Jesus! The day after tomorrow. Surgery? Surgery where?

I was overwhelmed with a feeling of despair and helplessness that I had never experienced before.

When we went to bed that night, I held her close and wept in her arms.

Cathy had her mastectomy and something like ten of the thirteen lymph glands were cancerous. She insisted on cooking Thanksgiving dinner two days after getting out of the hospital and for the first notice-able time, I realized with a force of a whack alongside my head, my life had changed. I never again mistook the trivia that encompasses our lives with the things that are reality. Losing a bill, ending up on the short end of an election, bad press, were all unceremoniously dumped into their proper perspectives. I couldn't imagine losing someone I loved so deeply and who meant so much to me.

If I had ever doubted the courage of my wife, and how much she meant to me and all that I was, it was all dispelled over the next eight months. Cathy started chemotherapy right after Christmas and, typical of her, she had the treatments scheduled for Mondays so I could go with her without infringing on my Tuesday through Friday legislative schedule. I don't know where she found the grit to go through what we could see were the lethal effects of the poison they circulated through her body each week. It was painful to watch. And, there was so little we could do to help the situation. The puppy was her constant com-panion, and they developed a love for each other that lasts until this day. It's been three years now and Cathy keeps coming out clean from her constant check-ups, but the next time somebody tells you life sucks because they were inconvenienced or didn't have happen what they had hoped for, you just tell them...

"Get it together, stupid. It's not cancer."

It wasn't something I found easy to talk to others about and I didn't mention anything to my friends in the legislature. As is the case with this dreaded disease, people were aware of it, but, perhaps because it was as discomfiting for them to hear about it, as it was for me to talk about it, they never mentioned it.

It was Murphy who finally brought it up as we were driving out to supper one evening. He related that his wife, Flora Belle, had been through something very similar and he felt everything would turn out just fine. I tried to change the subject and finally did, but not until after he said something I thought didn't make any sense.

Murphy always spoke in parables. It usually roots itself somewhere in the darkest recesses of your mind and then when you least expect, it pops out and the world becomes a brighter place, a tiny bit more understandable. But what he said as we were getting out of his truck to enter the Wayside restaurant, struck me as especially odd, even for a guy like Murphy.

"Check the closets, Mr. Speaker. Check the closets."

I didn't find her in the closet, but I went looking for her upstairs when the silence in the house caught my attention. You can't live in a house that had four kids and a foster child without having the infrequent moments of silence blare in your brain. This was one of those eerie moments, and I went upstairs looking for Cathy. She was in the extra bedroom by herself and she was crying. We said nothing. Holding her in my arms was sufficient. Murphy's words echoed in my head:

"Check the closets."

23. '...AND, SHE'S NO DICK SNELLING.'

I ran again in November, 1992 and was easily re-elected in my own district, being nominated as the Democratic candidate for Speaker, and beating Jane Mendicino, from Chittenden County, the latest Republican contender for the Speakership. She was not typical of the image of what a Republican Speaker would look like if one could get elected. A veteran of four terms, she had been my Chair of the Fish and Wildlife Committee. It was a job she coveted, and no matter how unlikely a candidate she might appear to be to others for that post, she had done a good job. Some may have thought she was a woman in a man's position, but Jane had a lot more talent and spunk than others were inclined to give her credit for.

Here is how "arrangements" between a Democrat running for Speaker on a secret ballot and a Republican whose vote will help decide the winner come about. Nothing was sinister about it.

Actually, lots of Republicans crossed over and voted for me. A mere check of my margin of victory against Democratic numbers made that quite clear.

My opponent only received 37 of 150 votes cast, thus about 24 Republicans crossed over during my fifth race. I knew who each was as they had called to tell me. All they asked in return was a committee assignment they could live with for two years. My so-called "hockey team" of Republicans seldom demanded anything. I know of no Speaker who has ever handled this phenomenon differently.

The problem I had with the whole scenario was I agreed to make her the Chair two years previously. This came about after I ran into her during one of my infrequent visits to the State House during the summer. She offered to cut a deal. I would get her vote for Speaker if she in turn could be Chair of the Fish and Wildlife Committee. I quickly accepted as it wasn't often I had a chance to add to my "hockey team." Jane never really became a member of the so-called "hockey team", as she feared her party's reprisal, but I assume she had kept her word and cast a vote for me against my opponent that year, Wally Russell of Barton. I kept my promise and named her Chair of the Committee. Loyalties are fleeting in the political world, and two years later she was reaching for new stars.

I was surprised as her ambitions drove her toward the podium. It was my easiest race as Mendicino had trouble with a lot of her own Republicans. Some suspected she had "cooked" a deal with me and I received a heap of Republican votes on the secret ballot I had never gotten before. It wasn't so much they had all suddenly fallen in love with me, the warm and cuddly Speaker, as it was they had trouble believing Mendicino stood any type of chance to pull off an upset. If they don't believe someone is going to win, they'll jump ship pretty fast. Power is often perception, rather than reality.

Barb Grimes from Burlington, my new recruiter, knocked them dead. She was everywhere and as tireless as Micque Glitman had been. She is a street smart woman who had been kicked around by life. She wasn't ever going to take any more guff from the world without giving it back in spades. She did a terrific job. Barb tore a path all over the state, recruiting and driving 15 additional Democrats home to victory. The Republican party never knew what hit them. I did. It was "Grimesy."

We rode the wind as Vermont was turning out to put an end to the Reagan/Bush era, and Bill Clinton was going to carry the state by the third largest majority in the country. Only Washington, D.C., and California topped the 19 percent victory margin Vermont gave to him. The Senate lost its Democratic majority, but I blame that on the Senate Democrats constant refusal to recognize they would have to join the political world and organize to the point of running competent campaigns. It always seemed the Democrats in that austere body trusted their fortunes to luck, rather than hard work and organization. No one wanted to take charge of recruiting, or put their neck on the chopping block in direct confrontation with the Republicans.

Consequently, the voters of Vermont were lending landslide majorities to us in the House, while the Democrats in the Senate saw their numbers drop to 15. The Senate, consisting of 30 members, now would be controlled by the Republicans, as they did manage a single victory with the constitutional offices by electing Barbara Snelling, Dick Snelling's widow, to the Lieutenant Governor's post. This meant Barbara Snelling would be the tie-breaking vote on a number of issues that would prove fatal to us and, in the long run, perhaps to her. Mrs Snelling rode Dick's coattails into the second highest office. There is no doubt in my mind about this. She dispelled any doubts of how crucial her vote would prove to be when she cast the tie-breaking votes to dismiss several hard working volunteers from the Environmental Board.

It was a five-week period of confrontation that was an extremely unattractive period for Vermonters who lived through it. The Press saw it as a flashback to the McCarthy witch hunts of the fifties. I hoped it was just a quagmire Mrs. Snelling and her Republican cohorts had stumbled into. They were more frightened of what was transpiring through the whole period of turmoil than anyone else.

They didn't wise up, as they placed the Lieutenant Governor in a second confrontation when they forced her to break a tie on raising the minimum wage. She did it, but immediately regretted it, as a member of the Press labeled her "cheap and mean" on a TV program. She carried the water for big business at every opportunity. Snelling who held a position with the Chittenden Bank, didn't do a very good job at hiding this type of singlemindedness. She eventually back-tracked on giving a 25-cent raise to the working poor, but for all the wrong reasons.

I'm sure Mrs. Snelling has her attributes, but let me paraphrase one-time Vice Presidential Candidate Lloyd Bentsen: *"I knew Dick Snelling and she's no Dick Snelling."*

I never fully blamed her for what would turn out to be a disastrous final two years for me in the legislature. Mrs. Snelling rode into office on a politically correct horse. She was the highest elected woman on the scene. The Press gave her the benefit of the doubt, at least in the beginning, and she survived her errors where others might not have. The real problem was she tried to muddle her way through her political initiation using unsound political advice.

24. GOING SOUTH

I had an overwhelming majority in the house (88 Democrats, 57 Republicans, 5 Independents). I had a Democratic governor with whom I could work most of the time. I had a Democrat in the White House. *And I had the worst two years of my political career.* Go figure.

The first advantage was the root of my problem. I had 25 more Democrats to please than when I started ten years earlier and I didn't meet the measure. I was like a deer caught in the headlights, frozen with indecision. When I did jump, it was too late, as I no longer cared enough to make the giant effort that it would have taken to escape the inevitable.

It promised to be the biggest of years. We were making every effort to be the first state in the nation to push through a health care bill that would offer coverage for all Vermonters through a "single payer" system. It was a revolutionary move to be sure, but one we had set the groundwork for two years earlier when we passed the preliminary measure setting up a health care authority to offer three different options. The Authority was made up of three very talented people, one of whom was Paul Harrington, my former Chair of the House Commerce Committee. The Authority spent nearly a million dollars doing the necessary research and compiling their analysis. It all sat waiting for us when we reconvened.

I felt it was time to face the massive problems we had in trying to find an equitable, fair source of funding for our struggling educational system. It was obvious we couldn't continue trying to raise the money from the already-beleaguered local property taxes. The property tax was, without any doubt, the poorest measure of a person's wealth. The dilemma was how to get it changed. I wasn't the first to make the effort, as people a lot more talented than I, had tried, and failed in the past.

These efforts went back all the way to Phil Hoff in the sixties, and efforts were made by succeeding Governors Snelling and Kunin. None of them ever got much further than the floor of the two houses.

I made the announcement the first week of the session at an editorial board meeting of the *Burlington Free Press*. It received an amazing amount of coverage over the next two years and we did an equally amazing amount of work.

The health care bill initiative was taken by the governor, as he had been the energy behind the effort right from the beginning. It certainly helped that President Clinton was pulling out all stops on the national level to bring about a health plan. We were giddy with enthusiasm, and it became a matter of who would accomplish it first. We were certain the President was going to be eating our dust as we crossed the finish line. We were to learn that the race doesn't go to the swift.

The first thing I did was repeat what I had done with the Environmental Act 200. I appointed a special committee, called the Universal Health Care Committee. It was made up of 11 members and I appointed the Democratic and Republican leaders to it. I made Sean Campbell, my Democratic leader, Chair. He was extremely competent. It was bi-partisan, as I let Rick Westman, the Republican leader, help me name the other Republican members, and it was made up of talented people who were truly committed to getting something done.

The only obligation I held the Democratic members of the committee to was that after all the fighting and shouting was over, they were to go with their Democratic colleagues on the final vote. This guaranteed whatever the Republicans did, I would be assured of a 7-4 vote coming out of committee. All I wanted was a chance to get a vote on the floor of the House. As for the Senate, I didn't dare think about the damage they would do.

I handed the Educational Bill to Dave Larsen from Wilmington, my Chair of Education, and turned him loose. That committee was one of the best I ever appointed, and I knew they'd get the job done. They did it unanimously with Republicans and Democrats alike voting to kick it out a year later with an 11-0 vote. I was accused by some of having stacked the committee and the accusations were well-founded. I had indeed placed each and every one on the committee with the hopes they would accomplish the goal.

The bill eventually died on the last day of the last year of the biennium, but H541 as constructed by the House, was the answer to the problem.

It showed a way to fund the entire cost of educating our 103,000 children—a cost of over $600 million—without the primary homeowners paying for it out of property tax. We simply shifted the share of the primary homeowner onto other broad based taxes, and created a statewide property tax on business and second homeowners.

This was a drastic, and truly revolutionary, proposal that would have worked and freed us from the constant hand-wringing of always raising local homeowner taxes to fund the ever-increasing cost of education. It would have allowed us to get back to actually educating, rather than continuing the never-ending struggle over how to pay for reaching for excellence.

In addition, H541 provided for a statewide teacher's contract that would have brought all 7,000 teachers pay up to the highest level over a ten-year period. More important, it would have rendered mute the constant fighting between unions and school boards on a local level. Thousands of hours were consumed in the 250 communities hassling over dental plans and the rate of this year's pay increase. This all would have been settled in the same way the state employees' contract had been settled since the early seventies, a single collective bargaining unit.

The teacher's union, which had grown stronger with each passing year, went into obit over their right to bargain locally. They argued it was unfair labor practice. I was, and still am, a card-carrying member of that union, but I never bought it for a minute. They simply wanted to negotiate where they had the decided edge, at the local level. It was here the inexperience of the small local boards gave the unions the upper hand, if in experience alone. It also was at this level a strike was not out of the question, whereas a statewide strike would have been more difficult to bring about. Everyone knew what devastation a strike could bring into a community, and how important this bargaining chip was.

Both efforts were destined to fail, but it wasn't because we didn't work hard. I can't recall any bill that taxed the entire body as each of these did during that session. The case was made, that we simply tried to do too much at once. I agree with that only to the degree the effort was never able to mobilize a populist front, but not because the plans for both wouldn't work, or that we couldn't do the job legislatively. They would and we did. Our eventual demise came about because we never got control over the politics of the fight. I take the blame for that. Politics was my job.

If the whole thing didn't kill us physically and mentally, it served to drive a spike into my political heart. We didn't get out in the second year until June 12, two whole months beyond deadline, making it the longest session since 1965. Everybody raised hell, and they knew who to blame. *Me.*

The whole affair had so many moving parts it is still difficult to analyze politically. Of course, there was the opposition. The Republican Senate not only abhorred the idea of shifting the primary home tax onto the backs of the commercial interests of the state, but they didn't want to see us solve the most pressing problems or the citizens of Vermont paying for schools and health care. It would have been the end of them as a viable political entity for a decade and they were determined to block us in any way they could.

The Republicans long ago had stopped considering any solutions, thus they had spent all their effort in developing obstructionist muscles. They simply were going to hang together and just say no. I often reflected during those tumultuous times at how success was so hard to bring about, because it brought *change,* while failure was so easy to understand because it left things as they were. In the perverted world of politics, it was so much easier to *kill,* than it was to *create.*

The Republican Senate hung together to maintain the status quo. There was nothing we could do but try to find a way to force them to bring it on the floor and debate the issue. I was confident if we were successful in seeing that happen, it would have passed. The arguments and benefits of H541 would have proven too great for them to publicly oppose and politically survive. The only reason they were able to hang tough was we never could manage to bring the average person to our aid. We simply didn't have the horses.

Almost every organization in the state went on record as opposing our plan and many had unlimited resources to spread their gospel of doom and gloom over the possibility of our bill passing.

Something else was going on while all this was occurring. I wasn't minding the store, as I had become so involved in my own issues, I had forgotten about everyone else's.

Many members were idle while the handful involved in the two major bills were in high gear right up until the final gavel. Anyone who has been responsible for a group of people, knows the danger of having people sit around waiting for a handful of others to get something done. By now, a majority of the 88 Democrats had become less than enthusiastic about the whole process. Republicans had always felt shut out and justifiably resented it, but I didn't owe my job to the bulk of them. I did owe my Dems, and that's where my trouble began.

If there is one characteristic cherished by a member of the legislature, it is trust. This is the glue that makes the bond of any relationship work, but it is especially vital in a legislature that deals in 30-second conversations and constantly changing alliances. Sure, issues and agendas drive a majority of the members, but a fear of loss of self is underlying in all but the very few who rest their case on getting elected.

Insecurity runs rampart in any governing body. That's the only way I can explain why members do the things I saw them do over the years. I was no different.

I satisfied my need for love and acceptance by accruing power. It was power to do good things as I saw it, but nevertheless it was there for all the world to see. Hell, I wore it on my sleeve. I never remember feeling lonely or unloved. I was active and even if I had to force myself into a situation or onto a scene, that's what I did. That wasn't the case with the group of Democrats who were now holding regular and secret meetings to bring about a leadership change. They had their own motivations for what they were doing. They would later explain all they wanted was to bring a sense of civility to the process and be more inclusive towards all the members. There is no way we could include all 150 members into the decision-making process and expect to get anything done. The effort at grass roots Democracy (or, being all-inclusive), was just a perception that belongs in a seventh grade civics class.

The best we might do, and then not with all the members, was to leave them with the illusion they were part of the process. That's all it would be, an illusion, as the process forced all the gut work and micro decisions an issue demanded to be made by those who were willing to roll up their sleeves and had the ability to make the tough and smart decisions. Not everyone wanted to be in those positions, or was capable of being there. So people had to trust other people to do the right thing at the right time and in the right manner. Easier said than done.

I can only guess the true motivation of these 'cabal' members. The truth probably lies closer to "we felt left out" or "leadership wasn't listening to us."

We may have been wrong and were pushing our authority beyond what we had a right to do, but none of this would have mattered if we had passed a universal "single payer" health care system plan, and if we had done away with local property taxes to fund education. Had we been successful in one of those endeavors, our friends would have been erecting statues in our honor. We would have been proclaimed as the greatest legislature in memory, and those who thought it was time for a change, would have been writing our testimonials. But we failed, and that is the ultimate political sin. Nobody loves a loser. As they say, "Victory has a million friends, while defeat is an orphan."

They were an interesting group with ties beyond a mere desire to change the process. Some had personal ties that satisfied their inner feelings of guilt or inadequacies. I had an old saying: "If your wife couldn't trust you, then why should I?" That was the common bond for a couple of them and they couldn't be trusted by me or their wives. You can't fight that type of bond with a "plush" committee assignment.

Others just didn't like my style. I didn't like their styles any better, but I wasn't going to execute them over it. I never passed judgment on how others led their lives. Until I could walk in their shoes, I would leave the morality bit to their priest or pastor.

If anyone bothers to try and piece together just what went wrong, they wouldn't be too far off if they started with the word "everything." I was the primary victim of my own undoing. As a student of history, I saw it coming but failed to do anything about it for a variety of reasons.

Here are the reasons:

My committees were breaking down. I allowed five or six committees to stop producing. This was an overload of the system that represented the "critical mass." The Democratic machine "tilted." Bob Harris' Committee ceased to function almost from the day I appointed it. I made the mistake of assuming leadership in the form of a chairmanship would force Harris to rise to the occasion. It didn't. It wasn't all his fault. His committee members were in constant rebellion. I spent a lot of time trying to smooth things over, without success. The committee actually would have periods lasting weeks when they wouldn't even meet. Promoting him to a chairmanship against almost unanimous advice to the contrary was a case of my taking care of my friends in spite of what it might do to the orderliness of the process. It was a strong hint I had become one of the "good ole boys", whom I had set my sights on toppling 15 years earlier.

I lost my right hand in the Commerce Committee when Barbara Grimes accepted the job of Commissioner of Housing and Community Affairs, and left at the beginning of the year. I was happy for her, not simply because I felt she deserved to run a department of state government. (She was one of the most competent people I have ever had the pleasure of working with.) But for the first time in a lot of years, she would be in a position not to have to worry about how she paid the rent or bought the groceries. A single mother of two teenage boys, it had not been easy on her. Kathy Keenan, my choice to replace Grimes, was another single mother who struggled through her first session. The fact the Commerce Committee had an unusually high number of complex and important bills, coupled with the petty jealousies that accompany the naming of a new Chair, added to her problems. She eventually got her feet set and the committee became as productive as it had ever been. But, it was a rough initiation for Kathy.

I had the three so-called "dump" committees which spent most of their time harassing the Democratic Chair at every twist and turn. It reached a point in Fish and Wildlife that David Deen was just happy to finish the year alive. I hatched this bad egg and now was going to have to eat it. The Agriculture Committee had a slightly less calamitous time, in that Bobby Starr was a veteran Chair and a whiz at power politics. He usually could get even the most recalcitrant committee members to come around and vote to pass legislation out that met the needs of the agricultural community. But, even in this committee I had to formally reprimand two of the younger Republican members for conduct best described as "juvenile."

I had been faced with replacing Chuck Ross, my highly competent and well-liked Chair of the Natural Resources Committee, right in the middle of the session. Ross opted to work with U.S. Senator Patrick Leahy in his Montpelier office. It was a great opportunity for Ross and Leahy's gain was my loss. To compound matters, Curt McCormack who had been the Chair prior to his run for Mayor of Rutland, received a promise from me if I ever had the opportunity, I would rename him Chair. I did this as he went into a pretty deep funk after getting badly beaten in the mayoralty race. I didn't ever think I would have the opportunity to fulfill my commitment, but the surprise departure of Ross gave me the chance to keep my word. I did it over the loud and persistent complaints of some of present members of the committee who were now vying for their own appointment or that of one of their friends to the chairmanship.

The sniping and back-stabbing that went on during this period was certainly not attractive. Still McCormack was my man and I reappointed him. The four or five members sitting in that committee who were also members of the "cabal", had another reason to want to change to a more civil process.

Six of the 14 committees were now preoccupied with extracurricular sideshows and the process suffered.

The formation of the Universal Health Committee had been necessary if we were going to pursue universal health care for all Vermonters. That was the good news. The bad news was it forced me to have my "right arm", Sean Campbell, heading that committee. It required someone who was not an ideologue either way, but who could lead the committee to its goal of getting something out. I knew Campbell, my Democrat leader could do the job. I lost his services for better than two months.

Campbell was my closest ally in the House and he had everything a leader needed to be successful. He was an exceptionally smart guy who amazed me with his ability to be a "quick study." He was a lot like Poirier, in that no problem was too big for him to grasp. He was a hard worker who put in as many hours as it took. And, he was loyal. These were all the ingredients I could not afford to be without for a moment, let alone two months.

This made me even more of a control freak, and it proved too much for even a powerful Speaker to maintain any semblance of order with all we had going on. I ended up making a jerk out of myself trying to keep all the dishes up on the sticks. It was a mess when the act was over. Broken dreams everywhere.

And finally, I had become bigger than the issue. People were simply setting their sights on me rather than the issue. They couldn't get beyond my personality, even when I tried to get their attention to the issue at hand. I noticed this years before, as I had become a powerful figure in the State House. I glowed in the light of my reputation, but like Wyatt Earp, I soon became the legend every young gun fighter who rode into town wanted to find. There are only so many "high noons" in a politician's life. Eventually the sun is destined to set and shine in your eyes.

The Republicans in the Senate didn't need any reason beyond their great need to protect the money interests in the state when they set out to kill property tax reform and health care.

All these factors put together led to failure, but if that wasn't enough, we were relying on a governor to provide the leadership in our march toward universal health care. Unfortunately, Howard Dean didn't carry the same commitment.

25. DR. GOVERNOR

Howard Dean never walked into a room with the slightest doubt that everyone who gathered there loved him. He just exuded that type of relaxed confidence. I never walked into a room without immediately spotting the single figure who hated my guts. He or she might be far to the back of the room, slouched behind the crowd, but I could spot him or her a mile away.

Dean can say the dumbest things, and it will be taken with a grain of salt. Others can make the slightest slip-up and the Press will rush to blow it way out of proportion. I don't think this is something that can be attributed to a tint of favoritism on the part of the public or the Press. It has nothing to do with what is said, but rather, with who is saying it.

Howard Dean's a "rich kid", who has been successful at everything he has ever experienced throughout his life. He was raised to achieve, and though he could decide the avenues he would travel for himself, he was not left with any choice between success and failure. That's the way it has always been for Dean. Winning starts with the idea that you're not going to lose. Governor Dean has never spent any significant amount of time mulling that possibility. More important, he isn't afraid to lose. Like everyone else, he's happy when he wins, but unlike everyone else, he isn't going to jump off the roof should he lose. It's the ingredient that is an absolute must in the warrior. And if Howard Dean is anything, he's a warrior.

Here's a kid raised on Park Ave., who goes to the best private schools, summers in the Hamptons, attends Yale, and after taking a year off skiing to "find himself", decides he doesn't want to spend his life making money on Wall Street, and goes off to medical school and becomes a doctor, where he can heal those in pain and extend life. Horatio Alger is alive and well, and he's Vermont's Governor.

One might think this would all lead him to a massive ego. It hasn't. Dean is one of the most humble men I have ever met. It isn't that he doesn't take himself seriously, it's just that he doesn't think what he's achieved is anything extraordinary. It's what is, and he accepts it the same as he accepted getting through medical school. He knew he could do the job. It's what makes him such a lovable figure.

He's been characterized as the "Teflon Governor", and that may be true. Who's to argue with the reality that nothing lastingly bad sticks to him for long. But I think this has a lot more to do with who he is than it does with whether he's ever made bad decisions. He certainly has and I was there to attest to them. But Dean has the unique ability to admit his errors and to literally change the prescription. To take the medical analogy a bit further, a patient or two may die, but he'll learn from the experience.

I'm sure young Dean, like any kid, got into the devil. If he wandered into his mother's flower garden, he was corrected, not cracked along the side the head. If he smoked a little pot, it was just a "phase", and he was encouraged to talk about it. When he experienced the dreaded indecision of what to do with his life, he was sent to Vail to ski for a year.

We couldn't have been more different. Where I come from, if we couldn't decide what to do with our life our fathers signed us up in the Marine Corps. It was an honorable occupation and the pay wasn't bad.

I'll bet if Albert Einstein School of Medicine offered a course in "bedside manners", Dean got an "A." He's an absolute delight to be around, and I've never seen anyone who can deny you what you came to see him for with such cordiality. I often left his office thinking I had been granted my request, only to find out differently down the road.

It's difficult to depress or discourage someone who has experienced the saving of lives and the sadness of death. A doctor can't fall to pieces when a patient dies. No matter how traumatic the moment, he or she has to keep wits and composure for there's another room and another patient that is going to make it. And that patient has needs now, not after a three-day grief period. Howard Dean has all this as part of his everyday life as a doctor, so as governor, he is not going to come unraveled because he just lost some bill in John Murphy's committee.

I first remember Dean on his feet on the floor of the House arguing some losing cause as a freshman. He was brief, articulate, and unrattled at his loss. I didn't really get to know him until he became the Assistant Democratic leader during my first term as Speaker. When he served as Democratic Whip, he tended to be under our feet all the time while he was learning the "ropes." Being more distant from the Whip as Speaker, I would laugh at Paul Poirier raising his eyes to the heavens anytime I would ask, "How's Howard doing?"

Dean still had a medical practice to tend to and he would leave by mid or late afternoon each day to conduct his rounds at the medical center. We didn't complain, as we were used to running the whole show anyway, but I think Poirier was always somewhat relieved when the doctor departed for rounds.

The first serious encounter I had with Dean was when he announced that upon my winning the Speakership, he was going to run for the

Whip's post. This struck both Poirier and me as somewhat brazen, as he announced this before I had won. Poirier, especially, took exception to Dean's move, as it was not at all certain I was going to overcome a six vote disadvantage and grab the brass ring back in 1985. If I lost, we had arranged for the leadership races to be held after the election, and therefore I was guaranteed my leadership post. The same was not the case with Poirier, as my defeat would have forced him to run for Whip against Dean who had already announced.

It didn't seem to bother the future governor as he was racing around the state searching for votes from our fellow Democrats, possibly against the very guy he would have to work with if I won. I did win and the question became moot, but I often wondered what the future would have held for him if I lost, maintained my Democratic leader's position, and Poirier had maintained his Whip's post by beating him in caucus. No doubt, that would have occurred.

The world wouldn't have been "according to Howard." He probably would have tired of the legislature and either returned to his full-time practice or ventured off searching for another political level to make a re-entry. What it does show was what I pointed out earlier. Dean has no fear of losing, and politics is something one doesn't get too attached to or take too seriously. If someone had to lose (and he never believed for a moment it would be him), one just pulled the sheet up over his or her head, and moved on to the next bed. He would be sad, but under control, with a deeply set commitment that life goes on.

It wasn't long before Dean was on the move again. This time it was in 1986.

Having moved out of his legislative district, Dean announced he would take on Peter Smith, the incumbent lieutenant governor. It was an uphill fight to say the least, and a lot of inside experts wrote him off almost from the moment he announced. Smith was no lightweight and the post was his, many argued, for as long as he desired. None of that seemed to bother Dean, and he paid little heed even when his closest political allies wrote him off as a political shooting star that was soon to disappear over the horizon. Politics is based on luck, or as we Catholics would say, fate. Fate was Howard Dean's companion once again.

Smith surprised the political pundits several weeks later when he held a press conference and declared his intention to take on Madeleine Kunin for the governor's office. I remember thinking, "What is it with this guy, Dean? He seems to see the future." It was, at worst, an uncanny coincidence Dean was the only announced candidate for the lieutenant governor's office in 1986. No one at the time thought he would be a strong or viable candidate, and certainly more formidable candidates would emerge now that Smith had created the opening and the opportunity. My only worry was Poirier would jump into the race and I would lose my "right arm." I had enough hints Paul wasn't going to sit in one place for too long because that wasn't his nature.

The question was when would the opportunity present itself for Paul to move on to the natural next step and become Speaker. That depended on what I had in mind as to my future. Poirier, sensing I was having too much fun in the Speakership, didn't see himself hanging around for another four years or so waiting for me to go somewhere. He made it known he was seriously considering running for the open office. It sent a shock wave through me as I couldn't imagine life without Poirier as my sidekick. I couldn't even imagine me remaining Speaker without him.

I did everything I could think of to explain all the drawbacks to Poirier's leaving the House, but it wasn't working. He wasn't worried about a primary with Dean as the future governor graciously announced that if Poirier decided to run for the lieutenant governor's job, he would defer to him and stay in the House. I gave a lot of thought to the possibility of Poirier leaving, and Dean becoming my right hand man as Democratic leader. That would have been an interesting scenario. I went for the groin and preyed on Poirier's soul by questioning his loyalty to me, his dearest friend. "How can you even think of deserting me, your best friend, to preside over that stuffy Senate? It's treason. You'd be shot in the Marine Corps for such an act."

It worked, as Poirier decided to stay put, and Dean was off to the races again, searching for his third promotion in three efforts.

Think about this: Poirier says, "Out of my way, Dean." He runs for the lieutenant governor's post, where he would have been at least as strong a statewide candidate as Dean turned out to be. He takes on a weak Republican foe in House Republican leader Susan Auld and beats her, as Dean did. He enjoys the benefits of the incumbent in an office that takes a special effort to get into political trouble (which shows how hard Barbara Snelling has worked at it), and gets re-elected twice. It would have been Poirier who the troopers run down on the Barre golf course on that fatal August morning in 1991 to tell him he was now the Governor of Vermont.

Ah, well, "Governor Poirier" just doesn't sound right.

I only saw Howard Dean out of control a few times. This was to be one of them.

"He's a no good son of a bitch. I swear, if it takes me a lifetime, I'll get the bastard." Dean's face was the color of the inside of a ripened watermelon as we stood in the waiting room outside of my office.

"Whoa! Hold on, Howard. Calm down a minute, and tell me what the hell's going on."

"Corcoran! That's what's going on!" he sputtered.

"Why the hell are you screaming at me?"

"Because you must be behind all this. He wouldn't do anything like this without your OK. I know him. It just wouldn't happen if you hadn't given him the green light." I saw no sign of him calming down.

"Well, you're wrong, Howard, as he does as he damn well pleases. Tell me what he's done?" I was getting a little indignant.

"He cut my budget up in the Appropriations Committee. He's cut Jane's (his assistant) entire salary and the entire office expense budget. It's a bullshit act and I swear he'll pay for this. I'm going to have to send her home, she's so upset."

"Why'd he do that? " I asked.

"I don't know. Since when does that mean little son of a bitch have to have a reason to do somebody in? You sure you don't know about this?" He was slowing calming down.

"I swear, I had no idea what he was up to. But, I'll fix it."

"You can't. They've already voted it out," he said, angry again. "And you know that they won't change it. He's a mean-spirited little bastard."

"How'd he get the vote in the committee to do something like that?" I asked, wondering if it could be something that could be repaired before the bill got out on the floor of the House

"I don't know how he got them to do his bidding, but the vote was 8-3 to cut the entire budget of the lieutenant governor's office."

"Apparently he's not the only mean-spirited little bastard up there. There are seven others." I was trying to be constructive. "You know it isn't going to stick. Corcoran can't do away with the lieutenant governor. You can fix it in the Senate. Don't worry, when it comes back in Conference Committee, I'll see to it that it stays in. OK?"

As he turned to leave, a last minute thought came to him, "And, when Jane leaves, she takes the coffee pot with her." With that, he stormed down the hallway.

"Holy Smokes," I thought, "I've got to do something about this. We can't have the Senate without their morning coffee."

The lieutenant governor's office is an awful place to be if one wants to get something done in government. The only duties are to preside over the Senate when it is in session, and to be ready in case the governor dies. Both could be considered morbid endeavors. There is a moment of empowerment at the beginning and end of each session as the lieutenant governor is automatically a member of the Committee on Committees. That's the three-member panel the Senate utilizes to pick committees during the opening days of the first year of the biennium, and to select the committee of conferences that enjoin the House's delegation at the end of the session to hammer out compromise solutions to the differing versions of bills. Beyond that, the lieutenant governor might as well be on another planet.

It is a great place to campaign from, however, as one has a wealth of free time to wander around the state pressing the flesh. Dean must have received his Master's degree in pressing the flesh. He was everywhere, speaking to anyone who would listen. A lot of people thought it was just great "to have a real lieutenant governor come visit us." They loved him wherever he went. He was handsome, bright, and refreshingly honest, at least for a politician. To meet him was to remember him.

It didn't hurt he was a medical doctor. It seemed every time I turned around, there was another little blip in the press about, "how lieutenant governor (Clark Kent) tore off his suit and the mild-mannered lieutenant governor became Dr. Dean (Superman) and came to the rescue of so and so who was choking on a chicken bone."

His first Battle Day Parade in Bennington saw him come to the rescue of a little girl who was accidentally hit by a vehicle. The rest of the world saw it on the front page of the morning newspaper. He wasn't looking for great press, but he sure knew how to get it. It is one of the political side benefits of being in the life-saving business.

Dean always impressed me as a man who was having the time of his life presiding over the Senate and as a man-in-waiting. He got his best shot in 1990 when Kunin announced she had enough after being governor for six years. Everyone would have expected Dean to be the heir apparent, except a month or so before she announced, the old Republican warrior, Dick Snelling, proclaimed he had been on the sidelines long enough and was going to make a comeback and run for a fifth term. King Kong was back.

Dean opted out, explaining his young family necessitated his foregoing the opportunity to serve full-time as a governor. He left the challenge to Peter Welch, the former President Pro Tem of the Democratic Senate, a lamb to the slaughter.

Welch is an extremely bright and issue-oriented kind of guy. We had our differences when he was in the Senate, but I admired what he stood for, and respected him as a person. He has a good sense of humor. Welch had to be upset with me as I had worked hard to help Poirier upset him in the Democratic primary for Congress in 1988. Paul's margin of victory in my district almost equaled the number of votes that Peter had been beaten by, and I knew it had hurt him.

But he surprised everyone with the competitive run he made against Snelling in 1990 and the former governor's margin of victory was a lot smaller than anyone predicted, or that he liked. But King Richard was back and it proved to be the most rewarding eight months of my entire time in the legislature. To this day, I gladly would have given up the first six years for this brief window of opportunity to get to know, work with, and befriend Dick Snelling. It was a special time and I'm still struck by the irony of it all.

Within eight months, Dick Snelling was to fall over dead while cleaning his pool. A massive heart attack was to take one of the most colorful and effective leaders the state of Vermont had ever known. I don't remember where I was or what I was doing when the news broke. I do know I met with new Governor Dean for an hour-long session within a 24-hour period. I can't remember whether it was the day of the governor's death or the next day. What I do remember is the grace the new governor showed in an immensely difficult time. It was like his whole life had been lived in the unpleasant anticipation of this moment. My only small effort at being a positive force was to offer whatever assistance I could. There wasn't anything that I could think of to do other than to just be there.

It was sometime during the next few tragic days that Dean offered the vacant lieutenant governor's post to me. He probably made the same offer to a number of people. The whole overture, as far as it concerned me, was out of the question. It would have presented more problems than it would have resolved. Besides, there were people who were constitutionally questioning whether there was even an opening. Some said the lieutentant governor was simply "acting " as governor, and therefore there was no opening in that office. Others hinted strongly any appointment would be construed as a blatant political move to give a friend, and presumably a Democrat, a leg up on the next election by making the 16-month temporary appointment. This murmur from the Republicans promised to rear the ugly nose of politics in the midst of a period of grieving.

As far as my anticipating the so-called "move up", I didn't. It was an office that would have bored me to death, and I was convinced those who occupied it were merely people in waiting. I also pointed out to the new governor I didn't think it was a smart move to remove me from the Speaker's chair, as this would require that the House reconvene to elect a new Speaker. Dean would be faced with a double whammy, in that not only would he be removing a presiding officer that had a proven track record of getting things done, but of greater possible consequence, there was no guarantee the House Democrats could put forward a candidate who could win.

We were still in the minority in the House as far as numbers were concerned, and I was convinced my Republican friends who had supported me in the past speakers' races might not support another Democrat. My ties with them were based on a friendship and a mutual respect for each other and I was not convinced these bonds were transferable to another Democrat, one who couldn't possibly win without at least a half a dozen Republican crossovers. In effect, we would have given up the Speaker's post to maintain a post I didn't think warranted the sacrifice. Dean saw the wisdom of the argument and we never spoke of it again. Several months later, it came up again, but this time it proved to be just an embarrassment.

I was confronted by a reporter wanting to know if the offer had been made and I answered the question honestly. "Yes, I had been offered the lieutenant governor's office, but it was one of those remarks that are made in the midst of a tumultuous period and was dismissed for a variety of reasons almost immediately by the two of us."

That would have been the end of it, but Dean denied to the same reporter the offer had ever been made. I was confronted a second time, this time with some question. It angered me as I felt there was a limit to how far on the sword I would fall for the new governor. Though I could see how this renewed story could present itself as an embarrassing moment for the governor, I also felt to be presented as a liar on the front page of the next morning's newspaper wasn't something I could tolerate. I told Dean that. He corrected his previous version of his recollection and the whole thing faded away.

Howard Dean dealt with the role of governor much as he did with his role as a doctor. He did the best he could and didn't get fancy. He went with the cards that were dealt him. He kept the same appointed people Snelling had brought on to ride out the deficit. This was an obvious sign to the Democrats that the fatal changing of the guard was not going to bring about a cleaning of the political house. He found new opportunities for Snelling's friends and allies. This new king wasn't going to make any waves. He kept all of the sitting commissioners and department heads on board and told them to go about their tasks. "We've got a government to run." He did bring in Cathy Hoyt, a trusted friend, who would provide the same confidence and trustworthiness she provided for Madeleine Kunin, first as commissioner and then as her administrative guru. She was experienced and had proven herself an invaluable asset in the front office.

Most people saw the lack of turnover in the staff as an effort by Dean to maintain a sense of security through the maintenance of the status quo. It was that to be sure, but it also was a clear and obvious sign to me these were also the types of people with whom Howard Dean felt most comfortable. These were the staff members at his first medical assignment that had operated the hospital just fine long before he got there and would carry on just fine now that he had arrived. Howard had no intention of changing course, philosophically or politically.

The deficit was the overriding problem facing the state and the plan to pay it off was in place, thanks to Dick Snelling, and that's what he would do. This certainly gave him credit for carrying on not just the deceased governor's plan, but also his memory.

Should it all fail, that would be time enough to admit failure of the Snelling Plan, and for him to venture forth with the Dean Plan. This never came to pass as the deficit retirement package pushed through by Snelling and the legislature was to prove adequate to move the state from the red to the black. It would take time, but not a drastic change in course. Failure didn't have the odds on its side in this one. Dean wasn't going to risk failure, no matter how disappointed the old Kunin Democrats longed for the days of creativeness and vision. Remember, he was the stockbroker's son, the off-spring of sound investments and slow dividends. Liberal Democrats raised their brows of suspicion this was a wolf in sheep's clothing; while Republicans raised their tolerance level for a Democratic governor who began to look a lot like them. This was a different kind of guy, to be sure. Several weeks after being thrust into the highest office in the state, Dean's popularity rating topped 70 percent. Five years later, it's gone up five points.

Dean had an agenda. It's just that his agenda was unknown to the rest of us, and was subject to change. He didn't believe in fighting the "good fight" just for fighting's sake. That wasn't his style. If failure seemed imminent, then just go on to the next item on the agenda.

26. A Finger to The Wind

The health care issue is a classic example of Dean's ability to put his finger to the wind. I never doubted the governor was committed to universal health care for all of Vermont's citizens. After all, he was a medical doctor who knew full well the crucial nature and need of people to obtain treatment for themselves, their children or their elderly. It was a measure of his ability to see into the future in his political crystal ball. He jumped out front on the issue. Because of him, Vermont was to move as close to the cutting edge of getting it done as any state in the nation. His timing was uncanny. None of this would have happened without his unique relationship with the President of the United States. Ironically, I was the matchmaker who first got them together.

My connection to Bill Clinton came out of the blue.

Obviously, I had heard of Bill Clinton, but it was a rather obscure awareness of a small state governor who I remembered carrying on for what seemed like hours at the 1988 National Democratic Convention. After that rather sorry effort, I had not given him another thought until the phone rang one Friday evening in December, 1991. I was sitting in my den watching the Celtics. It was early in the second period, and I couldn't believe that someone actually had the nerve to disturb me during a Celtic game. This call couldn't have been from anyone who knew me very well. Maybe it was a nuisance call, and it was with that frame of mind I answered in a rather terse voice.

"Hello," Larry had the ball.

"Hello. May I speak to Speaker Wright, please?" The person on the line had a thick southern drawl.

"Speaking. Who is this?"

"Mr. Speaker, this is Governor Bill Clinton, and I'm calling from down here in Little Rock. I wonder if I might have a moment of your time, if you don't mind." And as if he had a premonition as to just how much I minded, he added, "I hope I'm not bothering you at this hour at home."

Absolutely convinced that this was one of my friends screwing around, I jumped right on his case. "Who is this?"

"My name's Bill Clinton. I'm the Governor of Arkansas and I'm running for President."

"Yeah, sure! And I'm going to be the next Pope. Pro choice and all."

He added quickly, "I believe we have a mutual friend in Boston: Peter Lucas, the former newspaper columnist for the *Boston Globe*. It's my understanding you met with him recently and according to a friend of mine, you let him know you might support my candidacy for President. At least, I hope my friend heard it right. I'm calling in hopes that I might get your support."

That much was true. I recently had been to Boston and I had made my usual visit over to the State House on Beacon Hill to say hello to Peter. We had gone to high school together, joined the service at the same time, and met again four years later as freshmen at Boston University. Peter and I separated for years after graduation. He went into journalism where he gained a national reputation as a hard-hit-tling, talented columnist for both of the Boston dailies. I recalled I told Peter I liked Bill Clinton and I intended to support him. If the caller on the other end of the phone now had asked, I would have had to be truthful and added, "But, I don't believe he has a prayer." Not only was Clinton a little-known governor from a small southern state, but nobody would have guessed that George Bush was going to be vulnerable. I was convinced Harris or Corcoran were up to one of their tricks, and I answered in a slightly angry tone.

"Look. If this is you Harris, or Corcoran, ya better stop screwing around. The Celts are in the middle of the second period, and I'm in no mood for practical jokes."

"I beg your pardon," came the southern drawl again. "How are the Celts doing, Mr. Speaker? Larry's my favorite."

"Is this really Governor Clinton?" I asked, beginning to realize even Harris and Corcoran weren't this good.

And then the convincing comment, "I've got a good friend who plays for the Celtics, Joe Klein from the University of Arkansas. How's he doing?"

I knew Corc and Harris wouldn't have had the faintest who Joe Klein was. Sports wasn't their thing. Christ, I was really talking to the Governor of Arkansas. And the poor guy must have been wondering the length a candidate has to go by talking to some rude nut from Vermont who happened to be Speaker. I hit the mute button on the clicker and apologized.

"Jeez, I'm sorry, Governor. It's just that I have these friends who think Friday night is as good a time as any to call and play jokes. I never expected to be getting a call from the Governor of Arkansas. It's 8 P.M., Friday night. Shouldn't you be at a mall or something? What are you doing calling me here in little ole Vermont?"

"Well, Mr Speaker, I know it's early, and there are still lots of people that aren't even aware I'm running. But I'm just trying to touch base with as many state Democratic leaders as I can and hopefully get them on board early. Peter informed me you endorsed Governor Dukakis in 1988 from the Well of the House. Would you be willing to do that for me?"

"Sure, no problem, but I've got to warn you I did it for Dukakis and he immediately fell 20 points in the polls." Clinton laughed and said he wasn't worried about that happening again, but he did want to know about my governor.

"Do you think you might be able to get him to support me?"

"Well I don't know, Governor. I don't know that he has endorsed anyone since it's still pretty early in the game, but I'll be seeing him when we reconvene in three or four weeks and I'll be happy to see what I can do for you. All he can say is 'no'."

That was it. I was committed to a little-known governor from a small backwater state and the only measure of insurance I had I wasn't publicly backing another loser, was he probably was going to prove to be so inept a candidate his campaign was going to fold before it even got off the ground and before I had to tell anyone he was my man. So much for what I know about politics, right?

I got Dean to jump off Senator Kerrey's ship and onto Bill Clinton's in January and we both agreed to announce our endorsement at my fund-raiser during the second week in February. This seemed convenient as we were aware Clinton would be campaigning in the New Hampshire Primary almost on a daily basis and it would be fairly easy for him to skip on up to the evening gathering in Montpelier.

Besides, we argued, it was likely he would have dropped out by that time and our hectic lives wouldn't have to be interrupted by this inconvenient sideshow. Little did we know that, by the second week of February, 1992, Clinton would be in such deep trouble. It didn't help George Bush was being hailed as the conquering hero as he saw the Gulf War success sky rocket his polls to over 90 percent favorability. I didn't know it then, as I never considered myself lucky, but I was standing with a guy who probably plays through during thunderstorms.

My Speaker's Soiree was scheduled for a Wednesday night during the second week of February, and though I had invited Governor Clinton to be my special guest, I was relieved when his staff called to inform me that because of the governor's heavy hits over the Genifer Flowers fiasco and his "Draft" problem, he wouldn't be able to make it to my fundraiser, and his endorsement. That was the good news. The bad news was his wife, Hillary, would be there on her husband's behalf. Terrific.

I teased Dean a lot the week or so before the event, as to how he had finally allowed himself to be dragged into a no-win situation. I reminded him just how bad the kidding and abuse would be about our timing for supporting a guy who was dropping off the charts.

Sometimes he thought it was funny; sometimes he didn't.

Hillary Clinton showed up that evening with her head high. It was a wonderful display of public courage. She knocked them dead. I made sure I stood on one side of her, and Dean on her other, the entire evening. I had Julie Peterson, everyone's favorite legislator, in reserve, just in case. Nobody there that cold and dark night could have left without feeling the highest admiration for Hillary, and indirectly for Bill Clinton. These were not run-of-the-mill political people. She was extremely bright, committed to her husband's cause, and showed not the slightest sign of defeat. Unfortunately, only about 300 Vermonters bore witness to this profile in courage. The rest of America saw only a candidate down for the count.

"If you can keep your head when all about you are losing theirs and blaming it on you..."

It was a good night, fund-raising wise, as we sold over 250 tickets for $100 each for cocktails, and nearly 40 tickets at $500 each to the dinner. All told, I raised over $40,000 for Democratic House candidates. I still couldn't shake the sad feelings I had for the disaster that had befallen Bill Clinton. Nobody deserved what he was going through and certainly nobody would have been surprised or blamed him if he had simply called it quits and thrown in the towel. It was a measure of the man and his wife they got up and carried on against a seemingly unbeatable foe. I did something I had never done before.

I had never spent more than $150 in any campaign that my name was on a ballot. In fact, I had never given any other candidate anything larger than a $25 check in all my life. But now I sat down and wrote Bill Clinton a personal letter in longhand, and in it, I enclosed a money order for $100. Not a very large sum to many, but a fortune to me.

"Dear Governor Clinton," I wrote:

"I just wanted to write a brief note to thank you and Hillary for making my fund-raiser such a success last evening. I know how difficult it must have been for you and your wife to be concerned about other people's matters at such a time as this. I also feel certain this must surely be the low point in your political career. Nevertheless, simply let me say, 'don't let the bastards get you down.' You are going to be President of the United States come November. Take my word for it, and the proof is I'm willing to put my money where my mouth is with the enclosed check for the entire Wright estate, $100. Spend it wisely.

> *Warm regards,*
> *Ralph G. Wright*

P.S. Hillary knocked them dead. You can be proud of her, especially under fire."

The rest is history.

If the new President of the United States had a favorite governor, it couldn't have been anyone but Howard Dean. Within months after being inaugurated, the President announced it was time to do something about the health care problem. And he meant to do it now.

Dean, meanwhile, had already prepared Vermont for sweeping health care reform by passing a Universal Health Care bill a year earlier. I had sponsored that bill, an unusual move for me, and the momentum with which it flew threw the legislature was surprising to all of us. The bill didn't do anything to change the antiquated and costly system America had learned to live with all these years, nor did it provide a single additional Vermonter any trace of a health care package. It mandated the newly created Health Care Authority study the issue from soup to nuts and return with a choice of plans the legislature could act upon. To be fair to Dean, I never felt he recognized the full and sweeping impact his initiative could mean to Vermont's largest industries, especially if the legislature chose the most sweeping choice of reform. This, of course, would be the so-called "single payer" system that would provide a guaranteed basic package to all Vermonters. The cost was to be divided between employers and employees, which would come to more than $720 million. This was a phenomenal sum that was greater than the state's total general fund budget.

The "single payer" plan presented no problem for me, as I had no feelings of compunction or regret of laying these astronomical costs squarely on the shoulders of those who should be paying for the services, the guy carrying the lunch pail and his boss. The payroll tax was the only place one could look in order to raise this amount of money, as surely few could advocate raising the other taxes that were without the sources of money required. Only in payroll could enough be found to cover the amazing amount necessary to deliver the vital health services. Like Willy Sutton answered when asked why he robbed banks: "Because that's where the money is, stupid."

I may have had no problem with the "single payer" system, but Dean could break out in a rash at the mere mention of the smallest increase in the most obscure tax. To propose raising, by over $700 million, the one tax that had an impact on all working Vermonters, probably brought him to the edge of a stroke. He seldom said anything about it, at least the possibility of the "single payer" system as being one of the alternatives, but I sensed he felt the extraordinary heavy financial burden the "single payer" system would place on the state's fiscal condition would be enough to scare even the most radical of the proponents of change. In other words, I felt he was confident it would never come down to having a choice of a "single payer" system over some less revolutionary proposal. Once again Dean would not be making waves.

His dilemma was that he was gaining a national reputation as this extraordinary young governor in the little state of Vermont who was poised to set the pace for the entire nation in the quest to bring about universal health care for all its citizens.

It was a heady experience, indeed, for a guy who had just several years earlier been on the brink of political extermination. He had moved out of his district and found a new place to live before he found a new office to run for. I'm convinced it wouldn't have mattered much what office was available, as Dean would have said "fine with me" and jumped into the race.

It happened to be luck that Peter Smith took on a sitting governor and the lieutenant governor's office opened up. It was beyond anyone's imagination that Kunin's successor, Dick Snelling, was going to die not eight months into his two-year term. That, with Dean's willingness to listen to my advice and to throw Senator Kerrey over the bridge and join me in an early endorsement of Clinton. A smart player just might have Howard Dean buy his next lottery ticket for him. It would probably hit.

There's just so much that can be chalked up to luck. Howard Dean is more than lucky, he's good. I believe in addition to his phenomenal "bedside manner", he's blessed with an extraordinary ability to move with the flow. He can read what the polls are going to say long before the survey begins. He's shown this ability time after time for those who pay close attention. And, remember, he's never been a prisoner on the "locked" mentality of an incestuous legislature.

His world is a much broader arena than the average legislator's, as he reads the mind and concerns of the guy in the street extremely well. This has angered the political "wonks" who walk the legislative halls on a daily basis, especially the liberals, but he doesn't need their constant reassurance he is a good man doing good things. He knows this already. Besides, he's the one who's at 75 percent in the favorability polls, and the legislature is sucking up the weeds at the bottom of those polls.

This was a period of existential "highs." Our governor was appearing on national news shows on a fairly regular basis, and he always handled himself in an extremely effective way. He could be a "klutzy" sort from time-to-time in the privacy of his office. He told me "once the cell doors slammed shut behind the convicted, then they lost all of their rights as an American." I warned him he probably should not say that at his next press conference. But once the camera lights flashed on, he became the handsome young governor from the romantic state of Vermont. I once told a friend of mine it was not beyond my comprehension to envision Howard Dean in the White House. Envisioning him as governor once brought a chuckle, too.

Actually I did see him once in the White House and he appeared as comfortable there as he might be when cleaning his cellar. The event was the Health Care speech to a joint session of the Congress that President Clinton delivered early in 1993. Dean, as the President's favorite governor, received a special invitation to sit directly behind Mrs. Clinton in the Gallery of the Congress. He was nice enough to invite me to attend the event with him.

I was not going to be as privileged, but I was one of the 200 or so allowed to view the speech from the East Room of the White House. I had been in the White House once before as a legislative leader back in the Reagan days. In fact, the President had actually spoken to us in the East Room. Anyway this was something very special for me and I sat through the speech, displayed on the giant screens, certain I was part of history.

Earlier we had ridden to a pretty austere motel in Georgetown where the governor's staff managed to find me a room. I hadn't seen Dean throughout the day as he left the airport for the White House, where he would travel by limousine to the Capitol for the evening's event. It was at the reception following the speech that I ran into him as he accompanied the President and Hillary back to the White House where the crowd of dignitaries and I awaited. Everyone had been impressed with not only the message of the President's speech, but also with the delivery. The crowd was high with emotion, and at my less-than-humble urging, I got the governor to introduce me to the President and Hillary personally. I was in seventh heaven at just being in the same room with a President, thus it was with sadness someone announced the party was over and we would have to leave.

"Governor, am I riding back to the motel with you ?" I asked, certain the answer was yes.

"Where are you staying?"

I was getting a little confused, "I'm staying in a Holiday Inn, or something, in Georgetown at the same motel you are booked into."

"Uh, actually, I'm not staying in the same place as you."

It seemed a somewhat hesitant answer, and I thought, "Could it be my governor's got someone special he stays with here while he's in the Capitol? Can't be. He'd have to shake his body guard and I didn't think they'd let him do that. But, maybe. The world's full of little surprises. He must have guessed at what I was thinking, as he added:

"I'm staying here for the night." He looked embarrassed as I looked around re-verifying we were still at 1600 Pennsylvania Avenue.

"What the hell ya mean, you're stayin' here? This is the God damned White House, Howard." I was controlling the first sign of envy in my voice.

He showed a faint blush and I could tell he was truly embarrassed.

"The President has asked me to stay over for the night. I guess I have to. He'll feel insulted if I turned him down."

"Ya mean you're actually staying here at the White House? And, I suppose, in the Lincoln bedroom?" There was no concealing my envy for the man I had to convince to get off Kerrey's bandwagon and join Clinton's over a year ago.

"Well, I don't know where they're putting me up. It may not be in the Lincoln Bedroom."

I'm happy to report I slept in a room that had running water. The only other difference between the governor's accommodations and mine was I paid $80 and he paid nothing.

We were up bright and early the next morning in order to pick up the governor at the back entrance to the White House. I always enjoyed riding with the governor, not so much for the pleasure of his company, as for the thrill of being with the cops. We rode in a big white van especially equipped for VIPs and I felt like a big shot riding shotgun, hoping people might mistake me as a cop.

We entered after being cleared and the scene that struck me was right out of Norman Rockwell. Awaiting our arrival was this boyish looking guy, looking for all the world like he was waiting for a bus to take him to summer camp. My governor. He had a suitcase I'm certain was made out of cardboard. His hair looked like he had simply run his hands through it and was pronounced by his huge cowlick sticking up in the back. He had buttoned his shirt unevenly, and the knot in his tie was closer to his shoulder than it was to his Adam's apple. "Boy, we can't take you anywhere, Howard," I thought.

I jumped out, but before I could let him in the front seat, he had already struggled through the sliding door and plunked himself in the very rear seat of the van.

"Well, how'd your night go?" I asked.

"Just great." That's it? Just great?

"What happened when we left, and you and the President went upstairs to the family quarters? Did you get a chance to sit and chat for a while?"

"Not really, as I had a servant take me to my room. I don't know where the Clintons went. I was tired. I went right to sleep," he said in a matter of fact voice.

"Did you see them for breakfast? Ya musta had breakfast with them. Didn't you?" I felt disappointed in the lack of excitement to Howard's stay, at least up to this point.

"Actually, I didn't see anyone. I just got up, showered and came down here to wait for you guys." Now, he was going too far, and I turned almost 180 degrees to face him.

"You mean to say you get invited to stay overnight in the White House and you go to bed without a nightcap with the President, and then you wake up in the morning, and just get up and leave?" Now I was talking to a governor like he was a kid I sent somewhere to get a job accomplished and he had come back empty handed.

"Well, I showered before I left. Jeez, I'm hungry. I hope we have time to have a muffin at the airport. Think we will?"

"Governor," I said, "you didn't even get to have a cup of coffee this morning?"

"I don't drink coffee, besides I wasn't sure where I was exactly, and I didn't want to bother anybody that early."

"For Christ's sake, Governor, there's more servants in that building than there are Marines at Camp LeJeune. Didn't you have a phone in the room with buttons on it?"

"Well, er, yes, but I didn't want to bother anyone that early," he repeated.

"Christ, Governor. That was the White House you stayed in. A glass of juice isn't exactly a request for a navy base in Burlington. Why didn't you just keep pushing those buttons until somebody showed up?" I kept thinking of all the missed opportunities that come a man's way but once.

He laughed nervously. "I guess I should of, huh?"

Now I knew why he was the most popular governor in America.

I took one more trip to Washington with Dean. This time we attended a special fund-raiser put on for him by the President. We re-arranged our schedules to fit into the fierce health care fight that was raging in the Senate. Actually, things weren't looking very good for the issue that we had put so much of our time and energy into over the past two years and we were barely hanging on to the smallest semblance of the revolutionary measure that had struck such excitement in our hearts two years earlier. Time, cost, and complexity of the issue had been our greatest enemy.

In the Vermont House, I had at one time counted 88 votes for a sweeping "single payer" system. This was over the weekend preceding the Tuesday vote on the floor of the House. But the members were scared, as the revenue numbers the taxes would raise were huge in comparison to anything we had ever endeavored to push through in the past. This was accompanied by the biggest lobbying effort I had yet seen in my 14 years in the legislature.

We were goring lots of oxen, and they weren't rolling over for any of it. They pulled out all the stops realizing Vermont just might be small enough, even innocent enough, to do the right thing and provide a universal health plan for all its citizens, and do it with the fairest form of taxation, the income tax. We were David without the slingshot, and I realized it when I returned to the State House on Tuesday morning. I went into caucus and told them I had spoken to damned near every last one of them over the weekend. It took me 40 hours or so to dial and talk to each of them personally. They had committed to voting for a "single payer" system.

"Now we've got to put up or shut up," I said. "I know you've been lobbied with a fierceness seldom seen in this State House, but we've run out of time. It's time to go upstairs in a few hours and decide if we're going to get run over by the special interests, or we're going to do what's right by the people. I've got to know if we still feel strongly about what we're about to do. I say this because several of you have come to me and asked if we can't find another option, or at least not take this option. I respect those people's honesty, but I have to know how the rest of you feel. I don't want to go up on the floor and be embarrassed. Do you want to go on?"

A few of my more liberal members stood to speak in favor of pushing the "single payer" system. The rest sat silently. They said nothing, but revealed everything with their silence. They were terrified of the radical nature of what we in Vermont were about to do, and though they didn't want to have to vote to do it, they were creatures of that special institution, the legislature, that says that if you give your word, you keep your word. They weren't going to risk embarrassing themselves in front of their colleagues here in caucus. They would wait until they could grab me or Sean Campbell, the Democratic Leader who probably earned the title "Father of the Single Payer System" through his monstrous effort as Chair of the special Health Care committee. This was upstairs and out of ear shot of their fellow Democrats. Sensing this, I ended by saying, "If you've changed your mind, please, let Sean or me know."

Within an hour, 30 or 40 members came to us and we dropped into the mid thirties, vote-wise. Significant change in the way we deliver health care to some, and not at all to others, was lost. The next day we passed a watered down version of a health care plan, but the dike had broken and it was only a matter of the Senate drowning the whole idea.

I wasn't smart enough to realize the jig was up as I hoped the die hard Senate supporters of significant change would be able to get done what we had failed to get done in the House. I never dreamed of giving up. It wasn't in me. Besides, we still might pull it all together, for even though we didn't have a majority of Democrats in the Senate, the public demand still seemed to be there and we had the doctor/governor who had gotten this whole thing started.

We were 10,000 feet above New Jersey when the end came.

The governor and I arranged to attend a Vermont products conference at Killington Ski Resort, and immediately following the luncheon, we hopped on a small executive jet owned by Grand Union to fly to Washington for the fund-raiser. The governor and I were sitting across from each other, enjoying the privacy a small plane affords. He was reading the *New York Times* and seemed to be a man without a worry. I was holding on for dear life. The governor must have noticed my intensity, as he looked up from his paper and asked, "I thought you didn't fly, Mr. Speaker?"

"I fly, but I don't like it much."

"Well, there's nothing to it. It's safer than driving the New Jersey Turnpike."

"Well, that may be but, Governor, if hurdling along at 300 miles per hour, two miles up is so safe and sane, where are the pigeons?" I asked in a very serious tone.

"I beg your pardon. Pigeons?" He was totally confused by what must have seemed like crazy talk from me.

"Yeah, pigeons. If this is the place to be, where are the pigeons? Maybe they're smarter than both of us, cause they aren't here. They're safely perched on some ledge or on a statue of people like us. The pigeons, like the poets, know." He smiled faintly, more a confused than humorous smile, and slid behind his paper once again.

This time I interrupted him.

"Governor, what are we going to do with the Health Care Plan in the Senate?" I was prepared for a lengthy dialogue on a strategy carefully outlining an advance to final victory. I didn't have any such plan, but this was the governor's baby, and I had the hope of a child that father would now outline how to get the job done right.

He barely looked up from his reading and he nonchalantly answered, "Nothing, it's dead."

That's it? It's dead? Two years of grinding and fighting and it's dead? Everything went out of my mind, as the only visual I had was the Governor in a hospital room, pulling another sheet up over a patient's face, and turning to look at the charts on the patient in the next bed.

We had little to talk about for the rest of the flight.

It was to prove to be a memorable trip in more than one way. The event was held in one of the fancy downtown hotels that Washington seems to be loaded with, and I hung around watching the Secret Service dogs tug at their leashes as they sniffed things. There must have been 400 people at the reception who each paid $1,000 to be in the same room with the President. Since I had absolutely no role in the whole event, I had taken a place standing at the very rear of the large room. The President entered and stood patiently as Dean introduced him. I'm a great admirer of Bill Clinton and I was as honored to simply be in his presence. I had no misconception I would get to meet him this time, or that I had any special standing with him. Getting to be President in a nation of 250 million people is a campaign that boggles my mind. I was well aware that even my willingness to commit to him early, and to stand by his wife's side on his darkest political night the previous February, didn't mean much in the bigger scheme of national politics.

Still I had been arrogant enough to write the new President another one of my handwritten letters back in January. In it, I told him off as I had never received the smallest note of "thank you"for what I thought was loyalty on my part in his quest to capture the White House. I ended the saucy letter with the lecture that "where I come from, Mr. President, people at least learn to say thank you." I actually worried for a brief moment it might be turned over to the Secret Service and labeled for the 'nut' file. I sent it off and about two weeks later I got a pair of Presidential cuff links in the mail. My distant love affair was getting to be expensive as now I would have to go out and buy a shirt with French cuffs.

So it was with a sense of shock I thought I heard the President mention my name from the stage. A few seconds later, one of the corporate lobbyists who knew who I was, turned and said, "Mr. Speaker, he's asking you to raise your hand so he can see where you are."

"You gotta be kidding." I was confused as I was certain that it was all some sort of a joke, though a quicker mind would have come to the conclusion a room filled with corporate VIPs wasn't exactly a hot bed for humor. Maybe Corcoran or Harris had smuggled their way down here.

The room quieted as the President stood waiting for a response to his inquiry and then I heard it. "I know you're here, Ralph. Would you please? Where are you, Mr. Speaker?" And then, like a wave at Fenway, the heads slowly turned until it seemed, at least to me, that all eyes were on me at the back of the room. I raised my hand sheepishly, and the President made eye contact.

"Ah! There you are, Ralph Wright. I just wanted to take a moment before my formal remarks to say thank you, Ralph, for your support when things seemed darkest. I very much appreciated your willingness to hang in there with me, and I want you to know I will never forget you for that loyalty. You're a very special person. Thank you."

Andy Warhol once said that God's saddest soul, if he lives long enough, will have his 15 minutes in the sun. I had just had my 15 seconds.

I remember someone once told me the reason we so totally misunderstood the conflict in Vietnam, was we never came to grips with the fundamental difference between Oriental religious beliefs and Western culture. Americans place a great deal of value on "this life", while the Eastern world thinks what matters most is the "next life." We're terrified of dying, even for a cause; the Vietnamese felt how you died was more important than when you died. Life was, in a relative sense, expedient as it led to something better and certainly more lasting.

I remember sitting for hours listening to the "old salt" Marines tell their war stories to younger kids in the barracks at night in the early fifties. They were just young men themselves, but they had lived a lifetime on the beaches of Guadalcanal, Tawara, Iwo Jima, Okinawa, and other islands of human destruction during World War II.

The stories fascinated me as they served to reveal the extraordinary acts of human suffering and fright these men had endured. The thing that always went beyond any of their abilities to explain was the willingness of the enemy to give their own life for a cause. They simply dismissed it all as the acts of crazy men doing crazy things. The Marines I knew and listened to with the interest of a child hearing scary stories, always managed to speak of the willingness of the Japanese to lay down their lives with both admiration and confusion of these uncommon acts.

They never went any further in an effort to explain why. But I sensed they had great respect for the character of their foe, and his willingness to fight to the death. I also believe the entire Corps compensated in some small way for this by adopting the principal that Marines also carried out their dead and wounded, no matter the cost. I accepted that with pride. No man's dignity deserves abandonment.

I guess this was the one thing I never could understand about Howard Dean. He always seemed so ready to abandon his cause at the first sign of defeat. Maybe it was his medical training that toughened him to the certain failures that awaited us all. Maybe it was an unwillingness to have any cause at all, at least any cause for which he was willing to risk his political skin.

Thus it was a surprise he abandoned health care, the one cause he could have justifiably taken credit for. Even in defeat, he could have held his head high, but to me a lot of the pride and glory was sapped from the whole affair by his willingness not to fight to the very end. He was too quick to run up the white flag. It wasn't just causes he was willing to abandon, he was capable of acting the same with people.

27. Sometimes It Isn't Any Fun

The Press referred to the Environmental Board affair as a throwback to the McCarthy era, the "great Red scare" of the fifties. That was indeed an accurate description of the conduct of the Republican Senate during a five-week period in the session of 1994.

The impetus for the Senate's action was clearly political both while it was happening and in retrospect. Vermont's reputation for being on the cutting edge of the environmental movement in America was well-deserved, and the legacy of environmental bills Kunin and the Democratic legislature had passed between 1985 and 1990 cemented our standing as a state that cared. We wore the badge with pride.

The corporate interests never stopped whining and complaining about how the business community had been hamstrung in its constant effort to turn a profit through development. Neither side backed up and the only recourse the Republican Senate could see to begin the reverse of what they termed "environmental elitism", was to change the board that oversaw the Act 250 administration. It didn't matter to them Act 250 was a piece of legislation that had gained national acclaim and, in fact, had been enacted by Deane Davis, a very business-oriented Republican governor in the seventies.

This was a masterpiece of protective law that presented a maze of "hoops and hurdles" for anyone who thought Vermont was to be an easy mark for a quick buck. Vermont is known for its natural beauty of green valleys and undisturbed rolling hills that made us the envy of the multitudes from urban areas. Governor Davis and Act 250 recognized this and set out to preserve it. That was the principal on which the members of the Environmental Board operated. Senate Republicans, backed by the vast majority of the business community were determined to change Act 250, or at least the board that oversaw it.

Three board members were in front of the Senate awaiting the governor's recommendation for re-appointment by the Senate and the Natural Resources Committee, which was responsible for taking testimony and forwarding a recommendation to the full body. The three names were hardly new faces: Chair Elizabeth Courtney of Rutland, Terry Ehrich of Bennington and Nundy Bongartz of Manchester. Two of the three were Republicans, including the Chair.

They cared about Vermont and its environment and they ruled on each request for development permits with that as a primary consideration. It wasn't long before the Republican-dominated committee began asking "are you now, or have you ever been, an environmentalist?" to each of the candidates who found themselves fighting for their reputations and their re-appointments. It turned as ugly as anything I ever witnessed in the State House.

The Press slowly, but surely, saw the ugliness of the committee's intention to sink the three nominations, and began three weeks of delivering the worst "press" I ever saw. It didn't deter the committee, however, and they brought the recommendation to the full Senate the three ought to be fired. Republicans held a 16-14 majority in the Senate, but few really believed they could hold their troops together for the final public assassination.

We were all wrong. They axed the three by a small margin. In at least one case, they had the help of a tie-breaking vote by Lieutenant Governor Barbara Snelling to fire someone whom her late husband had appointed. It seemed the height of political stupidity to me as I was certain the public found the whole affair repugnant and adverse to their own deep belief that the special quality of Vermont was directly tied to our willingness to protect this aura of cleanliness and beauty.

But the Republican Senate hung tough, and even though we in the House had no Constitutional authority with the "advise and consent" prerogative of the board's appointments, we watched with deep interest and fascination as this was a very basic and fundamental struggle between unbridled development and conservation of that which we felt vital. Good and evil had met, and evil had not succumbed.

I still felt no sense of alarm as I was certain the Republicans were finally displaying the ugly side of their nature and the Press was doing a good job making it evident to the public. It seemed reasonable there was a political price to be paid by them somewhere down the road. No one, it seemed to me, could withstand the constant slamming the Republicans and, especially, Barbara Snelling was taking on a daily basis. It was just a matter of the governor re-submitting the same three names and forcing them to do it until they got it right. My alarm bell went off when the rumor ran through the State House the governor was going to cut his losses and not re-submit the three for a second time. I went ballistic. Sean Campbell did everything in his power to keep me from going to see the governor personally. It was good advice, as I'm sure it would have erupted into our first public fight. Even though I had an unwritten rule I wouldn't ever get into public and open conflict with a democratic governor, his refusal to hang tough with his three recommendations would have driven me over the edge. I did the next best thing. I talked to Anya Rader, his bright and tough aide. I relayed my strong feelings he simply had to "carry out his dead and wounded" and re-submit their names. The Senate wouldn't be able to withstand the abuse they were getting from all fronts forever.

There was a long moment when nobody knew for sure what Gov. Dean was going to do, but finally he sent the names to the Senate once again. I was proud he had stood beside his people and for the first time I had liberal Democrats who had developed a great dislike for the governor, come to me and relay "he's finally stood tall; he's finally used some of that political capital he so easily accrues to benefit someone and something we believe in. There may be hope for him after all."

This should have been a no-lose situation. The three nominees were good people who served competently and honorably and deserved re-appointment. The wolves in the Senate hadn't found a scintilla of evidence to the contrary. It was a witch hunt. The only better thing would be to hope the Republicans in the Senate got even dumber and refused to approve the appointments a second time.

Well, that's exactly what they did.

This time the Governor failed to re-submit. Another sheet was drawn over the bodies of three dedicated and long-serving public servants. I don't think I've ever been more disappointed than I was at the moment. It bothers me to this day.

In this one, Lieutenant Governor Barbara Snelling, I think, had the opportunity of a lifetime. She could have done the right thing and move to re-appoint the three, and to emerge as the true leader of the Republican party in the Senate, and the state. She let the opportunity to display a profile in courage pass her by. She even had the perfect excuse as far as so-called "political correctness" was concerned. As her deceased husband's appointments, she could have made the case to break the ties in a positive manner by saying that she was doing it if only in her husband's memory. "That's what Dick would have wanted." No one would have taken her to task over it.

Instead she stood by her party and its primary goal to play havoc with something important. She already had made a name for herself, and was labeled "cheap and mean" for her refusal to allow a quarter on the minimum wage. Now she simply reinforced her reputation as "mean." That's how a lot of the members in the State House felt. It was becoming increasingly clear she was resting her political reputation on being against everything and for nothing, a hostage to big business.

The whole event concerning the Environmental Board was tinged with a human sadness that didn't fit into anything I could understand. Loyalty to me is merely a sub-category of love, and here I witnessed the political discarding of that very vital principal. I felt I missed something and it crossed my mind maybe it was time to wrap up things and get out. There were times when politics wasn't very much fun, and this was one of those times.

28. Knocking On Doors

Campaigning is like love. There are certain principles involved that are undying and eternal, but they are measured by the temperament and personality of the candidate. The would-be "Hizzoner" molds his or her campaign to fit what he or she feels most comfortable with. Vermont, with its small population and reasonable district parameters, makes it unique from other states in that anyone can enter it.

A massive war chest isn't necessary, nor does there have to be an entourage of help to get elected. If someone dedicates approximately seven weeks of work, a minimum of brain labor, and a budget that can reach as low as a couple of hundred dollars he or she can, everything else considered, get elected.

I never spent more than $250 on any of my campaigns. In my final campaign, that ended in my only defeat over a 25-year political career, I was outspent 75 to 1. I was defeated for a multitude of reasons, however, being outspent was only one.

The major component of any successful campaign is basic person-to-person contact. That is necessary no matter what office a person runs for or from what area they're running. Obviously, a Texan can't just roll out of bed in the morning and start a door-to-door campaign. Too many doors. Districts in other states contain so many constituents one could spent years trying to meet each and every person and still come up way short of that goal. That's not so in Vermont where a district is only 3,700 people and that's men, women, and children, not just voters. Eligible voters might number 2,200 or so. If the turnout is unusually high, perhaps 80 percent, only one more than half are needed. This means victory can be achieved by accumulating 900 or so votes. It gets even better than that when the "anybody but" vote is factored in. These are the people who would vote for Donald Duck, rather than the opponent.

A normal incumbent might have 500 voters who would vote for any name on a ballot, rather than his or hers.

In my case, I had been around long enough to alienate almost everybody at one time or another, so the "anybody but Ralph" number rose by slow, but sure, proportions with each passing term. Like the law of averages, the end begins at the very beginning.

I literally had run from one end of my district to the other, as it was only six miles from its most northern point to its most southern. I felt good and the weather permitted it, but my point is if a casual jogger could traverse his district without collapsing, then it was no great task for a candidate to systematically walk from neighborhood to neighborhood knocking on each and every door. I did it nine different times during my political career, and I found after six or seven weeks of knocking on 30 doors a day, I could fairly well cover all of the district I needed to reach. I "maxed out" of places to go at about 1,200 or so houses. Of course, there were doors I chose not to knock on, as I became fairly adroit at knowing where the voters were. I kept a record for several terms. After that I got lazy and stopped doing the necessary research that was required after each election by going to Town Hall and recording those who had voted, and those who hadn't. Failing to do this chore systematically and precisely was one of those signs of over-confidence or, perhaps, weariness, that if paid heed to, eventually would have predicted trouble.

I'm not sure I learned an awful lot about issues during my door-to-door travels, but I did learn, or had reinforced, that which I already knew about people. I was always met at the door with utmost courtesy. People were always pleasant and polite. They obviously weren't all intent on voting for me, but that didn't keep them from greeting me with a friendliness and hospitality that would have made their mothers proud. Every house seemed to have at least one of man's best friend, but once I made my peace with an ill-mannered canine, I was home free. I tried never to go into the house itself, as that would have set the schedule back considerably. I had "miles to go and promises to keep" and to get into any lengthy dialogue in somebody's kitchen would have meant less territory covered. It was my experience people had better things to do than to philosophize with their local representative. Usually time itself was enough to curb my "visiting", as I went to their doors when people would most likely be home, from 5-7:30 P.M. weekday evenings; 10:30 A.M.-5:00 P.M. Saturdays, and noon until 5 P.M. or so Sundays.

During the week, people were just arriving home from work or picking the kids up at the day care center, and with the routine of preparing supper and analyzing each other's day, they didn't need me perched at the kitchen table. Saturdays were best as long as I didn't arrive too early and roust them out of bed. More than once, I happened upon some late risers who weren't exactly dressed to meet me, and I would apologize and beat a hasty retreat.

The season from Labor day until the first week in November was the ideal period to be moving about the district. The weather was neither too hot nor too cold, and many people were working in the yard. I might have been stuck carrying in groceries or moving a ladder, but these were "neighborly" efforts I didn't mind doing and helped my image as a guy who would roll up his sleeves and pitch in.

After a trip or two around the district, I got to know who lived where and whether they were friend or foe. I didn't have this down to a science, but I was 90 percent accurate. In fact, I made a point to try and recall what my last experience was at each house as I worked my way up the driveway.

I could see things only the traveling salesman's trained eye could detect and it kept me in good stead in preparing for whomever opened the door. People's yards are filled with tell-tale signs of who lived here and what they were like. The easiest clues would come from the vehicles in the driveway and the bumper stickers. I could tell whether they were of a liberal bent (Save The Whales) or a conservative bent (NRA). I wouldn't change my beliefs to suit the constituent, and if asked questions by them, I would answer honestly, but there were subjects I wouldn't bring up.

It was easy to spot a house that had children, as toys and bikes would be strewn about and if an issue was brought up, it generally would concern education. People care about their children and I feel confident there weren't too many exceptions. There weren't many doors in my district I didn't know who lived behind, based on past visits or by simply taking the time to observe.

It was a good experience knocking on 1,000 or so doors, as I came to respect people's struggles to merely keep their heads above water. The fact they would interrupt their busy lives to show me the high degree of courtesy they did, was a reward in itself. I have pleasant memories of meeting a lot of very nice people.

There were exceptions, but they were so few and far between, they magnified the rule. I was able to walk by those few I didn't want to get involved with. These also would include those I knew wouldn't vote. This was the type of information that could be extrapolated from the little bit of time that it would take to go to Town Hall after the election and record those who voted in the last election on my master voter check list. There was no way of knowing how someone voted, nor if they voted for each elective office on the ballot as some people voted for a single candidate in a single race. The people who gave me the hardest time at their door, or who boasted as to how valuable they were to the entire elective process, were always the ones that would turn up as non voters.

Too often I would have spent double or triple the time at their door, listening to their multitude of gripes, only to find they couldn't be bothered to exercise their franchise. I even had cases where the person at the door would swear they had always voted for me, when having just checked my list in the car, I knew they never voted in their lives. I actually had people profess their deep conviction to the electoral process when I had a checklist in my hand that was living proof they weren't even registered. People often acted like this in self defense, as no matter what we hear about the apathy of the average voter, I'm convinced that given less hectic lives, or more hopeful alternatives, people do care about their government and know more than we think about what it's doing. On the other hand some people just outright fib about their participation, rather than display a disregard for their lack of participation.

I understood their predicament, but I never felt comfortable with their commitment to rush out and vote for me. This was just another reason I feared placing my name on any more secret ballots than I absolutely had to. I felt strongly that registering them was the first step in a long process of getting a vote out of somebody. I would register them, but I wouldn't tell them what I knew about their lack of commitment to participating in the process. Instead, I would simply shift the onus on a mixed-up computer at the town clerk's office and offer to register them again. In either case, these were people to avoid if I could.

Sometimes people, like parents with too many kids, simply got confused. They knew they loved me. They were even certain that my line of work was doing good things through government service. But they weren't often sure how, or where, I did these things.

One especially hot summer day, I was cruising on foot along Main Street in Bennington and ran into Mrs. Wheelman. Knowing she was one of my strongest supporters, I took a minute to exchange pleasantries.

"It's gonna be a scorcher, isn't it, Mrs. Wheelman? How's everything at home?"

"Well, Ralph Wright, how are you? How's your family doing? I haven't seen you in a dog's age. I guess it is hot. Too hot for me, anyhow, " she answered.

"I don't think I like it when it gets this way either, but it beats winter," I responded, feeling pleased she knew who I was and the important effort I was making in Montpelier to better her life. It was nice to have well-informed constituents.

"Oh, I feel sorry for you," she said, not missing a beat. "I bet it's a lot worse than this where you work in Congress."

I took a chance. "Mrs. Wheelman, I'm not Speaker in Washington, thanks anyway. I'm just the Speaker in the legislature here in Vermont."

"Oh, that's right. How stupid of me. You're in Burlington. It's a lot cooler there with the breeze off the lake an' all."

I wasn't going to take any more risks, and didn't respond to that. But, I did move on down the street with a little more humility.

Dick Pembroke, my friend and district mate, (I was in a two-member district) didn't quite have the same patience and understanding, at least on one occasion. When we would go door-to-door together and get into one of these situations, he would get upset.

We had a pretty organized setup in that we shared duties each evening when we hit the pavement. One of us would be in charge of the physical aspect of the routine. He would be the first out of his truck and up the stairs leading to the door. Vermonters, you see, never use their front doors. Don't ask me why. It's an historical thing. It was never difficult to decipher which door they used, as there would be a myriad of clues to lead us to the payload. The obvious sign would be to pick the door closest to the family vehicle. If there was no vehicle, we'd look for where the kid dumped his bike, and if that wasn't evident, we'd look for the chain that held the 2,000-pound family pet. Pembroke was great with dogs as, unlike me, he never showed any fear of them.

His job was to nonchalantly push himself by the dog and tap on the door. I was in charge of the paperwork, which always included the most up-to-date checklist that provided the valuable data of whether the Jones or Smiths had voted in the past couple of elections; a clipboard that had an assortment of forms, including registration forms, and absentee ballot requests. It was a handful to manage without dropping all over the driveway, but usually I would be able to tell Dick who lived there as we waited for the door to be answered. We had made the circuit often enough that, between the two of us, we would have at least some faint recollection of who lived here and if this was a "good" or "bad" door. If I could fumble through the 4,000 names on the checklist fast enough, I would be able to report to him before the door was opened whether they had voted or not. This was the piece of information that determined whether we would spent seconds or minutes with the person who answered the door.

"How's it going, Joe?" Dick would be casual when a familiar face opened the door. "It's that time again. We're looking for support come November." The leaflets would be thrust into Joe's hand through the half-opened screen door.

"Hey, no problem in this house. You guys get my vote every election.

And I know my wife votes for you, too. Myself, I never miss an election."

"Great! Just wanted to make sure we showed our face, and that you wouldn't forget us." Dick was now convinced this was one of those "good" doors. I hadn't said a word as I was still fumbling desperately through my checklist, searching for Joe and his wife's name, to verify what I felt was certainly a voter who participated.

"OK," said Dick, moving down the steps. "We'll be on our way. Thanks for the support. See you at the polls down at St. Francis Parish Hall."

"Don't worry. Me and the Mrs. never fail to vote. We'll be there bright and early."

I had no sooner climbed up into Dick's big pickup and he was backing down the driveway headed for the next house, when I finally realized I must not have Joe's right last name because I couldn't locate it on the checklist. I wasn't going to say anything, as we were pulling into the next driveway, and besides I was certain Joe was a voter and what he had told us was money in the bank. But something piqued my curiosity and I asked.

"Isn't Joe's last name Jones, Dick?"

"Yeah! Why?"

"Well, I can't find any Joe Jones or his wife on the list."

"What the hell ya mean he's not on the list? You heard him. He's a big supporter and he votes bright and early. He's gotta be there somewhere. You gotta be looking in the wrong place."

"Look, I'm telling you the son of a bitch isn't on this checklist. He's connin' us. He's probably never voted in his life. Ya live and learn, Dick." That was the end of it as far as I was concerned. But not for Pembroke.

He had principles he wouldn't compromise, and being "taken" was one of them. He reacted like a man who had just discovered his wallet had been stolen.

Pembroke threw the truck in reverse with such ferocity, my head snapped back as we spun out of the driveway and headed back to Joe's house. Before I could get any more out of my mouth than "Where we going, Dick?", we were in the driveway we had just left and he was out of the truck. Pembroke is a giant of a man who towered over me and I usually didn't worry about his temper, as he was generally easy going. But I was worried as he pounded extra hard on the door and stood red-faced, awaiting Joe's arrival at the door. "Oh! Oh!" I thought.

"Hi, again. You forget something?" Joe had no idea his small sin had struck my running mate with such force.

"No, I didn't forget anything, but apparently you forgot to tell us you're not even registered. You or your wife aren't on the checklist. You can't vote if you're not on the checklist."

"Well, it must be some mistake. I know I'm registered. Can I see that?" Pointing to Dick's handful of leaflets, Joe just verified to Dick that he didn't know a checklist from his Adam's Apple. Pembroke was as angry as I'd ever seen him.

"Never mind, it's a mistake. Mary isn't the one who made any mistake (referring to Mary Hodeck the well known and revered Bennington town clerk who had been on the job since the 1920s). Mary would've had you on the list if you had registered. You're not registered and you couldn't have voted for anybody, let alone us." We're sure winning friends and influencing people today.

"Well, where can I register?" he stammered.

"It's too late. The deadline for registering has passed." With that, Pembroke stormed back and got into the truck. I wasn't sure I should say anything as he had said it all, but I did manage a smart retort.

"Another couple of hundred houses like this, Little Brother, and we'll finish second to Hitler."

Pembroke's only answer: "The guy's a liar. He lied to us."

These were the exceptions, as we didn't run into this type of indignity very often and occasionally the reverse happened. I would take some satisfaction at pestering a few of my own who couldn't even stand my presence at their door.

There was one gent who told whomever would listen I was the world's biggest jerk. The feelings were mutual, and I don't believe that we ever spent two minutes in each other's company, except for my bi-annual visit to his door. I timed it so I would arrive in his neighborhood shortly after 8 P.M., making sure his was the last house I visited that evening. I made certain I would appear at the front door, a door that hadn't been used in the big old colonial since the turn of the century. I would tip-toe across the stately front porch and rap on the outer storm door. Peering in, I could see John and his wife of over 50 years comfortably settled in for the evening, absorbed in their preferred reading matter. Both were a little hard of hearing, so it would take several taps on the door for his wife, who was not quite as deaf as he, to bellow she heard a knock at the door.

"What are you deaf, John? There's someone at the door." She had perfected her nagging tone for over a half century.

"I hear it. I hear it," he shouted back telling her his little white lie. He put down his paper, obviously annoyed, and headed in the opposite direction from where I was observing on the front porch, out into the kitchen, and answered the door customarily used by all but kids on Halloween.

I would wait until he re-appeared several minutes later, muttering to his loved one she was the one hearing things, and then watch as he would re-seat himself. When he got comfortable once again, with his paper hiding his visible anger from a wife who carried on she had not been hearing things, I would knock again .

"There, John, I told you there was someone at the door, didn't I?"

"Well, I'll be a son of a .....", the expletive trailed off as he rose once more from the overstuffed chair and lugged himself out to the kitchen door again.

"I swear, John, I don't know what I'm going to do with you. You're getting so absent-minded. You can't even answer the door anymore. I think someone's at the front door." John, by now, had disappeared once again into the darkened kitchen.

Again, I would wait and enjoy his re-entry into the turn-of-the-century parlor, this time mumbling in a louder than conversational tone there was nobody at the damned door, only to be interrupted by the Mrs. saying that someone was at the front door.

"They can't be. We never use the front door," he'd say. And, he lifted himself wearily from the chair again and began the trek toward me from the far side of the expansive room.

"I told you they were at the front door, but I'd be the last one that you'd listen to," she carried on.

"OK, OK! Who the hell would be using the front door at an hour like this? Probably some trick or treater kids." And he began to struggle with moving the table that had been placed smack in front of the door. This had to be done slowly and carefully so the Tiffany lamp did not get jostled to the floor.

I knocked again, even though I could see he was struggling as well as he could to get to the point where the door would open.

"I'm coming, I'm coming!" Then, in just a low enough tone he assumed she wouldn't hear, but I could, loud and clear, "Hold your God damned water! I'm coming! Who is it?"

I muttered fast, "It's Ralph Wright. I just wanted to leave my leaflet."

"Who?" He was struggling with the multitude of latches and chain locks that had to be grappled with, and finally said, "Dear, where the hell's the key to this damned door?"

"It's right where it should be," she said. "In the top drawer of the table you just pushed across my beautiful hardwood floor. And I wish you wouldn't use those words. You sound so vulgar."

Finally, all the locks were unlatched and all the keys turned. He swung the door open and with disappointment that couldn't be hidden, looked into my face.

"Hi, John. I hope I'm not disturbing you, but I wouldn't think of walking past and not stopping to drop off one of my leaflets for you and the Mrs." With that I peeked my head around the corner and accompanied by my biggest and most genuine smile, waved hello to John's suddenly pleasant and poised Mrs.

It would be a cold day in hell before John or his wife would have put an X next to my name, even if I was the only one on the ballot; but you could have pulled their fingernails before you would have gotten the slightest hint of their true feelings towards me. I knew it, he knew it and she knew it to be true. This was the classic composure of that group of Americans I refer to as the permanently disgruntled.

"Well, thank you, Ralph. We always vote. You can be sure of that." But not for me. I reflected with amusement. I can be doubly sure of that.

"I'm sure I get your support, as we liberals have to stick together."

John and the little lady safely could be classified as to the right of Attila the Hun, but a politeness I didn't have prevented him from rebuking my outrageous characterization of where they stood politically. I continued on with my spiel, "I didn't want you hearing from the neighbors in the coffee shop tomorrow I had been by their places and not yours. Some politicians take their supporters for granted and skip right on by their houses. Not me. I think it's important to ask even those who are certain supporters. Anyway, here's my little leaflet. You can go back to relaxing and enjoying the little woman's company. Thanks in advance for the support."

I know it's a convoluted measure of reward for the small amount of abuse and back-biting all politicians get during their campaigning, but my visit to their house brightened what might otherwise have been a long and arduous day.

Dogs, not people, were the most distracting facets of anyone's door-to-door experience and though I had never been outright attacked by any, they were always foremost on a my mind until I was sure that no dog existed, or it was under his or her master's control. I'm convinced 95 percent of all Vermonters have a dog and 94 percent have about as much control over their dogs as they do over Saddam Hussein.

Tim Corcoran, the consummate campaigner, was always visiting with someone in his district. It didn't have to be the election season to have him show up at a door because he might come bearing gifts any time of the year. He didn't campaign like a normal person. He had his own itinerary and the seven weeks before an election were just the final stage of an on-going 12-month, 365-day sequence. Bennington has no "Welcome Wagon" so to speak, but in lieu of that gesture of hospitality, there was the "Corc." He could detect a Mayflower moving van miles from the Vermont border and it was inevitable he would be the first to greet newcomers in their new town, and always with a small welcome token. It might be a *Vermont Life* calendar he had procured or it could be a Bennington Battle flag, depending on the number of new voters following the van. It didn't matter, nobody escaped his Irish charm.

He paid special attention to the elderly, as they were most likely to vote by absentee ballot. He knew where they lived and he would check in on them periodically to see if there was anything they needed or that he could get done for them. Most of them watched him grow up as he had been their paperboy 35 years earlier. They not only knew him, but they liked him and he was, for many, their only access to the outside world. He never let them down as there was no task too heavy or no job too time consuming "Timmy" couldn't carry out. All he ever wanted in return was the small sense of loyalty that took the form of a vote.

One warm September day found him opening the screen door of Mrs. Denehy's home. He would tap, and without waiting for an answer, cautiously enter.

"Hi, Mrs. Denehy, it's Timmy. How's everything?" By this time he was several feet inside the living room.

"Oh! It's you, Timmy," she'd reply, as she came from the kitchen, paying no attention to the little poodle who was yapping at a safe distance of several feet from Corc's inviting shins. He was an older dog, graying around the mouth, and stood in an arthritic pose at Corcoran's feet. "Yap, yap, yap."

Tim knew the dog to be nothing more than a nuisance and got on about his mission.

"Mrs. Denehy, I'm sure you want to vote and I have your request for your absentee ballot with me that you can sign. It'll just take a second." He knew this was wishful thinking as Mrs. Denehy, anxious for any company, always insisted he have a cup of tea while she asked about his family.

"Oh, yes. I certainly wouldn't fail to vote after all these years. Are you up again for re-election? It seems like we just finished voting for you, Tim. Let me get you a cup of tea. Now you just sit there on the divan and make yourself comfortable." Corcoran sat with a groan.

Corc wasn't here to drink tea. In fact, I don't believe in all the years

I had known him, I ever saw him take a cup of tea or coffee. But this was a time for sacrifice, and if he had to fidget with a cup of something to get an absentee ballot, that's what he'd do. His problem at this moment was little Fifi, who had kept up a constant flanking of Corc's shins from the moment he entered the house. Fifi now was positioned just on the other side of the coffee table with his head and body about half way under the table, yapping incessantly at what he considered an intruder to his private domain.

His master paid him no heed, but the dog was a big aggravation to the Corc, to say nothing of a danger. The dog kept up the constant barking, which was interrupted from time-to-time by a less than forceful lunge at Corc's pant leg. Corcoran meanwhile would retaliate by thrusting his foot at the ever-encroaching Fifi. The dog was merely an unsettling distraction in his quest to carry out that which he came for: Mrs. Denehy's vote.

As Fifi made one last lunge at Corcoran's shins, Father Time rang his bell. For Fifi it was the end of the day, in fact, it was the end of all his days as his last effort at harassing the Corc had strained the poor creature's 15-year-old heart beyond its capacity, and he fell over dead right there under the coffee table at Corc's feet.

Now, to Corcoran, a death usually meant an opportunity to attend a wake and press a little flesh while, all the time, showing a deep respect for the deceased. But this was the first time he had to deal with a dead dog. To make matters worse, Fifi had done what came natural, and with his last breath, peed all over the rug *and* Corcoran's shoes. It was all too much for him to bear, and he got up totaling unraveled, explaining on his hurried way out, he just remembered an emergency appointment and he left, perhaps for the first time in his long political career, without the precious absentee ballot form.

Upon Corcoran's next visit (which was before the deadline for absentee requests), Mrs. Denehy had managed her period of grief, helped greatly by her acquisition of a new puppy with a young and vibrant heart. Corcoran breathed easier, too.

Campaigning held many experiences. One of the great political lines in my entire experience was from the mouth of one of my most dedicated foes: Dwight Lorenz.

The Press was morbidly fascinated with the possibility my demise was inevitable, and if there seemed little chance the Republicans in the House were going to bring me down, perhaps my adversaries in my own district just might do the trick. So, it was a routine thing for me to get a call from one of the members of the Press with a request they come to Bennington and accompany me on some door-to-door visits.

I never encouraged this as I felt embarrassed with a reporter tagging along behind me as I went knocking on doors, but they were insistent, especially if they were taken with the propaganda pumped out on a regular basis by the state Republican party that I was especially vulnerable, or had a strong challenger.

Everything and everybody has a shelf life. I've said that before. When it's up, it's up. The problem politicians have that prehistoric artifacts don't, is nobody thinks enough of politicians to scientifically measure the shelf life. We find out how long we're going to live the day we die.

It was an inevitable call I received from Meg Dennison of the Associated Press, asking if I would mind her coming down and spending a few hours with me traveling door-to-door. I did my best to get out of it, but Meg was a decent sort who explained her bosses were going to have her spend the day in Bennington anyway, and since she'd be talking to a lot of people about my campaign, I might as well let her accompany me to 30 or 40 doors so she could get a feel for how the ordinary people felt about me. I caved in, knowing if I didn't, they would have their own twist to the story, noting I was so worried about the outcome I wouldn't even speak with them. It would be one of those "The Speaker refused to participate in this effort, or the Speaker made himself unavailable for comment" things.

I allowed Dennison to pick out any neighborhood she wanted to do our canvassing in, and it was a happy coincidence she picked out a section that included the Village of North Bennington. I had always done extremely well in the Village since it was noticeably liberal in its outlook on world affairs; in no small measure due to the influence of Bennington College. I had numerous detractors, and few people remained neutral about me. They either hated or liked me.

If they liked me, it was in spite of my reputation for wielding power; and if they hated me, it was because of my reputation for wielding power. Somehow that seemed normal and fair to me. It wasn't I was afraid Dennison would find 51 percent of my constituency were done with me, but that I was going to have to endure the false chest-beating of a Republican leadership that made a living misleading themselves and their devoted followers.

The Press' stake in this had nothing to do with whether they cared who won or lost, but they just wanted to drum up a story. If that meant giving credence to something they thought unlikely, or remote, so be it.

Dennison and I did 20 or 30 houses and the best that she could get was the old saw, "Ralph may be a SOB, but he's our SOB and we're going to vote Ralph." I was pleasantly surprised, not at the unscientific poll unfolding on Dennison's note pad, as I was attentive enough over the years to know that this was liberal country and I would do just fine here, but at how little inhibition my friends and neighbors had in talking with Meg. They were nowhere near as apprehensive of the Press as I was, but, of course, they had never experienced "bad" press. I was a shell-shocked veteran of combat and I reached the point I didn't care if my name ever appeared in print again. Politics, like war, is hell. Especially if you're the one being fired upon.

It got to the point that Dennison was ready to give up in her effort to find an outspoken critic when we turned out of Cora May and Bob Howe's drive. I easily could have turned left, as I'm sure she would have taken me up on the offer to drive her back to her car and call it a day. Instead, I turned right and continued down the narrow dirt road to the last house on the lane.

"Meg, I'm going to take you to a house where I guarantee the person who resides there absolutely hates the ground I walk on. You'll get your juicy quote yet."

"Yeah, sure," Dennison said, "You've said that before, but they inevitably say nice things about you." My comment did perk her up a bit. It had been a long day for her, too, and I could tell she didn't feel she had gotten what she came for.

"I'm not kidding about this guy. He absolutely hates my politics and doesn't think much of me personally either. You'll see. Dwight Lorenz won't let you down. I've never knocked on his door as it would do about as much good as trying to convince my mother-in-law her daughter married well. You'll see. You'll see." We pulled up in front of the Lorenz house.

I knocked on the door with hope Dwight might not be home, but much to my chagrin I heard someone say, "Dwight, there's someone at the door." Simultaneously, a huge Doberman pinscher came sliding and crashing out into the kitchen from the rear of the house.

"Who is it?"

Dennison didn't like the snarling teeth of the dog any more than I, but with the experience of a wizened old veteran, I placed the toe of my foot up against the outer screen door.

"Just in case the latch isn't working," I assured Meg.

"It's me, Dwight, Ralph Wright knocking on doors. I have someone with me I want you to meet."

Dwight suddenly appeared around the same corner that the dog had

245

skidded out from and as we were on the other side of the door, he couldn't see it was me standing outside.

"Who is it?" he repeated.

"Ralph Wright, your favorite politician," I answered.

"Well, my goodness, if it isn't the great one himself. What brings you over to my humble abode?"

"I'm just knocking on a few doors and I have a reporter with me who is tagging along for a story. I thought I'd drop by." His voice so lacked the normal dislike I had grown accustomed to, I actually began to have the faint thought this might turn out better than I thought and poor Meg wasn't going to get that great negative quote after all. I was wrong, as Dwight, blessed with a good, if somewhat misguided mind, came back with the quote of the season.

"Well, you come right on in here, Ralph. The dogs haven't eaten all day."

Those words, of course, appeared prominently in the lead of Dennison's story.

I hated to get started on campaigning as it took a sucking in of the gut and a discipline that was uncomfortable. It had to be done, but not because the bulk of the community would miss if me if I didn't drop by. They wouldn't have, as most never expected me at their door to begin with, at least until your presence reminded them they did. My appearance in front of them seemed to raise a subconscious need they had for this one small moment in the American political process: a reminder they were in charge. Their vote was what I was there for and it was now their decision. They were the boss, if only for this snapshot in time.

The great majority of the American public never even got this much of a moment in the sun with higher level candidates, as they simply don't go door-to-door. There was no eye contact, no polished pol with his hat in his hand, praying someone liked him or her. But they could nearly always depend on this Vermont state rep appearing at their door. Even if I'm wrong about their sub-conscience need, I felt strongly I, at least, needed this moment of humility. A reckoning, with the origins of all political power in a democracy.

It wasn't easy, as no matter how much confidence I had in my own abilities, or the degree of great affection I felt they held for me, this was "humble city." A place where $30 haircuts and $500 suits were a liability. In the General Assembly, we simply dressed for each other. Unless we had an extraordinary attraction to the voters, door-to-door campaigning had to be done in Vermont.

I used to remind myself of the Jack Kennedy/Mrs. O'Brien story.

The moral is "Everybody likes to be asked," and it goes something like this.

Kennedy, upon his triumphant return to Boston after his election as President of the United States, asked if he could return to the Alston /Brighton area that had served as his first home as a child. The President-elect's request was met and a tour of the old neighborhood was laid out in great detail. They even got lucky and found Mrs. O'Brien who, as a young girl, had spent a good deal of time as a babysitter for the future President.

She was a much older women now and had never traveled very far from the house in which she was born. It was not a chance happening, as Kennedy knew they had located Mrs. O'Brien and he looked forward to meeting up with her once again. He remembered her fondly and she cherished the ground he walked on. Upon meeting and embracing while the cameras rolled, they got around to how well the little Kennedy child had done over the years since their last embrace.

"I couldn't have done it without you, Mrs. O'Brien, and millions more just like you," the President said within earshot of all the cameras and mikes.

"Yes, ya could, Jack. In fact, ya did just that."

The President-to-be, curious, asked what she meant. "I don't understand, Mrs. O'Brien. It sounds like perhaps you didn't vote for me."

"Well, now the truth wins out, Jack, as God is at my door. I didn't."

"And, how come?"

"Because you never asked."

If you were going to vote against me it wasn't going to be because I didn't ask.

Knocking on doors was like eating pistachio nuts, once you started, you couldn't stop. I had to be careful, as no matter how energized I might be, there was a time and place I had to stop. I was careful not to stay out too late, as in lots of houses with kids, I ran the risk of meeting a very upset parent if I arrived just after they had managed to wrestle the little ones into bed for the night, only to be lured downstairs by some politician at the door.

During my first campaign, I was edging along the boundary that separated my district between Bennington and Shaftsbury, the next town north. I never had the availability of the assistance we would later provide for all our candidates and I was campaigning on instinct alone. It was getting late, perhaps 8:30 P.M. or so, but I was pushing to get this one last section done. I left my leaflet after a brief chat with the residents, but I began to notice I didn't seem to recognize anyone, nor did they appear to recognize me. This was unusual, as I seldom went more than a couple of houses without some sort of recognition. About the tenth house up what seemed like an endless road, I finally came upon a fellow school teacher.

"Geez, I was beginning to think I was in Canada. I don't know a soul on this road." I confessed among friends. "Anyway, I'm nearly done for the night. Hope I can get your support, Steve."

"Well, I'd love to Ralph as I am really rooting for you to win this thing, but I'm afraid that I can't vote for you."

"Whatta ya mean, you're not going to support me?"

"I would, Ralph, but I don't live in your district. You're deep in the town of Shaftsbury. It's against the law."

Of my nine campaigns, I enjoyed the luxury of being unopposed only once. I usually felt sorry for my Democratic running mates, because I was obviously the one that the Republicans were after. The fact I was on the ticket placed Pembroke in the inevitable position of being at risk. He never said too much about it all, but my having opposition meant he, also, had opposition. Actually, Pembroke always topped the ticket as he was extremely well-liked throughout the district. Though this was mostly due to his warm, friendly personality, there was a vast difference between us when it came to status and power. As Speaker, I determined the fortunes of all the Republicans in the House. Therefore, their fondest wishes were directly connected with my political demise. Actually I'm quite sure their fantasies went beyond politics on occasion.

I have nothing but the greatest admiration for the vast majority of the people I met over the years. They were polite and kind almost to a person. Beyond that, I couldn't help be overwhelmed by their constant effort to "hang tough." It seemed the only thing that mattered to them was that I do what I thought was right, and give it my full effort. That's what they did every day, and though they seldom pretended to know more than I did, they often gave me credit for doing what they professed to have no desire to do. In turn, I held them in high esteem for whatever small part their busy and tumultuous lives allowed them to play in the democratic process. Some had such great odds stacked against them, I wouldn't have blamed them if they refused to ever vote again. Too many bills and too little money never seemed to stall their hope things were bound to get better, if not for them, then hopefully, for their children. If there were times I needed reinforcement for why I was doing what I was, then campaigning more than provided the impetus.

I was able to deal with the few boobs who thought the world owned them their every desire. I'm sure that it adds to the multitude of reasons that led to my defeat. I know my propensity to stand and fight with the very same people from whom I was hoping to get a vote, cost me. How greatly really doesn't matter, because I don't believe I would have reacted any differently if I was aware they might be the decisive vote in my re-election. I found it harder and harder to put up with the constant complainers, especially when all the visible signs of having so much more than the vast majority of their neighbors was so evident.

I looked around one day before entering the screened in back porch of a local businessman I knew "retired" at an earlier age than most of us expect to retire. "Kally", as he was called, was not someone I knew well, but I always had managed to get "in and out" of his house without too much conversation. I knocked on the door and stood admiring the armada of "toys" he managed to accumulate. If the old adage the "one with the most toys wins" has any ring of truth, Kally is sure to be a medal winner. There was a boat with a 30-horse Johnson engine, a Scamper camper, a three-wheeler, and an antique automobile covered with a canvas. This ensemble didn't include the brand new Chevy pickup and a late model car that sat in the driveway. Kally had it all, at least as dictated by Detroit.

He answered the door and didn't say a word, just stared at me. I tried to dismiss what I sensed was a very hostile attitude by spewing forth my normal introduction.

"Hi, I'm Ralph Wright and I just wanted to drop by and leave my leaflet. I'm running for re-election to the House of Representatives and I wanted to let you know I care enough to be here."

"I know who you are," he said with obvious contempt.

This wasn't going to be pleasant. Knowing Kally had a huge family residing in my district and more than likely he was relied on by them for economic and political advice, I counted to three silently and finished what I had to say.

"Well, I'd be happy to try and answer any questions you might have concerning the legislature. If you're busy, I have my number on the other side of the leaflet and you can feel free to call me anytime." I was trying to get out, as he looked down hastily at the leaflet I just handed to him.

"What the hell you characters gonna do about VSAC? They ain't worth a damn." It was a statement not a question.

I knew Vermont Student Assistance Plan (VSAC) to be a highly reputable, non-profit organization that distributed millions each year to kids who needed financial help in their efforts to go to college. Its funds were limited, but it had helped tens of thousands of Vermonters to realize their dreams. Of necessity, it had criteria that determined those in greatest financial need. Some didn't qualify.

"I beg your pardon," I said. I could feel the Irish rushing up my spine and gathering in columns of two in my neck.

"You know what I'm talking about, and if you don't, I guess that doesn't surprise me either. I'm gettin' to think you guys don't know much of anything, anyway."

"I don't understand. What about VSAC? What's the problem?" My patience was about at the end.

"They give it to all these bums and welfare cheats. Normal people can't get any help. Normal people being the people who pay the taxes. Like me. I'm sick of it all, and I'm sick of all you characters with your promises to do this and do that. Ya don't ever do anything. We're just wasting our money. Might as well just go out there and throw it down the sewer."

I had already made the decision I no longer wanted his vote, and as it was unlikely someone who thought as I did had ever gotten it in the past, I concluded I probably wasn't going to lose anything anyway. As for his family, I'd try and make that up somewhere down the road.

I stood in front of this ingrate hearing little of his specifics, but absorbing his tone of hate and animosity. I was desperately trying to put in perspective how anyone who had accumulated all the toys this guy had managed to collect, could possibly feel they were still owed.

His problem wasn't more material gathering, but a vacuum in his soul. He was missing in action. He didn't like himself, and consequently he couldn't find compassion or understanding for anything or anyone else. He was a tragic figure of the contemporary American who, through selfishness and lack of social feeling, found no meaning for what this country had afforded him. His search for meaning and happiness constantly spanned the horizon when all he had to do was look closer to home to discover what was missing.

I realized suddenly he had apparently spent himself as he stood there in front of me awaiting a response. My anger had subsided and I realized there was only one proper response. I had no trouble with it either.

"Ya know, Kally, in some South American banana republics, they shoot people like you." I reached out and took my now sweat-soaked and crumbled leaflet out of his hand and left.

The thought re-entered my mind that perhaps I had overstayed my time in the Vermont legislature.

29. THE LAST SUNSET

1994 proved my inner feelings were detected by my constituents. A host of Monday morning quarterbacks have analyzed my defeat and each brings a different perspective. I still cling to the reason I gave in my concession news release the night I learned the results.

I thanked the community for allowing me to serve them and stated it had been their decision 16 years earlier to send me to Montpelier, and having accepted their decision then as good judgment, I would be less than honest to feel their decision to send my opponent in my place now was anything less. It was time for a change and the people knew it.

When one is beaten by 160 votes, one looks back to see what could have been done differently to switch half that number, thereby snatching victory from the jaws of defeat. The simple answer is I didn't do any of the things that would have brought this about. Gerry Morrissey, my opponent, had raised a huge amount of money to mount his very effective campaign, reported around $13,000, and I persisted in keeping the bragging rights to my claim I had never raised or accepted a penny for any of my efforts toward getting elected or re-elected. The fact the Republican party made me their top target and solicited contributions for Morrissey from all over the state (as well as out of state), never worried me in the least. I never credited money as the deciding factor in my previous victories. Jim Williams, four years earlier, raised at least an equal amount and I still won. I still held to the ninth grade civics class notion the heartbeat of democracy was something of a higher value than the almighty dollar. Money might help or at least prove to be the great equalizer, but there were too many other ingredients that went into victory. Gerry won it on his own.

It wasn't that I hadn't been offered a ton of money over the years. I had. The title "Speaker" was like magic when it came to hitting on lobbyists or other potential contributors. I had proven that by raising unprecedented amounts for my house Democrats over the period I was Speaker. In 1994 alone, I raised and spent nearly $80,000 in seeing that the national landslide that put Newt Gingrich into power, didn't have an impact on our majority in the Vermont House. We had lost two seats, but it was a small miracle we withstood the tide and still had a very comfortable majority.

There was no doubt we were never again going to be out spent by the Republicans. I knew how to raise money, and though I found it the most uncomfortable responsibility of being Speaker, I never hesitated in doing it, except for my own race when I stubbornly drew the line. I could have matched my opponent's fund-raising dollar for dollar. But would it, and all the things it would purchase, have helped get me another 80 odd votes? Probably! Then why didn't I just cave in and do what I had to do? The straight answer is I never thought for a single moment I could lose.

Perhaps of greater significance than the money, was a certain neglect I gave to my district. *All politics is personal.* That's been a theme of this book. History is chock full of examples of the high and mighty becoming absorbed *"in the big"* scene, while neglecting those closer to home.

I was into "great" issues. I was trying to bring property tax relief and health care reform to Vermonters. These issues dominated my every waking moment during the previous two years. Once the 1994 session began, sensing success, I turned up my efforts on all the notches that were left. I was certain both were finally within our grasp and I was prepared to do whatever I could to make them reality. If that meant staying in session "until the leaves turned", so be it.

The Press had a field day with my seeming disregard for the protocol and tradition of the "citizen legislature", and since I had never mastered the art of the public relations, handled the fallout in every conceivable wrong way. I kept the legislature in session longer than any Speaker, with one exception, throughout Vermont's long history. My arrogant response to the mountain of criticism was "we'll stay until we get the job done." It took its toll, not just politically as my popularity ratings fell to, even for me, an alarming low level, but physically as well.

It wasn't that I didn't have a deep and profound respect for the "citizen legislature." I most certainly did. But I had my own viewpoint on just what constituted and was vital to maintaining such a grass roots assembly and it had little to do with how long we stayed in session.

The fact is we often served without pay during my years as Speaker, thus the criticism surrounding the "outrageous" cost of over-extending our allotted time was greatly exaggerated. It made good press and went far to incite the populace, but it was money that had to be spent if we were going to be allowed to do our jobs.

Legislators, with the exception of the Speaker and the President ProTem of the Senate, had no staff. This was the crux of this thing we call the citizen legislature. A member must do all his or her own constituent work and this prevented him or her from having a paid campaign manager. That's what "staff" soon become. It's the tonic of "self perpetuation" in all the full-time legislatures across the country.

I never once adjourned when we were supposed to. And I caught holy living hell. It was like I was single-handedly holding up adjournment for a frivolous cause. I didn't see it that way as the opposition, whether the Republicans in the House, or the Senate, saw a distinct advantage to getting out before the other side's agenda was moved to completion.

Their whole game plan was to wait us out. If the pressure from the public, aided by the Press, grew strong enough, then our only option was to defy the clamor or leave our agenda behind. The latter alternative was repugnant. The legislative process wasn't a football game where the end comes at a pre-determined time whatever the score. Didn't there have to be a winner? Wasn't someone's agenda worth fighting for? If not, why were we bothering to meet? And, what if the opposition had no agenda at all? Did it mean our agenda didn't deserve to be fought for? Just go home? Give up the fight for what we believed in? If we did, we would ignore the terrible burden of the vast majority of Vermonters who had been brought to their knees under the weight of a brutal and unfair property tax, or the worry of wondering how their family medical bills were going to be paid, all in the name of promptness and expediency. I didn't think that was the right course to take. But there was a price to be paid for standing and fighting for the things in which we believed. I paid it.

I lost it all. Health Care, property tax reform, and my credibility, too. Five months earlier, I was sitting with Sean Campbell in the Speaker's office, having adjourned early Sunday morning, June 12. Our silence, sensing the early rising of the Montpelier sun, said it all. I don't know what Campbell's inner thoughts were that morning, but I couldn't help reflect this would be the last time we would enjoy each other's company in this surrounding.

We said good-bye as we exited into the empty parking lot and I went back to my apartment to grab a few hours sleep before heading down the road, home to Bennington. I awoke around 10:30 A.M. and stopped to get the Sunday morning papers. Both statewide newspapers front pages barely mentioned the story of our long and bloody fight over the two most important issues facing Vermont. Instead, they mocked and ridiculed the length of the session, and by inference, the souls who had been so much a part of it. There was no mention as to how close we had come to resolving the tremendous issues.

The drive down Interstate 89 seemed an eternity as I reflected how long and hard my fellow members, the Cillos, Friedens, Powdens, Larsons, and Campbells had worked, only to come up short. By the time I got home, all I could do was to climb into bed and toss and turn the night away.

Monday morning I set out to drive to Florida. I had made previous arrangements to meet Cathy at my daughter Cathy Marie's home in Orlando and after spending a few days, we planned to drive leisurely up U.S. 17 and home. I hadn't set any definite arrival time, but she knew the legislature had adjourned and I would take my time driving South, while visiting some of my favorite Civil War sites in Virginia. I had never visited the site of Lee's surrender at Appomattox, and I made certain I didn't miss this opportunity.

It is a wonderfully peaceful site, and I eerily noted a place of such beauty should turn out to be the end of such carnage. It was the off season for tourists, and I was the only soul there. I sat overlooking the grassy knoll Lee must have ridden up to relinquish his sword to Grant, and it dawned on me it was time for me to do the same.

I always wanted to see Cape Hatteras, so I took a circuitous route and started down the long series of bridge connections that make it up. By the time I got to Ocracoke at the very tip and rested in the beautiful sun-drenched little park while waiting for the ferry to North Carolina, I had made up my mind. My political career was over. It was time to move on. I went to the pay phone to make the call to Corcoran so he could arrange to make the release available to the press and the members. My decision was irrevocable and I knew my isolation on the road would serve as a buffer to the reaction of my decision. Perhaps it was the magic of the sun and the ocean, but I felt a deep sense of relief that it was over for me and it was now somebody else's turn.

"Hello, Timmy?" The phone rang only once at the town clerk's office in Bennington.

"Yeah. Where are you?"

"Never mind where the hell I am. I've got something to tell you."

"Oh, ya already heard, huh? Morrissey's announcement?" Corc always enjoyed somebody else's political bad news.

"What announcement?"

"Really! He announced yesterday he's running against you. Announced it right up in your bailiwick at Power's Market in the Village. Had a pretty big deal. Press from all over. Says it's time for a change."

How quick one's life can change. I was in a fight and so much for my retirement plans.

The rest of the conversation was made up of a casualness and bravado neither of us believed for a moment, as Gerry, I was certain, was going to be a formidable foe.

The ferry ride didn't hold the same enchantment I had anticipated.

I spent the summer and fall racing around the state recruiting, training, and bolstering 135 Democratic candidates. My trusty side car partner was Steve Howard, who I had hired to help me in my efforts to keep the House safe for Democrats. Steve was elected Democratic Representative from Rutland Town in 1992, while still a senior in college. Already a political junkie, he took to hanging around the Speaker's office and I took a liking to him. I had infinite respect for his energy and intelligence.

Steve was invaluable, as he was a tireless worker, bright as hell, and an absolute captive to the political world. I was amazed at how much he knew at age 23. There wasn't anything he wouldn't do, and few things he couldn't do. Need a news release? He'd bat it out. If somebody had to be in the Northeast Kingdom at 7 A.M., he'd be there. It got so I began to worry about his health and would take care not to casually mention any chores less than absolutely necessary because he'd insist on doing them.

We spent a lifetime together in the car or on the phone over the next six months and there is no doubt in my mind any less of an effort would have spelled disaster for us when the results were tallied in November. We worked seven days a week, often 18 hours a day. Because I didn't get paid, I kept exact mileage numbers, for which I did get reimbursed. Come election day, I added them all up and found I had put over 28,000 miles on my car in little old Vermont. I was absolutely worn out while Steve looked like a man possessed and ready to do it all over again. Ah, youth!

The non-stop express we were on nearly killed me, but it was actually Steve who came closest to dying. We had just spent 12 hours wandering around the northern part of the state visiting with our candidates, when I remembered I hadn't eaten all day and was famished. As we passed through Barre on the way home at about 8 P.M., I suggested we stop and grab some Chinese food. Steve agreed with whatever I suggested. I could have said we were going to stop and bowl a few strings and he would have brought out a bowling ball. About half way through my boneless fried chicken, I sensed something and looked up to stare into the most terror-filled eyes I had ever seen. Steve was choking, and he was frozen in fear.

The last thing I wanted to do was to react in panic as I knew that would only leave the possibility to him, at least, of getting up and bolting to who knows where. In as calm a voice as I could manage, I asked if he was choking, "Just nod, Steve, if you are."

He nodded. His eyes were bugging out of their sockets.

I rose and at the same time told Steve to get up and turn around. At first he resisted, and I had to grab his arm and tug him to his feet. He stood staring at me, helplessly.

I managed to get him turned around and get my arms around his chest cavity. This was no small chore as Steve is a big man. I gave him a squeeze, but I could tell nothing had happened as I felt him try to break away from my grasp. I held onto him and the second time I did it with no concern for the potential of broken ribs. I smiled with relief as, if on schedule, whatever was lodged in his esophagus flew out and landed at his feet. He turned around and gave the best smile he could manage under the circumstances. Just as he was finally ready to go to the men's room to freshen up, the table of eight that had been watching all this broke into a round of applause. Their human spontaneity worked better than Steve's esophagus.

For the first time in a long while, I felt good about the world and the people who inhabit it. If nothing else came out of this grueling six-month period, I can take some measure of small satisfaction I left Steve Howard for Vermont and posterity.

When there are 135 people, over half of them running for office for the first time, they can get pretty demanding. For those who have never put their name on a secret ballot, it is impossible to reckon with the trauma candidates endure. The candidate often feels an isolation others can only imagine. This doesn't reveal itself during the period that leads up to the campaign. When one first announces, there may not be any announced opposition, so the possibility exists for what is referred to as a "free ride." That's infrequent, but it's possible for the more fortunate.

The other party seldom sits back watching with interest. The pleasant thought of a "free ride" conjures up illusions of grandeur in all but the most realistic that everybody loves you. This bubble bursts when your opponent announces he or she is going to take you on, and intends to administer a good beating to you. Thoughts of being "the people's choice" soon turn to wondering if anybody but your immediate family is going to turn out to support you. Your opponent suddenly isn't as dumb as a rock or as ugly as you remembered him or her. Actually he or she's looking more and more like an "I Like Ike" poster child with each passing day. Then you read there's a fundraiser, or that all the people at the plant are for your opponent, and your doubts as to why you ever got yourself into this mess begin to blossom and explode into sleepless nights. What if you lose? What if you get trounced? What will my spouse or the kids or the gang at work think? "God damned that Ralph Wright for talking me into this.

Where is he anyway? Haven't heard from him in days."

We tried to alleviate some of this by staying in constant contact. We knew what they were going through and it was our job to keep them focused on what we had tried to teach them. The last thing we wanted to happen was for them to get so discouraged at the endless tasks a campaign demanded they simply stopped.

This had happened too often in the past for us to be casual about the possibility. For some, the most terrifying chore was the door-to-door campaign we insisted was the one ingredient in their effort that was an absolute necessity. The most veteran among us found that meeting thousands of constituents at their door, often on lonely back roads wasn't something the majority enjoyed. This was especially difficult for a great number of our candidates who were women. You never could tell just who you might run into on those back roads, or their condition. It had to be done, but it took a measure of self-assurance in the candidate that he or she had not had to call on in his past experiences as frequently as the situation now demanded.

More than once during my checking in with them I would find people who, under normal circumstances, wouldn't think of participating in stretching the truth, now forced themselves to outright lie to cover the fact they couldn't force themselves to go door-to-door. When that occurred, there was little we could do about it, as like the fear of flying, it was only in their minds. But it was real. Almost without exception, this candidate and that seat could be written off.

I learned houses were like books in that it was dangerous always to judge them by their outward appearances. I traveled miles of back roads and saw houses that tempted me to keep driving. They looked like something out of Appalachia in the sixties. Junk cars, houses that looked more than run-down sheds, and the infamous chained-up dog. But their hospitality and friendliness seldom failed to come through. Better still they voted. It would take a pretty mean looking, unchained dog for me to pass by.

It took all the patience and time we could muster to make ourselves available for the seven weeks between Labor Day and the November election. We tried to schedule at least one visit into our candidates' district during this period and, in many cases, we found we would have to return several times.

I found the unusual demand on my time a God send, because it helped the time go by. But it cut into my schedule back in North Bennington, and that got compensated for by a tact I never pursued before. I skipped whole neighborhoods where I felt the residents had already made up their minds. This was a vital mistake, not because I would have turned that many around by appearing at their door, but it left the eventually fatal impression I didn't seem to have the same enthusiasm I had in past campaigns.

It was a realistic conclusion, as I opted to transfer the missing energy from my district to my candidates around the state. This culminated in my deciding to visit a candidate in Burlington, rather than to appear jointly with my opponent on local television. I dismissed it then as not symptomatic of anything of a larger threatening nature to a successful campaign, but in retrospect, it was.

The other crucial mistake I made was I informed my running mate Dick Pembroke he ought to get on with his campaign without me accompanying him. I sincerely felt my crazy schedule would make it impossible for me to be home each night by 5 P.M. for us to go door-to-door together. This had never happened before, as Pembroke and I always had gone to each and every door together through four previous campaigns.

It wasn't that it was going to cost him any votes, since he was by far the most popular of the two of us in the district. I had picked up more votes by being in his company, than I had ever gotten him. Beyond that, Pembroke is one of those extremely reliable and totally trustworthy people. If he said he'd pick me up at a certain time, it didn't matter how bad the weather or how tiring a day he had, he'd be in my driveway on schedule. More important, he didn't have the slightest apprehension talking to the most antagonistic voter. If someone lived behind a door, he'd knock on it. I wouldn't have been allowed to skip a single house, let alone entire neighborhoods if I had been with Pembroke. It would have made a difference, but so would a lot of other things that were happening.

I don't know how concerted the effort of the state Republican party was to "get" me, but there are those who swear that is all they had on their minds. As far as I'm concerned, it doesn't really amount to a whole lot because I never believed one person meant all that much in the scheme of legislative things. One person might make a difference, but he or she didn't make that big a difference. Besides, if I had amounted to all that much, I would have seen the heath care and property tax reform bills pass. I didn't. It does matter whether we win or lose, as the Press will make sure we play the game fair, and we hadn't gotten the job done. I suspect my enemies would have accepted an even worse situation if they could be assured they could get rid of me.

I knew something out of the ordinary was going on when a large number of my friends called to tell me they had received a call from a pollster out of Virginia and the poll itself appeared to have one aim:

"What do you think of that awful man Ralph Wright?", it seemed to be asking. No effort was made, so my informants claimed, to appear the least bit unbiased in questions or tone. The rumor was this was being paid for by the Republican National Committee and it was a statewide effort that cost $75,000. I don't know how much of that to believe, but it did give me a deeper sense of their determination to pull off the upset of the year.

They knew they had placed a tough opponent against me and that, just maybe, their decade-long campaign to disparage me, my liberal politics, and probably most important, my so-called "Boston-style politics" was finally going to bear some fruit.

Morrissey's money kept pouring in, and for the first time I began to see his TV ads. This was "big city politics" I never had seen in Vermont. It must have cost a great deal of money to put this together, and even though it was something I don't believe I would have done, it got voter's attention. The 30-second sound bite finally had arrived in little ole Bennington, Vermont.

To add to my myriad of problems, the "gun nuts" had come out of their caves and, though they weren't energized by any of my actions, I was to catch their fury. I had managed to escape their attention throughout my career, not because I was a Second Amendment advocate, but because I had made it clear to whomever asked that I personally wouldn't kill "Bambi", I'd have no problem blowing up any son of a bitch who came up my driveway with harm to me or mine in his heart. They knew I had done my hitch in the Marine Corps and as long as I didn't attempt to tamper with their guns, they lived and let live. I was never afraid of guns, per se, but I could work up a pretty terrific fright over what I might do if provoked or frightened.

They had their suspicions I was one of those "dopey do-gooders", as I had been embroiled in a major brouhaha over moose. Several years earlier, the state decided to bring moose back to one of their old natural habitats and turned several loose in the northern wilds. As one might expect, they proliferated and soon grew to a herd of 1,000. The hunting advocates realized this was another source of revenue for the Fish and Game Department, and before we could spell "Bowinkle", a bill was introduced in the House to allow a moose season. Normally, this would have been a matter I willingly would have left to others to grapple with, but as it turned out, one of my least favorite people became the chief sponsor. This, coupled with an incident created to embarrass one of my members by several members of the Fish and Game Committee, was enough to motivate me to kill the bill. When asked by the Press why I didn't want to shoot moose, I answered, "Shooting a moose is like shooting a parked car." That wise ass comment went coast-to-coast. I guess I was never going to learn to keep my mouth shut.

This wasn't what got them to sit in front of the polls election day with a sign that read, "Protect your Second Amendment rights: Vote against Mary Ann Carlson and Ralph Wright." Carlson, a liberal Senator from the county, had been brave enough to put her name as a sponsor on a gun control bill the previous session. It had no chance of getting even serious discussion, let alone an affirmative vote, but she was one of those legislators who did what she thought was right. She paid a big price for it, as the gun people came out in droves and she suffered a crushing defeat. This was a woman who had topped the ticket just two years earlier. It certainly didn't get me any extra votes.

I was already on the "hit list" of my fellow teachers, or at least the teacher's union, as I had called for a single negotiation for all 7,000 Vermont Education in Association (VEA) members in my property tax bill. I thought it was a good idea to eliminate the tens of thousand of person hours the 250 or so local school boards consumed in any given year, meeting on a weekly basis. My bill called for one single negotiation between the teacher's representative and the state, and a single contract. The teacher's union went ballistic, of course.

The fact I had been a card-carrying union member for my entire career as a teacher and that I was the founder and director of an innovative alternative school for dropouts, kept them from having me run out of state, but they let it be known that our romance was over. I'm not sure all the rank and file teachers disagreed with my suggestion, so perhaps I still received some support from my colleagues, but it wasn't going to be anywhere near the support I received in the previous elections.

The union agreed with every other part of the property tax bill, but they worked their butts off to kill the whole thing. I wasn't proud of their single-mindedness, and my feelings toward my profession forever changed. It's a noble profession and they deserve much more gratitude than the typical community gives them, but as a group, represented in Montpelier by their union, they took on all the characteristics of a street gang. They'll pay the price for that stance forever in the loss of their professional image.

Finally, there were the health providers. We're talking big money folks, and since our health care bill was going to change the system, somebody's fortune was placed in jeopardy. A Canadian-styled "single payer" system was the "black hand of Communism" for many of the hospital administrators, the doctors, and the insurance companies.

They spent hundreds of thousands of dollars lobbying to kill the bill. If it hadn't been against the law, they would have done the same to many of us who were fighting to bring about the change. They, too, could hardly wait to get to the polls on election day.

The revelation that shook me the most was the *Bennington Banner,* which had always supported me, suddenly had a change of heart and endorsed Morrissey. I sensed this was coming when I saw on the finance report Morrissey turned in the publisher of the paper had given him a pretty hefty contribution. I assume the board that made the decision was well aware the boss had a favorite in this race. I've asked around in the world of journalism since, and I can't find anyone who thinks this isn't an unusual action for a publisher to take, at least publicly.

It probably wasn't any single thing that led to my defeat, rather a decade-long accumulation of things that were just too much to overcome. If the Republicans, the hunters, the teachers, the health care providers, and my local newspaper weren't enough, the fact they had a competent and well-financed opponent running against me was sufficient to get it done.

But the truth of the matter was, it was time for a new face.

30. The End

Now it was time to go. I knew Barbara Agnew, my administrative assistant, was going to be angry, as I had promised I would not make my last visit without saying good-bye. Instead, I had left a dozen roses on her always cleaned-off desk. All the files she had so carefully packed away for me were loaded in my car in the parking lot. She knew, I suspect, that wasn't how it would be. I rose from my seat, walked along the back row to the light switch panel on the wall to the left of the big entry doors, and stood getting my bearings in anticipation of navigating the length of the hall in darkness. I glimpsed quickly at the full vista of the chamber, focusing on the center. The podium caught my stare and I was taken back by its appearance. How small and insignificant it appeared, a contrast to my first encounter 16 years ago. Then it was the centerpiece of a larger-than-life arena. It is a majestic room where the people's business is carried out in the best democratic traditions. As I walked through the chamber, the total darkness did not impede my steps. I had made this journey thousands of times. I went up the stairs, reaching out to feel for the podium, not for guidance, but for one last time to touch the seat of power for memory's sake. I went through the runway to the back of the building, only this time instead of going straight and into the Speaker's quarters, I turned sharply to the left and proceeded down the stairs leading to the parking lot at the back of the building. There was a lightness in my step as I pranced down the back steps. There, that feeling of guilt came over me again. I had this same rush the night I had my son, Rick, read the election results to me. He, his sisters, and mostly Cathy, had stared with expressions of hurt and anguish, perhaps anticipating some overflow of emotional hurt on my part. I felt guilty, as the only feeling I recognized now was one of relief. Now this same sense overcame me and I reflected that somehow I was rationalizing, or kidding myself. Hurt would come later as I drove past the Executive Office Building and turned right, I was aware of the State House, its illumination showing it in all its splendor. Never had I failed to be overwhelmed by its majestic stature as I entered and left the Capital over the years. It held the same allure to me now, but this time I fought the urge to look back. I officially had left the House. I was returning home.

Wright, Ralph

324.2   All politics is personal
Wri   JUN   '97

HARTLAND PUBLIC LIBRARIES
PO BOX 137, ROUTE 12
HARTLAND VT 05048